FIELD NOTES *from a* WATERBORNE LAND

'Parimal Bhattacharya's *Field Notes from a Waterborne Land* brings us a Bengal the rest of India does not see or even know of – a natural world of gorgeous yet threatened riverine, deltaic and forest landscapes, a social world of peasant and tribal communities struggling heroically for survival. These diverse landscapes and the people who inhabit them are sketched with tenderness and empathy. This is a richly readable as well as deeply moving book.'

— RAMACHANDRA GUHA

'In this moving and insightful travelogue, Parimal Bhattacharya takes leave of the sheltered lives of the bhadralok to discover the other side of Bengal and its own struggles to live, love and learn.'

— JEAN DRÈZE

'This is truly an unusual travelogue and "field journal" that weaves together history, sociology, politics, anthropology, culture and ecology. Written delightfully, it is a work of deep scholarship as well as a poignant commentary on the lives of communities missing from the usual narratives of West Bengal's diverse society. I found myself captivated reading it and finished the book at one go.'

— JAIRAM RAMESH

'Parimal Bhattacharya's book mixes history, anecdotes, memories, social insights and political observations in prose that has a touch of magic and is evocative, moving, wistful, and sensitive without being sentimental. A work of non-fiction that, like his earlier books, transcends narrow boundaries to follow the trails of the extraordinary stories of seemingly ordinary people that unfold along the dusty roads of Bengal. Bhattacharya records these with a detached intensity and empathy that leave a lasting impression.'

— MAITREESH GHATAK

PARIMAL BHATTACHARYA

FIELD NOTES
from a
WATERBORNE LAND

Bengal Beyond *the* Bhadralok

HarperCollins *Publishers* India

First published in India by HarperCollins *Publishers* 2022
4th Floor, Tower A, Building No. 10, Phase II, DLF Cyber City,
Gurugram – 122002
www.harpercollins.co.in

2 4 6 8 10 9 7 5 3 1

Copyright © Parimal Bhattacharya 2022

P-ISBN: 978-93-5489-437-4
E-ISBN: 978-93-5489-441-1

The views and opinions expressed in this book are the author's own
and the facts are as reported by him, and the publishers
are not in any way liable for the same.

Parimal Bhattacharya asserts the moral right
to be identified as the author of this work.

All rights reserved. No part of this publication may be reproduced,
stored in a retrieval system, or transmitted, in any form or by any
means, electronic, mechanical, photocopying, recording or otherwise,
without the prior permission of the publishers.

Cover photograph: Arati Kumar-Rao
Cover design: Twisha Mehta

Typeset in 11/15 Adobe Caslon Pro at
Manipal Technologies Limited, Manipal

Printed and bound at
Thomson Press (India) Ltd

❋❋❋❋ HarperCollinsIn

This book is produced from independently certified FSC® paper
to ensure responsible forest management.

'If we look into our hearts, we will have to admit that the India we know is actually the India of the bhadralok.'

— RABINDRANATH TAGORE

'There is no lie that does not have at its core some truth. One must only know how to listen.'

— J.M. COETZEE, *Age of Iron*

A MAP OF PLACES MENTIONED IN THE BOOK

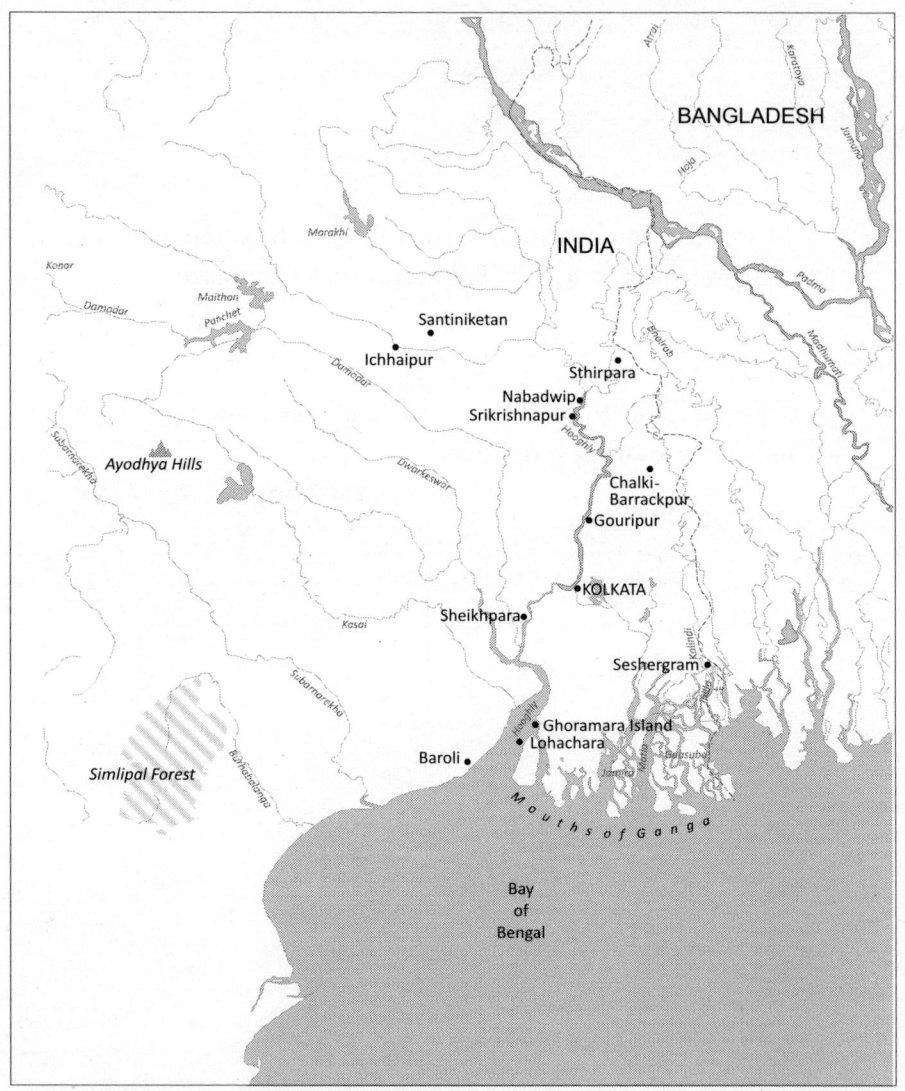

CONTENTS

Note from the Author   ix

I   Ganga, Ichhamati, Damodar   1

II   Ayodhya Hill   101

III   Simlipal   123

IV   Ajay   161

V   Raimangal, Kalindi   191

VI   Hooghly   241

VII   Bay of Bengal   267

Acknowledgements   297

NOTE FROM THE AUTHOR

It began with the mystery of the invisible children.

I read in a newspaper report that eight out of ten children who enrolled in West Bengal's primary schools dropped out before they completed secondary education. Where did they go? The statistical handbook of the state, from which the report had quoted, could not give a clue. But eight out of ten was a big number, nearly twenty times more than the official number of child labourers in the state. Where were they if not in schools? I couldn't remember noticing many out-of-school children except in the dingy crevices of my city, in squatter settlements and around railway stations.

I fished around for some time until I sensed that this required a formal approach. I applied for, and received, a grant from the University Grants Commission (UGC) for a research project. This gave me a passport to go to places not on tourist maps, visit institutions and interview people. This was in 2006. The Sarva Shiksha Abhiyan, the programme for universal primary education, was in its sixth year. I planned to complete the project in two years.

But I had more on my hands than I had imagined. Soon after I began my travels and talked to people, I discovered that universal primary education is a prism: it refracts a spectrum of economic, social, cultural and even ecological issues, which usually remain muddled. Thus, what began as a straightforward enquiry grew into a labyrinth, my curiosity hardened into an obsession, I lost my tree in the forest. After two years, I was still making trips to out-of-the-way places in south Bengal and also in eastern Odisha. I couldn't complete the project and returned the grant to the UGC.

But what I think I learnt during that time was how to listen to stories, extraordinary stories told by seemingly ordinary people, about themselves and about the land on which they lived.

Deltaic Bengal is a young landmass built by silt-carrying rivers – a waterborne land, which is still being made and unmade. Its fertility and accessibility through its rivers and the sea have always drawn people – agriculturists, artisans, merchants, freebooters and colonizers – making it one of the most prosperous and historically significant regions in the subcontinent.

However, all that is in the past. The majority of the people who now live on the ruins of a once highly commercialized land are either tied to subsistence farming or are transiting all over the country to work in its informal sectors. Battered by cyclones, floods, and the rough hand of history – Partition – their story is one of untold misery but also of remarkable grit.

How different these stories are from the one we have been telling each other and the world – the story of a lazy, argumentative, culture-loving community who love their adda, mishti doi and Tagore. This, I realized, is the story of my kind of people, a small segment of the more than nine crore who originate from the Indian side of the Bengal Delta and speak Bangla, the educated urban middle-class and mostly upper-caste Hindus: the bhadralok.

The realization made me undertake the most difficult of journeys: to my own space, my roots, without the blinkers of self-delusion.

When I began these journeys, the Left Front was still in power in West Bengal. But the formidable red bastion was being hollowed out, particularly in rural areas. It soon crumbled – sooner than anyone had expected. The well-oiled machine of a party society gave way to disorder and improvisation. But this also pulled down old walls for the winds of change to blow. Since then, several state welfare schemes targeted at young people and students, particularly girl students, have shown positive results. But, as elsewhere in the country, the shift towards privatization of education has accelerated; many state-run schools in urban areas have closed down for lack of students. Some of the descendants of the early settlers, those gritty men and women who built a life from scratch, have become dependent on government programmes. With the returns from farming dwindling, the labour migration has continued. As I write these lines, nearly two years of a pandemic and lockdown have pushed this population to the brink. The schools are closed, and an uncountable number of children have dropped out.

Meanwhile, the climate crisis has worsened. Four major cyclones have ravaged coastal Bengal in about two years, turning swathes of land practically uninhabitable. But people still hang on, bracing themselves for the quirks of nature and the state, for the next cyclone or the Citizenship Act, because they have nowhere else to go.

I have tried to tell their stories, stories rooted in their locales. I have changed the names of people, primary locations and institutions throughout the book. Names of organizations like Astika Agro and Maserio are fictitious. In some cases, I have fashioned a character out of more than one real person, bending the factual to be truthful. Thus, Amitava, Radha-Rokeya, Gouranga-da, Bishu, the Sens, the Guptas and many others exist only on the pages of this book. This also applies to places like Ichhaipur, Seshergram, Adivasipara, Dumurdi and a few others. Two of the hamlets I visited have since been washed away. In our waterborne land, this is in the natural order of things. What remain constant here are just some concepts, an imaginary line or a centre of power, the Border or the Party, always in uppercase.

I made the trips at different times, for over a decade, by boat, bus, train, toddy-palm canoe, vano (motorized tricycle), and a motorcycle on whose rear-view mirror was printed:

OBJECTS IN THE MIRROR ARE CLOSER THAN THEY APPEAR.

In the end, all that has remained with me are some objects – words and images, a glint in the eye and the murmur of a sigh – which got closer and closer until they seeped within me, and began to whisper with each other in the recesses of my memory.

September 2021
Kolkata

I

GANGA, ICHHAMATI, DAMODAR

16 VIDYALANKAR ROAD

'I want to go home,' said Ma, my mother. She had pancreatic cancer, stage four. By home she meant our ancestral house in Gouripur, a small old town forty kilometres from Kolkata, by the river Hooghly. She had spent three-fourths of her life there. 'I want to go home. Take me home!' Ma insisted, a new childlike obstinacy cracking her voice. We, her children and in-laws, debated the merit of her demand until we all agreed that she had a point. Ma had the right to spend her last few days in this world at a place she could claim as her own in the teeth of time. Nobody should snatch it from her. So we shifted her from the aseptic blue hospital to our old house at 16 Vidyalankar Road. We set up a critical-care facility there, as far as practicable, and got in touch with an agency for round-the-clock attendant service. They sent us two women who divided the day between them.

Bharati Das worked the day shifts. In her late twenties and married, she came from Mayapur, a small town one-and-half hours' distance by a suburban train. She was a lively, caring woman who did more than her assigned duty; she'd wash Ma's clothes and sometimes cook a special stew for her. Perhaps this was part of her professional grooming, but soon she wormed her way into Ma's enfeebled heart. And this really mattered. Bharati called her Mashima, aunt, and Ma would wait for her to arrive every morning with lucid expectancy. A rare calm would light up her pain-ravaged face when Bharati propped her up against a bolster and combed the few remaining strands of hair on her scalp and talked with her in a voice that one reserves for little girls.

Relatives and family friends around town were dropping in to see Ma. To see her off actually. A few of them were surfacing after ages. One day, I took out my Handycam to film such a reunion. But I also wanted to archive Ma's fading moments.

Bharati was greatly excited when she saw the fist-sized machine that could capture moving images and sounds in real time, and disgorge them on a tiny screen. But I think what attracted her was the camera's complete refusal to differentiate between the memorable and the banal, between a self-conscious face and a doormat, a well-modulated voice and a chair's leg scratching the floor. The fidelity with which it recorded the antics of our pet cat Ganga moved Bharati and, emboldened, she asked me one day, 'Can it show me as I am, Dada?'

Thus happened the film that I am transcribing here, word for word. I mounted the camera on a stool and turned the LCD screen at her, so that Bharati could watch the recording. This, I guess, prodded her on. It was as if she were speaking to a mirror, a mirror with a memory.

~

I was five when we crossed into India. They called me Alpana on that side. My father gave me this name, Bharati, when we got our ration cards. Bharati – because now we were in Bharat. [*Smiles.*] My two uncles had come before us. They were settled. Their children did their schooling here, they married here. A cousin works in Hyderabad, in the factory that produces Charminar cigarettes. After we crossed the Border, our first stop was at Netajinagar. Have you heard of Netajinagar? It's on a branch line in Nadia district. Netajinagar, Taraknagar, Bankimnagar – halt stations all. Earlier there weren't any, only endless fields and mango orchards. The stations came up when the rifus (refugees) moved in and built hutments inside the orchards. In the beginning, the trains didn't stop. But then men would pull the chain to get off. So what could the rail company do? A halt station with a ticket office is good for everyone, taina? There were snakes in the orchards. And floods. I have seen three floods at Netajinagar. Waist-deep water covered the fields. The *Party* (CPI[M]) gave us *GR* (government relief). We did face floods on the other side, but I have no memory of them. My father pulled a rickshaw there. One day, the Miyas set fire to it. They threatened to torch our house. So we sold off everything and undertook the crossing. [*Takes a pause, wipes her face with the end of her sari.*]

    I studied till Class 4 at the Netajinagar Free Primary School. Then the flood hit. It reduced us to a tarpaulin tent on the railway track. I never returned to school. And then we shifted to Natunpalli. It was a new settlement on a sandbar along the Ganga, of the rifus who came before us. At that time Natunpalli had no school, no road, no pucca building, nothing. Only miles of sand and tall grass everywhere. We built our huts with the grass. The riverbanks were teeming with jackals and monitor lizards. Once a jackal carried off a baby, a girl. I remember it well. The mother was sunning her in the courtyard. She went inside to warm some massage oil and, snap! Not a sign of the baby, only bloodstains on the reed mat. [*Shuts her eyes, shudders.*] There are five weaver families in Natunpalli, the rest are all farmers. Each family has a parcel of land. Land deeds too. Now there's electricity and brick-paved paths. Even a few pucca houses. We grow three crops a year. But these days the return from farming is low. So boys from Natunpalli travel south, to work in *centring* (shuttering, a part of building construction work). My two brothers are now working in Tamil Nadu. But wherever they are, they'll never miss a chance to return at least once a year, during the Baruni Mela.

    You haven't heard of Baruni Mela? [*Eyebrows arched, looks around the camera.*] You know nothing about the Matua? Well, we are the Matua. Call us the Namashudra if you like: low caste. But we were the Brahmins who got duped. It happened a long time ago, and I don't know that history very well. Let me tell you about Baruni Mela instead. Every year, on the tenth day of the month of Choitro in spring, all members of the Matua community, wherever they are, assemble at Thakurnagar, the birthplace of our guru Harichand Thakur. [*Shuts her eyes, brushes her index finger against her silently moving lips.*] It is our biggest festival. People throng from all corners of Bengal, Bihar, Assam, even from across the Border. We in Natunpalli would hire an open truck and set out before daybreak. My brothers would carry drums and rattles, and climb on top of the driver's cabin. No matter where they were, they'd always return to the bhitay (home) on this occasion.

Yes, bhitay. Of course it is our home! [*Sets her arms akimbo, glowers into the camera.*] My father's home was across the Border, in the land of Miyas. I have no memory of it. We stayed briefly in Netajinagar, but it was a transit colony. Where one has a roof of one's own and a plot of land to till, that's a home, taina? So much has happened since we set foot in Natunpalli, one has to see it to believe it. We built everything, bit by bit, with our hands. Now we even have a high school. Issh! Had it been there when I was young!

Can't read English. [*Smiles shyly, bites a corner of her lower lip.*] The school wasn't there when we were young girls.

Before I joined this centre, I used to work in a nursing home. They'd have given me a permanent job if I could read the medicine bottles. So many girls have donned the nurse's uniform after a two-month training. Even in this centre, those who read English have a higher pay.

No, that's not possible any more. [*Shakes her head, looks away from the camera.*] How can I? [*Turns her eyes back to the camera.*] I wake up at four in the morning, bathe, wash clothes, cook and pack my lunch. It takes two hours to reach the centre on a crowded train. Then they say – Go here! Go there! They give us only the bus fare. I return home between eight and nine, or later, if my reliever is late. Then again, a bath and washing the clothes, even in chilly winter, if it is a shitting-pissing case I'm attending. This routine goes upside down when I work the night shifts. How long can I carry on like this? Don't know. Maybe as long as this body will bear.

I stay at my father's place, but I was married once. [*Takes a pause, coils the end of her sari around her index finger.*] I've walked out, my husband has another woman ... This? [*Points to the white shell bangle on her wrist.*] But why shouldn't I keep it? The marriage isn't broken, he pops up from time to time. [*Narrows her eyes, an impish smile twists the corners of her lips.*] For money, what else? Besides, it has its uses. Wicked men are everywhere, even on a sickbed.

A family of my own? Never gave it a thought. But my nephews are growing; the little one is very sharp. I'll send him to an English-medium school, whatever it may cost. Last year, my mother had a kidney stone. I spent eight thousand rupees to get it removed. I hope to build a pucca room one day, so we won't have to move to the school building during a flood. That's all. I wish nothing for me. In this job we can't do ourselves up in style, the Madam will kick us out. She has a temper! [*Puckers her lips and bursts into laughter.*]

~

When Ma was drawing her final breath, Bharati was by her bedside. It seemed she could sniff the scent of death. She asked me to pour a spoonful of Gangajal between Ma's pinched lips seconds before the doctor lost the pulse. Ma was sinking fast, and yet she struggled to fix her pupils on my face. I leaned over her. She attempted to say something, but only a rattle emanated from her larynx. Then it stopped.

'Ma! Ma!' I cried, and each time, a tiny muscle on her brow twitched in response.

Then Bharati touched my wrist. 'Don't call her from behind, Dada,' she whispered. 'You can see, Mashima is faltering on her path.'

I stopped calling and let Ma set off in peace. Her eyes rolled towards the sunlight streaming in through a window and became still. Bharati pinched them shut with her thumb and forefinger, as if she were snuffing out a candle's wick.

Now as I replay the seven-minute recording, something strikes me. Bharati must have had a rich store of experiences that she had gathered in her line of work. But she didn't utter a word of it before the camera. Perhaps her professional ethics forbade her. Or perhaps, for her, the world of sickness and pain and appointments with death was like the dreams that visit us every night and leave with scarcely a trace. Transiting between them, keeping the two worlds apart, was her strategy.

I think of the bonding that had developed, although for a brief period of time, between Bharati and Ma, between a low-caste girl and an old Brahmin lady from an orthodox household. Though not overtly observant herself, Ma had lived almost her entire life in a family where certain codes were taken for granted. It wasn't easy for her to give up the predispositions that had hardened into habits – eating food cooked by a Namashudra woman, for example. Did the weight of approaching death crush these codes? Or was it something else?

Bharati was a rifu. It is an old nickname that people in western Bengal gave to migrants who had crossed the Border. Rifu is also a Bangla word; it means darning. The word has its origin in the Arabic word 'rafu'. Bharati was one among the millions who crisscrossed a land that Partition had torn apart like a fabric, darning it in inconceivable ways.

In a way, Ma too was a migrant who had found refuge at 16 Vidyalankar Road. It had been her in-laws' home, a home with a qualifier. She was not born here. And yet, she had wanted to come back to this address for one last time. Bharati lent a modicum of grace to her final transit.

THE CHORUS WOMEN OF NABADWIP

Oddly, the scene reminded me of a tableau from a Republic Day show on Rajpath: one depicting a flood-hit West Bengal, coming in the wake of a long-range missile and followed by Naga bamboo dancers. About two hundred men and women huddled with their belongings upon a narrow railway platform encircled by water. An entire village appeared to have taken refuge at the obscure halt station in the endless expanse of inundated paddy fields. Men, women, children, cows, goats, poultry, even the neighbourhood dogs. Cots, dressing tables, door frames, a thresher – all wrenched out of their setting and dumped on the concrete platform. The station's name was Samudragarh; it means a fort on the sea. The sight was too pitiful for us to savour the irony.

It was the third week of September, the final phase of the three-month-long monsoon in Gangetic Bengal. A photographer friend and I were carrying relief materials to Nabadwip, an ancient town one hundred and thirty kilometres north of Kolkata, on the west bank of the river Hooghly, also known as the Ganga. We were seeing the flood's havoc an hour after we had left behind the city's urban sprawl. Miles of russet water on both sides of the railway track, with clumps of hyacinths and torn straw roofs eddying about; tree canopies rising above inundated fields; groves of toddy palm dripping with empty weaver-birds' nests. Everything looked desolate. Ten kilometres before Nabadwip, we spotted the first sign of life.

'Look over there!' Nihar-da pointed out into the distance. He offered me the camera with the heavy zoom, with which he was scanning and capturing the scenes.

I could see a figure in chest-deep water: a woman, pushing a banana-trunk raft with pots of drinking water and a child on it, a daily chore constant in the middle of a disaster. And now I could see with naked eyes a few pucca houses, half-submerged, and people stranded on the roofs.

And then our train passed Samudragarh, the fort on the sea. How did it get this name? The sea was at least two hundred and fifty kilometres to the south.

There was no stoppage here, but our train crawled, alerted by the water standing an inch below the track. Scenes of domesticity rolled past the windows: of men lounging, smoking hookah; of women grinding spices on a stone bench, cooking; a girl braiding her hair with a red ribbon, training her eyes at a tiny mirror nailed on a tree; a grizzled old man on a red plastic chair, guarding a baby in a hammock tied to signal posts; children playing hopscotch on flagstones. A village without walls.

A hush fell inside the compartment; all the passengers were peering outside. Nihar-da fiddled with his camera and thrust his heavy torso over my shoulder to find a good frame. The dismal tableau receded slowly.

Nihar Sengupta had worked as a photojournalist with *Soviet Desh*, the Bangla version of the Soviet magazine published worldwide. He lost his job when the USSR fell. Since then, he had developed a passion for sites of disaster, wrought by nature or man. Sometimes I accompanied him on these trips. Over the years, Nihar-da had built an impressive dossier of disaster photographs. Portly, effervescent, with a flowing Karl-Marx beard, he had always been a staunch communist. But of late, perhaps because of the hobby he had picked up, Nihar-da was drifting towards a type of fatalism. Strings of crystal and rudraksha beads now jostled around his neck alongside camera straps.

Kazi received us at Nabadwip. We stepped out of the railway station premises into a ghost settlement. I have known this thousand-year-old town as a labyrinth of narrow lanes winding around decayed, moss-lined houses and unkempt garden plots. But now, the river was flowing right through its heart like an uneasy dream.

'It has been five days, but the water is still rising in some neighbourhoods,' Kazi said. He had come with a boat to take us to the interiors.

In his early thirties, Mushirul Haq, alias Kazi, was a university dropout and the secretary of Churni–Jalangi Bachao Committee. It was a voluntary organization committed to the cause of two tributary rivers of the Hooghly – Churni and Jalangi. His family owned a medicine shop in town, which Kazi manned when he was not busy with his activism. When most of his university friends were occupied with matters of 'high' culture – West Bengal has around thirty amateur cine clubs, two hundred amateur theatre groups and seven hundred amateur literary magazines – Mushirul Haq was running an amateur organization working to save two dying rivers.

∼

Sitting astride the narrow prow of a boat, the camera's protruding lens set off by the mass of grey beard, Nihar-da resembled a grizzled scavenger bird. The situation was worse than we had expected. As our boat glided into the old neighbourhoods, past bazaars and temple complexes, we found the town strangely silent and still. The houses were abandoned and locked. The residents had left or were leaving, on boats and makeshift rafts. Men with rolled-up trousers, bags and boxes around their feet, and women sitting on their heels, clutching their children, faces torn with anxiety. They had waited out a whole week for the water to recede. It hadn't.

'They are not the type who'll shift to a refugee camp,' observed Raghab, our boatman. 'They are going to their relatives' place in Bardhaman or Kolkata.'

'It's an annual affair here,' Kazi said. 'The Ganga floods the old low-lying neighbourhoods. Those who can afford it are leaving the town for good.'

The census reports confirmed his observation. Between 1991 and 2011, among the sixty cities and towns in West Bengal, Nabadwip was the only town that witnessed a negative population growth. The old, decrepit mansions told this story: crumbling brickwork held together by thick banyan roots, rotting wooden slats on balconies, gaping cast-iron railings. Some of the buildings had raised steps at their entrances in the shape of dykes. It didn't help this time. Pools of muddy water stood in arched passageways. As the boat picked its way through the cavernous lanes, the splash of oars echoed in empty, boarded-up rooms.

A wooden chariot of Lord Jagannath stood at a crossing. It was half-submerged in water. A mangy bitch and her three pups had taken shelter on the topmost tier. Kazi tore open a packet of Tiger biscuits and tossed them towards the famished animals. Nihar-da snapped the image.

'Did you observe the current, Kazi-da?' Raghab pointed to a trail of drifting hyacinths. 'The Ganga is flowing directly over this area.'

The Ganga flows south-east across much of north India until it forks near Farakka in West Bengal. One arm flows into Bangladesh, the other, the one that turns south, becomes Bhagirathi-Hooghly, or the Hooghly. But the people in south Bengal still call this distributary the Ganga. Nabadwip, the 'new island', had been the seat of the last Hindu Sena kingdom before Bakhtiyar Khilji established the Bengal Sultanate. It was the birthplace of Sri Chaitanya, the fifteenth-century mystic who started the Bhakti movement in eastern India. The head office of the International Society for Krishna Consciousness, or ISKCON, stood on the opposite bank at Mayapur. The flood had affected both banks.

In normal times, Raghab pedalled a cycle-rickshaw in Nabadwip for a living. From time to time, he was giving us a running commentary on the historical landmarks we were passing, as he did when he took pilgrims on a tour. Sri Chaitanya had spent the first twenty-three years of his life here, and the sites associated with his memory lay all over the town. But the flood had muddled the topography Raghab knew by heart, connecting lanes, squares and backyards in inconceivable ways. After some effort, he resigned to the whims of the water and steered the boat along the current.

For decades, the Hooghly's course had been shifting towards the town. Each year, the hungry river would nibble away at ancient terracotta ghats and temples, and inundate low-lying areas for a couple of days, or even a week, before it would return to its bed like an amenable drunkard.

What if it wouldn't this time?

This had happened before. Rivers in the Bengal Delta had devoured the towns they themselves had spawned and nourished over the centuries; or had moved away and abandoned them forever. Five hundred years ago, during Sri Chaitanya's time, the Ganga had veered away from its old course, leaving Gaur, the capital of Bengal during the Middle Ages, to die a slow death.

After an hour's wandering, the sun on the water and vapours rising from it wove a haze inside my head. I had a surreal vision of three bare-chested priests in a boat, cradling in their arms painted wooden images of Lord Jagannath and his siblings.

'What happened?' Kazi called out.

'The temple sanctum is flooded,' the elderly priest, his forehead smeared with sandalwood paste, said. 'It is now chest-deep inside.'

The plump, well-fed bodies of the three men were in contrast to the painted idols, faded and dressed in worm-eaten finery. After a century's residence inside a temple's dark womb, the idols were now contemplating the flooded town with startled, disc-shaped eyes. Nihar-da's camera recorded the scene: the evacuation of the gods.

We heard a shuffle of feet and prayers mumbled overhead. Five old women dressed in white saris leaned out from the first-floor balcony of a decayed two-storeyed house. They threw coins and touched their tonsured heads, dusted with grey like bur flowers, on the railing in obeisance. The priests fielded the coins and returned a grateful smile. The pious women, their faces luminous in the light reflected off the water, looked despondent.

The gods were departing. The neighbourhood was turning desolate. We moored our boat below the staircase.

'Why are you still here?' Kazi demanded.

'Where shall we go? This is our ashram,' one of them replied.

It was a hostel of eleven aged widows. They were living out their lives in this holy town, awaiting release from the cycle of rebirth. Floodwater had entered the ground-floor rooms; the boarders had shifted upstairs.

'They have evacuated everyone in this neighbourhood. Aren't you facing difficulties?'

Shrivelled faces cracked into toothless smiles.

'No problem here, bachha. A servant boy brings drinking water every day. And we have our stock of dry food.'

'Yes, child. We have enough chinray (pressed rice) to see us through a month. Then there's the boy who brings us the drinking water. What else do we need?'

'Hasn't a relief team come this way?' Kazi asked.

'Yes, it did. They wanted to give us relief materials, but we refused. We have enough. What more do we need?'

'What else do we need? We are old people.'

'Even then they insisted.'

'Yes, they also wanted to shift us to a relief camp. They said they'd return us when the water turns. But where shall we go? We have been living here for so long. The gods are here.'

'We don't have many years left. Why should we go now? The gods are here.'

'We have lived in this ashram for so long, seen so many floods. The gods are here, they'll look after us.'

They were like chorus women in a play: each picked up the thread of words from the other, added her own, and continued to string a prayer bead.

'The gods left just now,' Raghab quipped. 'On a boat.'

'Don't say that, bachha,' chided one of them, opening her mouth wide in mock horror.

'Never utter such unlucky words, son,' said another. 'The gods live here.' She touched a garland of tulsi stems around her withered neck. 'And there.'

She pointed her finger to an alcove cut into the wall. In it there were tiny stone images decked with vermilion and dried flowers. A fig tree growing outside on the cornices had shot forth a filigree of roots. Black moss spotted the limewashed plaster on the walls – it was dark and dank. Grass mats and rolled-up bedding lined the red stone floor. Pots of chyavanprash, religious books, a blue cloth-bound almanac, and terracotta water pots, their long necks capped with upturned bronze tumblers, were laid out on windowsills. A red telephone sat affectedly on a stool in the corner. It was out of order.

Many of them had children living in distant cities, we learnt. They also received money orders, but not every one of them. Interests accrued on deposits in the ashram's trust met their regular maintenance.

Electric-supply men had cut off the power lines when water reached the roadside transformers. One of the women had a fever. We gave paracetamol tablets. A tall widow with an aquiline nose proceeded to crush a tablet on a small stone mortar.

'What are you doing?' Kazi protested. 'She must swallow it whole.'

'That's impossible, son,' the woman said. 'She can't swallow any hard substance, doesn't pass down her throat.'

She mixed the powdered tablet with a drop of honey and smeared the paste on the sick woman's pinched lips. Then she leaned over her and whispered, 'Lick it up, Didi. It's medicine.'

The pale face remained motionless, the eyes were closed. Finally, the lips parted and the tip of a tongue slithered out.

The nurse and her patient looked the same age. But their physical features, and the fabrics of the white sari they wore, hinted at a division of class. This was also discernible among the rest of them. Perhaps this had to do with the subscription one could donate, or the frequency of phone calls one received. And yet, as the fag end of life closed in on them like floodwater, they held on to one another in an ardent embrace.

'Did you stock up the dry food in anticipation of the flood?' I asked.

'No. We keep a stock round the year. Sometimes the money orders are late. Sometimes the boy takes leave to go to his village.'

'Yes, we keep a stock. We are old people. How much do we need?'

'How much do we eat? It's like birdfeed.'

Ancient chorus women, well prepared to live out their twilight days, even in the middle of a calamity. We gave them biscuits and a phial of chlorine. Their faces beamed.

'How much do we need? But we'll accept your gifts. The gods sent you here.'

'Yes, lord Gouranga sent you here.'

They shuffled up to the head of the stairwell to bid us goodbye. The bony frames hunched forward, delicate and alert, necks craned. They resembled a flock of jacanas.

'Jai Gouranga Mahaprabhu!'

They raised their arms to bless us. The white saris flapped like wings.

'Jai Gouranga Mahaprabhu!'

A BOY'S STORY

Moments before her death, her eyes fixed on my face, Ma had called out the first syllable of a name that only she and I knew: Apu. It was the name she had chosen for me before I was born. But I wasn't given this name.

'That's an unlucky name,' Thamma, my grandmother, had declared. 'Boys with that name are fated to have an unhappy life.'

Apu, the fictional hero in Bibhutibhushan Bandyopadhyay's novels *Pather Panchali* (The Song of the Road) and *Aparajito* (The Unvanquished), is a poor Brahmin's son who grows up with his sister in the lush green surroundings of a village in Bengal. Unrelenting poverty marks their lives. His sister dies of malaria; the family shifts to Benares, where his father too dies. Apu, a callow boy now, returns with his mother to the village and begins to work as a priest. But he is bright and ambitious, and despite all the hardships, goes to Calcutta for higher studies. His mother dies, and a series of misfortunes hounds Apu throughout his adult life.

I never found out if Thamma had read the novels, or had seen Satyajit Ray's films based on them. But after my grandfather's death, Thamma was the unchallenged matriarch of 16 Vidyalankar Road. Ma's presence there was like that of a silent shadow. But she had built around her a world of her own with a few ordinary things: books from a neighbourhood lending library, a popular literary magazine named *Nabokallol* which the newspaper boy delivered every month, and a Murphy radio set. After I began to go to school, Ma assigned me the duty of going to the public library twice every week to bring books, mostly novels and travelogues, for her.

Even at that age, I could guess that the name I was never given, Apu, had come to her from a book.

Much later did I learn that my grandfather used to encourage Ma's passion for reading. There was much sourness between him and his wife, and perhaps that was why Thamma suspected anything that came from books. She had outright rejected the name her son's wife had wished to give her grandson.

But sometimes, in brief moments of intimacy during my childhood, Ma would address me as Apu. Those were exclusive moments between a mother and son, rare, and filled with a feathery light. Perhaps Ma had wanted to evoke that light one last time by calling me Apu. But she spent her breath before her lips could get together to intone the second syllable.

~

When it comes to naming children, Apu has never been particularly popular in Bengal. And yet, for nearly a century, Apu has remained the most popular fictional character in Bangla literature, more popular than Gora or Devdas, the eponymous heroes of the two famous novels by Rabindranath Tagore and Sarat Chandra Chattopadhyay respectively. Gora is a foreigner by birth, an idealist, and Devdas is a profligate, whose undying devotion to his childhood love cannot salvage his image. Apu, in contrast, is essentially a boy next door, and he best symbolizes the aspirations of the educated Bengali middle class. Generations of men have seen their dreams reflected in Apu's youthful ambitions. In his attachment to the beauty of rural Bengal, generations of migrants uprooted by Partition have found a home for their nostalgia. In his wide-eyed fascination for Calcutta, too, the cosmopolitan longings of middle-class Bengalis have found a mirror. Apu's move from the village to the city, his devotion to learning, his ambition to rise above his situation through education, even the muddle of his later life, sum up the story of the bhadralok – educated urban middle-class and mostly upper-caste Hindus that emerged in Bengal during the nineteenth century.

I come from this class. Like Apu, I am a Brahmin's son, and my father was a teacher. But the parallels end there. I didn't grow up in a village, nor did I face such hardships and loss so early in life.

My first encounter with Apu was through an abridged version of his story. Satyajit Ray, who would later make the famous Apu trilogy, had illustrated the book. It was titled *Am Antir Bhenpu*, A Mango-seed Whistle, and it is here that I met my hero for the first time. I had barely begun to learn the alphabet then. In a square tin box where I kept my drawing books, abacus and other toys, there was this illustrated storybook that someone had gifted me a little prematurely. But what fascinated me most during that unlettered phase of my life were the black-and-white drawings by Ray that I can still recall vividly, more black than white and drawn like woodcut prints. They depicted the adventures of a small boy and her older sister. I cannot remember exactly when that little book began to cast a spell on me. Perhaps it was during the long summer afternoons in the preschool days when all members of the household would be taking a siesta. I'd sit on the cool red stone floor of a shuttered room and turn the pages of the book, to kill the endless hours when the sun blazed outside and nothing stirred, until each detail in the pictures imprinted itself in my memory. The shadings became the shadows under the deep stairwell of our ancient house, through which the whiteness of the paper oozed, like light seeping through dust-coated windowpanes. There were trees massed up behind thatched mud huts, a hair-parting path rambling across village fields, with a bullock cart on it, and a row of toddy palms that resembled toy fans sold in fairs. There was also a goddess with a betel-leaf face glowing amid dark brambles. By the following summer, if I remember correctly, the rows of mute letters that had appeared like a marching army of black ants began to speak to me. I learnt to read.

I read the unabridged novel much later. Before that, I saw the movie, alternately perching on the knees of my mother and an aunt, and peering over a row of dark heads. It was a matinee show in a movie house in our small town. I was too young then to grasp the visual language of cinema, to make a story out of successive picture frames projected on a screen. What has stayed with me from that adventure, though, is the scene of pouring rain and a girl dancing in it and swinging her head full of long, thick hair, like a spirit. And then she died and morphed into a spirit, and her young brother was walking along a village path with an oversized umbrella tucked under his arm, like a grown-up man.

That is all I remember of my first viewing of *Pather Panchali*. It was already a classic, released nine years before I was born.

THE SWAMPS

Holding an oyster mushroom between his thumb and forefinger, feeling the texture of its flared hood, Anil uncle, whom I called Kaka, was reminiscing:

'There was a time when village women would pick these things in the marshes and bring them to the bazaar. They'd collect wild figs, a variety of greens, tortoise eggs and small fish. The types of fish we used to get in East Bengal, those you won't find here any more. Do you see those women now? You don't. Why not? That's because the marshes have vanished. The shrub jungles too, that once bordered this town. All gone. There was a time when these wetlands connected the rivers.'

Kaka was talking to himself.

'Is that when Kolkata belonged to the Sundarbans?' I chipped in.

'Oh no, not that long ago!' He turned to me and smiled. 'Waterfowl would nest there in winter. Sometimes we'd get their meat in the bazaar, sweet and decked with pearls of fat. I can still remember the taste on my tongue.'

For many years, Kaka's day would begin with a visit to the bazaar. Dressed in a lungi and a front-open vest, he'd drift around the honeycomb of the old market and the vegetable stalls that spilled into the lanes behind it. But for him, shopping was an excuse, and most of the time he didn't even carry a shopping bag, because Kaka lived alone and took his meals from a neighbourhood catering service. Perhaps the cornucopia of greens and fish connected him with memories of a village he had left during his teens, at the time of Partition. But there were other attractions. Kaka would chat with the shop owners, the fish sellers, the greengrocers, and more particularly, the farmers who brought their produce every morning from the surrounding villages. After about an hour spent this way, he'd walk to a roadside tea shop to have his morning breakfast of toast and poached eggs, and have another round of adda with the daily-wage labourers who'd assemble there at that hour. This way, Kaka would glean all the news of the world that he cared for the most, before he returned home to read four newspapers and keep tabs on the bhadralok world.

Two years ago, a stroke paralysed the left side of his body. It robbed him of this routine and confined him to his tiny, rented government flat. A caregiver came daily to look after him. Anil Kaka, my father's distant cousin, was in his early seventies and a bachelor. For most of his life, he had remained a card-holding member of the Communist Party of India (Marxist) (CPI[M]). He gave up his membership soon after his party came to power in West Bengal. That was in 1977.

When I was a young boy, these women were still around. I remember them sitting out in the open on their haunches, in a vacant lot behind the market, selling dried fish and other rare items. A gut-wrenching smell would hang in the air there, and I hated to go to that part of the market. But the women fascinated me. They reminded me of the woodcut images on the pages of *Am Antir Bhenpu*. Most of them were widows; they wore mud-coloured saris and garlands of tulsi stems, and had nicotine-stained teeth. During the rains, they'd hold broad arum leaves over their heads. To my immature eyes, they were the closest intimations of the village greens, fields of white kans grass, bullock carts rolling on hair-parting paths and toy-fan toddy palms that made up Apu's world.

When I was old enough to visit the marshes on the eastern margins of my home town, the shallow waterbodies that were connected to the endless lowlands of eastern Kolkata and stretched all the way to the Sundarbans, that ecosystem had almost vanished. The women who collected curious food items there had also vanished. Afterwards, when I tried to recast my childhood memories of them on the frame of my later experiences, I realized that these old women were outcasts who lived mostly on their own, without a family to look after them. These marshlands had existed for centuries, since land had emerged out of the network of rivers and creeks on this Delta. They were part of the village commons, a vital support system for the old, hapless people cast away by their families and society. Sometimes these places were also their last refuge, where they'd go to die, as Apu's aunt Indir Thakrun had done. During a famine – and there had been a series of famines in Bengal since the eighteenth century, since British rule began – the edible roots and clams that thrived in the marshes had saved entire communities, particularly the landless lower-caste people.

Following the birth of Bangladesh in 1971, the refugees who crossed the border set up their colonies on the lowlands east of Gouripur. The land that was left, where the women collected mushrooms and clams to sell in the local bazaar, vanished twenty years later when an expressway was built. Brick kilns, cowsheds, residential colonies and small factories took over. The dim outline of a new township rose in the distance.

Since last week, this lowland with its refugee colonies and parts of the new township had been under water. It was early October. The sky had cleared; the monsoon season was officially over. And yet, the Hooghly had swelled well above the danger mark. Like an accident victim recovering old memories, the river sought out the lost creeks and canals, revived reclaimed marshes, flooded the new settlements and attacked our river-facing town from the rear. A huge volume of water released from the barrage at Farakka had wreaked this havoc.

Every year, for around three months, Gangetic Bengal attracts heavy rains. By the end of September, all its rivers and waterbodies become full, and the earth turns soggy, like a piece of bread dropped in tea. At that time, if a cloudburst over north Bihar joins forces with a high lunar tide in the Bay of Bengal, it's a recipe for catastrophe – not only for the districts but also for Kolkata and its suburbs.

It was Radha, Kaka's caregiver, who brought the bad news. She lived in a slum on the edge of the marshes. She filled us in with daily updates on the flood.

I went one afternoon to see with my own eyes. It was a surreal scene: the sky was a pea-flower blue spangled with silver clouds, and under it roiled the floodwaters. A refugee colony was evacuating. Furious men and women were cursing the government for opening the barrage gates in the early morning hours. The evening before, there was a warning broadcast over the radio. No one knew what to do with a statutory announcement that measured water in cusecs – cubic feet per second. Nobody could figure how to uncouple volume from time in a unit of measurement; nobody knew which areas would sink first. So they waited out the long night as the drainage canals swelled and searched out the forgotten swamps and hollows. The men, women and children waited with bated breath and prayed to Shanidev, the blue-skinned god who rides a crow, the god of wrath. Many could hear a strange subterranean tapping as the Hooghly began to reclaim lost territory. They spent a sleepless night huddled inside flimsy hutments, raising cots on bricks and climbing on them. Then they clambered up on to the bamboo rafters and watched helplessly as the surging water gurgled around dug-out ovens, eddied and leapt across door frames, setting pots and pans adrift. And still, it was rising.

Now they were abandoning the site. They were taking apart the dwellings and packing everything, working like a disciplined army. The men had climbed on to the roofs and were dismantling the terracotta tiles. Women, standing in waist-deep water, were busy piling the tiles on makeshift rafts. An entire colony was being taken apart and stacked up in heaps, with children on top clutching live poultry, pet cats and green gourd creepers ripped from roof thatches. All were heading to a new colony site. Transiting. Transplanting.

I stood on a culvert and watched. An almost naked man was riding an inflated car tube. He had a gamchha, a rough hand-spun towel, wound around his head like a pugree. The man was driving the tube with his arms like a coracle, driving it towards the culvert. In the crook of his lap rested a cane basket full of tittering chicks and a bunch of mushrooms. These were oyster mushrooms, dark brown on the edges, a variety I hadn't seen since my childhood visits to the bazaar.

'Will you sell them?' I said, pointing to the mushrooms.

'You want 'em? Take 'em!' He beamed a cheery smile and began to dry his limbs with the gamchha. 'These were growing under the bamboo floor of my hut. I found them when I was pulling apart the frame.'

I gave him twenty rupees and took the mushrooms to Kaka's flat.

~

'Last night I had a dream,' Anil Kaka said. He was reclining on his bed, still holding the mushroom between his fingers, like a flower. 'I dreamt that the Hooghly had gone dry. There was only a wide sand bed with cactus bushes and skeletons of boats. A thin, black stream ran down the middle; animal carcasses were drifting on it. I saw people living under the Howrah Bridge, under upturned boats. I saw it all so vividly – even a paper kite stuck on a thorny tree. And hooch dens and burning tyres, and dark human figures sitting around a fire.'

Beads of sweat glistened on Kaka's forehead; his eyes were closed. The stroke had twisted part of his left chin and his lips flapped sometimes when he talked. But this couldn't rob him of his dusky good looks, which still marked his high cheekbones, thick silver hair, and a thin nose. Some men retained aspects of their early youth even in old age, and I could imagine Anil Kaka during his youthful years.

Anil Banerjee was seventeen when he came to newly independent India from a village in eastern Bengal. Although I had always been told that he was my father's distant cousin, the bloodline that connected them was tenuous. That was because all our relatives from my father's side were ghoti – that is, from the western part of Bengal. Kaka was a bangal, an East Bengali. He had been close to my father since their college days, but he came to stay with us in our house during the Emergency in 1975. Everywhere, the communists were being thrown into jails, and Kaka was offered shelter in our home. I was eleven, and I was thrilled to discover our house being turned into the *underground*. It didn't take me long to take to this mild-mannered man, wanted by the police and living incognito with us. Much later did I learn that my grandfather had sympathies for the communists. This was a discovery, because men of his generation in our town were deeply suspicious of the faith system developed by beef-eating sahibs, which corrupted the minds of bright men from orthodox Brahmin families and made them throw away their sacred threads.

This time, Thamma didn't disagree with her husband. That was because Anil Banerjee was also a Brahmin.

When the Communist Party of India (CPI) split in 1964, Kaka had joined the breakaway CPI(M). This was a mistake, because the theoretical ambience of the CPI, the parent party, suited his temperament. Kaka's intellectualism and growing cynicism alienated him from the Party after it began its rule in our state. He gave up his membership.

He now stretched before me on his back as the evening shadows gathered inside the room. There was a power cut, and Radha entered the room with a lighted candle. Kaka opened his eyes and turned to look at me.

'I guess I saw that dream because of the things I've been reading in the newspapers. Experts are warning that the Ganga might bypass the barrage at Farakka and find an alternative course to connect directly with the Padma. If that happens, our Hooghly will dry up. Do you think the squatters will then go and live right in the middle of the riverbed?'

Kaka spoke in a thick voice, as if he had just woken up from a deep sleep. He was still in the grip of that nightmare.

'They will,' I said. 'If they can live on a drainage canal, then why not on a riverbed?'

'Hmm. But why didn't they dredge up the canals? Parts of this town have been under water for six days now. Can you imagine the suffering? Radha has to wade through waist-deep water every day to reach here. Tell me, what is *your* government doing?'

Since I had joined a government college as an assistant professor, Kaka had made it a habit of hauling me up whenever he had an axe to grind against the system. Sometimes, this irritated me.

'Who can dare to touch even a single shanty to dredge the canals, Kaka?' I shot back. 'It was *your* Party that allowed them to squat there. And here you are, getting nostalgic about duck meat and tortoise eggs.'

'*My* Party?' Kaka looked hurt.

'Your *ex*-Party.' I gave him a wry smile. 'Who started the land reforms and settled these uninhabited lowlands?'

'Don't speak like an idiot!' Kaka shook his head slowly. 'Putting it that way isn't fair.'

He propelled his torso up from the bed with his right arm. In stark contrast to his limp left arm, his right arm was strong and muscular, like that of a tennis player.

'Don't mix it up with what was a historic duty thrust upon us. When Partition struck, the government in Delhi supervised a transfer of property in the Punjab provinces. Nothing of that sort happened here in Bengal. You have read about those harrowing times in books, but I was a victim. Millions were pouring in every day. Where would they live? What would they eat? The central and state governments didn't lift a finger for the hungry millions without a roof over their head. The Congress party did nothing, the Jan Sangh did nothing. Only the communists stood by their side. We helped them organize, demand basic human rights and cobble together a new life from the wreckage of Partition.'

I was impatient. 'But Kaka, land reforms also reclaimed all the low-lying wetlands.'

'It was a historic struggle,' he went on. 'Not just for a piece of land. It was a struggle for an identity, for a life of dignity. It was a struggle to build a new nation.'

I had heard him recite this litany before. Many times.

'But we were talking about the flood, taina?' I persisted. 'What about those floodplains? In normal times, they'd remain fallow and covered in shrub jungles, where the outcast women would go to pick mushrooms and clams. During a flood, these floodplains would save the surrounding villages and towns. They'd even save the poor during a famine.'

Kaka wasn't listening. His face was flushed and his eyes were focused on the grey mushroom between his fingers.

'In 1971, history turned a cycle. Another flood of refugees, another fight for survival, of organizing the people to get them justice. Nothing had changed in these years. Only the name they used to call these people had changed. In 1947, they called us rifus; now we were calling the border-crossers "shoronarthis", asylum seekers. This was our success. A change of perception, an element of compassion. And that was important. But this time it was more difficult. Already there was pressure on land, the industries were sick. And then, six years later, the Left Front came to power. Our first job was to avert a humanitarian disaster. The land reforms began right away. The amount of excess and benami land we distributed to the landless in the first ten years is a record of sorts. It was more than the sum total of land redistributed in the entire country after Independence. But that was not an end. It was only a beginning. It should have been a beginning.'

Kaka's lips flapped, his speech slurred. But he continued. He wasn't addressing his words at me, it seemed, but to a part of his own self, perhaps the part that had gone limp from shoulder down. It could not respond, but only pulsed in mute rage.

The power cut was over. Radha padded in and switched on the light. She then snuffed out the candle by pinching the burning wick with her thumb and forefinger. She saw the mushrooms heaped upon the bedside table.

'Where did you find them?' She beamed at me.

I told her about my visit to the flooded colony.

'All the ponds in our area have flooded. We caught some fish this morning with mosquito nets, mostly katla and koi. This big!' Radha indicated their size with her palm, and then turned to Anil Kaka. 'Let me change your shirt, Kaka-babu? You've been wearing this since morning.'

Kaka raised his right arm like an obedient child. Radha opened his shirt buttons with nimble fingers, daubed talcum powder on his shoulders with a puff, and covered the flesh, still flushed in residual excitement, with a white cotton kurta.

~

The road leading out of the Housing Board residential colony into the centre of town was under knee-deep water. I took Feeder Road. It was a Saturday and life followed its normal evening rhythm in the market area. People were milling around brightly lit shops, roadside food stalls were doing a brisk business, the air was heavy with the smell of soy sauce and fried onion. Who'd imagine another part of the town was reeling under a flood?

I collected my packed dinner from an eatery and plodded back to the desolate Vidyalankar Road. It was pitch dark; our neighbourhood had had no power supply since morning. A small grey serpent coiled around the doorknob, its beady eyes gleaming under the torchlight. I took a side door. Nobody was home. In fact, almost the entire neighbourhood was empty. Dogs barked in an empty house. These were mongrels; they had probably slipped inside through a window that someone had carelessly left open. Rows of shuttered houses amplified their howls. A yellow moon hung overhead, casting its reflection on standing water. The dogs fell silent for a few minutes, and then began all over again. Were they agitated by the ghostly moonlight? Or was hunger and end-of-season lust clawing at their mangy bellies?

I climbed to our first-floor balcony opening on to the road and lit a cigarette. Candlelight flickered in a few neighbourhood windows. The dogs were now hushed; I could hear the gurgle of water in roadside gutters. A low tide had begun in the Hooghly.

I attempted to recreate in my mind the nightmare Anil Kaka was narrating: of the Ganga changing its course, bypassing the big dam at Farakka; the Hooghly turning bone dry and dead; cacti on sands, and a frayed kite stuck in a thorny berry tree; a ribbon of black, scummy water and dead animals drifting on it; vultures roosting atop the Howrah Bridge and humans squatting under it inside abandoned boats.

My imagination failed to hold on to the murky images. The memory of Radha replaced them. I remembered her clean nut-brown skin, her cotton sari neatly pleated and pinned at the shoulder; I remembered her erect shoulder blades and her muscular arms covered with fine hair. I remembered the way she snuffed out the burning candle with her thumb and forefinger. I remembered

Bharati Das. She had closed Ma's eyes in exactly the same fashion, a second after her death.

Radha's actual name was Rokeya, and she lived in one of the canal-side slums. Kaka had once told me the story of her life. When Rokeya was fifteen, a group of men from a nearby slum kidnapped and raped her. The slum committee, a quasi-political entity that negotiated with various government agencies on behalf of the slum dwellers, called a meeting and married Rokeya off to one of her rapists. She gave birth to a girl. And then, within a year of the marriage, her husband melted away. He had slipped into Bangladesh, they said. Rokeya became a caregiver. She was much in demand in her line of work because she was a very efficient and responsible girl.

For nearly a week, swathes of our town remained waterlogged. But Radha never missed work.

A WATER SUTRA

Two months after my last visit to Nabadwip, I went there again. This time I was alone. I was working on a project on primary education, and I wanted to study the impact of a natural calamity on school dropouts. It was Kazi who put me in touch with the headmistress of Harishpur Balika Vidyalaya, a girls' school in a village on the outskirts of Nabadwip town. I had wanted to visit a school in Natunpalli, the village on the mudflats where Bharati Das, Ma's caregiver, had her home. These mudflats were called 'char'. But Kazi informed me that there were more than a dozen such char villages by that name around Nabadwip and Mayapur, and it was impossible to locate that village without more specific information on block or mouza level. There were Natunpalli, Natungram, Nabapalli, Nabagram, Nayachar ... all having the same meaning – a new habitat. In fact, Nabadwip itself meant a new island. Also, the name the settlers gave to a new village sometimes differed from the one by which the old residents of surrounding areas called it. After some enquiring, Kazi referred me to this particular school because most of its pupils came from settlements on the mudflats.

I rode a suburban train from Kolkata, the same train that had taken me to Nabadwip two months before. It was now November, the day was pleasant and sunny. Brown farmlands stretched to the horizon, splotched with blinding yellow mustard fields. The cottages set in them appeared newly thatched and spruced up. The flood seemed a distant memory.

But not quite. I found sixteen families staying inside the premises of Harishpur Balika Vidyalaya. This was the remnant of a refugee camp. The families were from a char village where the floodwaters hadn't receded. But the board examinations were a few weeks away, and classes had resumed for the girls who'd appear in the exams.

It was a disturbing sight. Patient rows of girls in blue-bordered white saris inside the classroom, struggling to figure out the workings of the human metabolic system from a diagram the teacher had drawn on the blackboard. The piercing cry of a baby and the aroma of cumin seeds sizzling in hot oil came from the other wing. There were also other smells – a cocktail of odours that included the stench of sweat, baby urine, rotting foodgrains, musty clothes, stale beedi smoke and other undefinable emanations. Two worlds, separated by a line of washing and salvaged things – cots, almirahs, terracotta tiles and bamboo screens.

'This isn't the first time we are doing this,' the headmistress said. She was a plump, pleasant-looking woman with greying hair and black-rimmed spectacles that lent her soft, round face a befitting gravitas. 'The flood affects the low-lying areas here, and we open our school building almost every year. This usually coincides with the Durga Puja vacation. This year, though, it's been really bad. Some areas are still waterlogged. But what to do? We must finish the syllabus before the exams, taina?'

Twenty-three girls were braving the noise and odour of a refugee camp to carry on with the business of learning. Not all of them were present, though.

'This is another problem,' the lady confessed. 'After every long recess or natural calamity, when the school reopens, there will be a fall in attendance. You can check for yourself.'

From a wooden cupboard, she pulled out an old attendance register and turned the pages. Rows of boxes marked with 'P' tapered off into dots and finally joined to become unbroken red lines. They resembled the terminal pulsing of a heart printed on an ECG report.

I turned to the names on the left column: Rekha Duley, Moumita Mondal, Baisakhi Halder, Jinnat Khatun – the surnames told the girls' backward caste and community origins. But nothing more. The headmistress, too, couldn't give more information.

The person who could, was present inside the building, in that other world across the line of washing. I was lucky.

Nitu Saha was the secretary of the school management committee and a leader of the local gram panchayat. A dark, stocky man with a shining pate and a big tummy protruding from his front-open vest, he looked to be around forty-five. When we searched him out, he was busy supervising the preparation of khichuri bubbling in a huge iron kadai. Sidekicks hung around him. Seeing Kazi with me, Nitu Saha's brows creased with suspicion. I introduced myself and explained to him the purpose of my visit.

Saha smiled standoffishly.

'You could have met some of the girls missing in the classroom if you had come two weeks ago.' He lit a cigarette and took a deep puff. 'They had taken shelter in *my* school. This year we shifted forty-two families. Most have returned home. Now they are busy – repairing the cottages, cleaning up homestead lands, preparing the plots for the robi crop. It's a lot of work. Some have lost their cattle, some have lost everything. Those who don't own land will find no work in the village for the next few months. They'll migrate to other states. These girls shall run the household. A few shall go to towns as housemaids. They'll return home before the month of Choitro. The money they earn will buy them a pair of goats, as investments, or a pair of gold earrings for their wedding. A few of them will never return.'

Nitu Saha reeled this out with a folkloric assurance. He knew *his* world inside out.

Kazi chipped in, 'The flood is an annual visitor here. Can't you spare the school and make alternative arrangements?'

Saha wagged his index finger at him.

'You see, *Mister*,' he snapped, 'you town-babus don't understand the realities. You run some fancy club with a fancy cause and think you know everything.'

Kazi flashed a wry smile and shut his mouth. He was used to the jibes that men such as Nitu Saha reserved for workers like him.

Saha turned to me.

'Our foremost priority is human lives. Then we'll think of livestock, then the lands, and then comes lyakapora.'

Being primarily a panchayat leader, lyakapora – reading and writing, or education – stood fourth in Nitu Saha's list of concerns. It was men like him who had established the settlements on mudflats and other vested lands, set up village-level communities, bargained with government agencies, and mobilized local resources to build schools, dispensaries and other facilities. This had given him the power to decide the sequence of priorities.

Some of the girls would never return, he said.

Back to school? Back to their homes? I didn't get the chance to ask Saha any more questions because the khichuri was ready. He gave directions as two men filled up plastic buckets with the steaming yellow gruel. The warm smell had stirred up the torpid air inside the school building. Children jostled to sit in a row in the corridor, on bare concrete floor. The clang of ladles scraping the iron kadai roused the old people curled up inside classrooms. They rummaged through their belongings for bowls and plates, and queued up before a handpump. Within minutes, the entire wing was transformed into a big, noisy household. A house without walls, wrenched out of a riverbank and planted inside a public building.

Or one could mistake it for a Kumbh Mela tent, packed with pilgrims waiting for a holy dip. Waiting: for the men and women here, it was not a stasis, not a suspension of activities, but a state of being with its own varieties of rhythms – waiting for the crops to ripen, for the rains to come, for kerosene or voter ID cards, for

Border Security Force (BSF) men at the border checkpost to slacken vigil. Waitings pulsed in the bloodstream.

Now they were waiting for the floodwaters to withdraw.

Kazi asked around to find out if anyone was from Natunpalli. I scanned the women milling about the courtyard, half hoping to spot Bharati Das among them. It had been three years since I'd last seen her. Perhaps Bharati had finally built a pucca room.

Two married women from neighbouring settlements greeted each other in the food queue.

'How are things at your place, Didi?' said one, pushing back the sari from over her head.

The other woman had a naked baby boy astride her lap. He had boils all over his body.

'My elder son went on the relief party's boat yesterday to have a look. The land around the cottages has risen, but the fields are still under waist-deep water.'

'Then it's not that bad, sister. In our area, it's still chest-deep.'

Water: chest-deep, waist-deep, knee-deep. The human body turned into a measuring scale. Also in various postures of stasis. Stretched on bare concrete floor, an arm folded across the eyes, curled up sideways, or sitting on the haunches with hands hanging against folded knees. They talked endlessly about the whim of the water, about when it would retreat – and how – and about when it would give them back their land. Cast away from it, the land was never far from their mind.

But the person who had the deepest knowledge on the subject couldn't be found in the rows of men sitting on the floor with empty plates before them. Kazi searched him out at the rear of the building, on a patch of lawn near the boundary wall. He was repairing a small fishing net. Dressed in a blue lungi, bare-chested, he sat hunched over the net, one leg folded up against his chest and the other stretched forward, with a coil of blue nylon thread around his big toe. He was a dark, wiry man of uncertain age, anywhere between forty and fifty, with shoulder-length hair and a furrowed face. His name was Nakul Sardar, and he was from Srikrishnapur village.

'Aren't you having lunch?' Kazi offered him a beedi.

Nakul tucked the beedi behind his ear. 'It's my fucking stomach. If I eat that khichuri, it won't give me time to bare my arse.' He remained silent for a minute, his fingers busy with the threads, and looked up at us. 'Can't these buggers just give us the provisions and allow us to cook? What's the harm?'

'Did you ask them?' Kazi enquired.

'Many times. But Saha-babu won't listen.'

'What are they saying?'

'Oh, they talk of fire hazards and this and that. As if we don't know how the relief money is being spent!' Nakul mumbled and, after a pause, added, 'That apart, the arrangements aren't bad. There's drinking water, toilets, and safety for women.'

'Isn't this your second year in this camp?' Kazi asked.

'Third.' Nakul twisted the corner of his lips.

I attempted to come up with suitable words of sympathy, but he cut me short.

'You see, babu, we are settlers on the char. Can we afford to be scared of a flood? Floods quicken the soil, give us a good harvest. But these days they rush in too quickly, don't give us the time to take down everything and move to higher ground. It wasn't like this before.'

'Why?' I asked him. 'Why are the floods behaving like this?'

Nakul pointed a finger at Kazi and, with a faint smile on his lips, said, 'He knows.'

'The irrigation department is building bunds everywhere,' Kazi explained. 'They often get breached. And since they began mining sand from the riverbed with pumps, erosion has increased.'

'Yes, bhangon!' Nakul declared. 'Chunks of land vanishing into the river in the blink of an eye.'

'Isn't the gram panchayat doing anything about it?' I asked.

'They are a bunch of gandus!' Nakul cursed.

'There's big money here,' Kazi said. 'Every day, two hundred trucks carry away the sand. All head to Rajarhat New Town. Those who lose their land in the river go there as construction workers. It's these sand contractors who get them the jobs.'

Nakul turned a pair of muddy eyes on me. 'Come to our village this winter. I will show you how we are being fucked both ways, in the mouth and up the arse!'

Then, realizing that he had spilled too much before a stranger, Nakul clammed up. I watched his deft fingers working the thread.

'Do you catch fish with this net?' I asked.

Nakul nodded vaguely.

'So you are a fisherman?'

'I farm when I have land, else I catch fish. I also work in brickfields. My plot of land is now under knee-deep water.'

'When will it recede?'

Nakul Sardar looked up and scrutinized me for a second. He laid aside the net, picked up the beedi from behind his ear, and lit up. Then, between swirls of smoke, he reeled out an astonishingly detailed jal-sutra, a water chronicle. He narrated how the flood had already withdrawn and parcels of land had emerged, how the ebbing had washed away the topsoil, rousing the dormant creeks and bogs, and how these waterbodies had re-established long-forgotten links with the river. Then he began to recount the specific plots that would remain flood-bound even after all the water drained out, and the channels that would have to be cut to steer stranded segments of the river back to its course, and the floodplains that would still remain marshy and would have to wait another two months until the fierce spring sun would bake them.

'Shabash!' I cheered.

'Didn't I tell you he's an expert?' Kazi chuckled. 'He'd give the irrigation department engineers a run for their money. But would they listen to him?'

For the first time, Nakul Sardar flashed a broad smile, exposing a pair of large upper teeth crossed like tentative fingers.

'Counting this one, I've seen eleven floods in twenty years. This bitch of a river won't let me be for two consecutive years.'

Nakul uttered the words with a thick vehemence and then, the deep lines on his face melting into an indescribably soft expression, he said, 'And yet, I can never imagine a life away from her.'

~

The Ganga commands a basin spread over ten lakh kilometres and eleven states, and serves four out of ten Indians. It flows east across much of north India until, keeping the Rajmahal Hills to its left, it curves south before it forks. One stream flows into Bangladesh as the Padma; the other, known as the Bhagirathi-Hooghly, flows down south for about five hundred kilometres until it debouches into the Bay of Bengal. These rivers are part of a complex system that carries not only water but also silt – about eighty crore tonnes a year, enough to erect a Great Wall of China around India's territory. The lower region, known as the Bengal Delta, is a young landmass built with this silt. For thousands of years, the Ganga and her tributaries have crafted the flat fertile lowlands and supported a rich variety of life.

Left alone, the rivers would continue to meander and create new land. But the Bengal Delta is one of the most densely populated regions in the world. With 2.7 per cent of the country's territory, West Bengal is home to 8 per cent of its population. Here people have always lived close to the river and have built their settlements right on the floodplains. Over the last one and a half centuries, railways and roads have damaged this region's natural hydrology; dams and embankments have meddled with the natural flow of the rivers. Floods, considered nature's boon since the beginning of civilization, which renewed the land with rich alluvium, have become a bane. They destroy life and property.

In Bangladesh, which shares a border with West Bengal, floods uproot twenty lakh people every year. For decades, a section of them slipped into the border districts of India. But that was until Bangladesh's economy became strong enough to relocate its own displaced people. The country now fares better than India on many social development indicators. The poorest among the ecological refugees squat in the peripheries of towns and cities. In Kolkata alone, more than ten lakh people live in shanties on four drainage canals that run from east to west across the city. Sometimes, they are pushed into ecologically critical lowlands, drainage basins and floodplains of rivers. This leads to more flooding and more evictions. Moving from place to place, without a permanent shelter, they are a most vulnerable human group. Every year, according to the National Crime Records Bureau, an average of four thousand girls go missing in West Bengal. Many of them are schoolgoing children.

Sometimes, it all begins with dots in the school's attendance register, that soon join to form unbroken red lines.

THE BLUE PIAGGIO

Late on a February morning, a thin mist dimmed the sun like a tea strainer. Sheikhpara was a blur across empty fields stretched pale yellow after a recent paddy harvest. It was a village with a large Muslim population. We headed there along grid paths of beaten earth. We were on a mission. Ananda Roy, a teacher in a local school, and I were going to enquire about one Rafiqul Islam who had not been coming to school for a month. Rafiqul was enrolled in Class 10 in the Khejurdaha Uchchomadhyamik Vidyapith, the only higher secondary school in the area. He was the only boy from Sheikhpara who'd appear in the upcoming board examination. Few boys from his village reached this far, and Ananda wanted to find out why Rafiqul wasn't attending school.

Khejurdaha was a large Scheduled Caste settlement, larger than Sheikhpara, and Ananda was a bhumiputra, a son of the soil. He was a swarthy young man of athletic build, with close-cropped hair and a ready smile. Unlike other teachers in his school who commuted from distant urban areas, Ananda, a commerce graduate, had an intimate knowledge of this world.

'That is a bhagar over there.' He pointed his finger at a patch of fallow earth under a palm grove. 'People from the surrounding villages leave their dead cattle here.'

Waxy milkweed bushes covered an acre of land. A date palm had shot through a banyan's trunk. Or was it the banyan sheathing the palm? A breeze picked a murmur in the fronds. The bhagar, desolate and vaguely sinister, stood like a sentinel between the two villages, Khejurdaha and Sheikhpara.

'When we were young, we'd often come here to watch the vultures. The big, clumsy birds would perch on the palm trees until the cobblers had stripped off the hide. Then they'd descend one after another and polish off a carcass in less than an hour. But nowadays we don't see the vultures any more.'

We stepped over the flinty levee across stubble fields for half a kilometre until we hit a trodden track. Four little boys were sitting around a fire they had built with twigs. They had scavenged potatoes left over on the field after a harvest, and were turning them over the cinders with jute stalks. We left the fields and entered a dirt lane fenced on one side with cactus bushes. Tiny yellow flowers had bloomed on them.

Ananda stopped and turned to me.

'Can you hear something?'

'Yes,' I said. 'Birds.'

Ananda chuckled.

For a few seconds, I thought we were near a deep wood. I could hear the staccato music of a colony of woodpeckers, punctuated with the rise and fall of serenading crickets. But no sooner did we enter the village than the bucolic orchestra fell apart. I discovered with a shock that the tapping of the woodpeckers was, in fact, wooden blocks being hammered on framed fabrics. The crickets' chirps turned out to be the whirr of a dozen sewing machines running together in frantic bursts. Around us, inside thatched huts and mud-plastered courtyards, behind bamboo latticework, dozens of girls were busy at work.

Tailoring workshops were being run from the village.

'They stitch the salwar suits and lehenga–cholis sold in upmarket garments shops in Kolkata. Here the girls do the embroidery, block-printing and brocade work.'

The cluster of thatched mud cottages was buzzing with activity. A hum of hand-driven implements, punctuated with FM radio channels, rose in waves and engulfed us from all directions. But we couldn't see much. Banana leaves, dry and tattered, strung on bamboo frames screened the courtyards. We caught glimpses of the girls sitting under jackfruit trees, hunched over lengths of cloth. The glittering fabrics billowing in the dark green shade under the trees gave the silent human figures an evanescent quality.

There appeared to be too many of them. I shared this thought with Ananda.

'Many are from the surrounding villages,' he explained. 'The wholesalers send the materials through middlemen. Earlier, they used to get this work done in villages on the highway. When the workers there demanded a raise, they came to the interiors. All they needed was a metalled road.'

Two years ago, Sheikhpara received a windfall: an asphalt road under the Pradhan Mantri Gram Sadak Yojana scheme (PMGSY). The informal sector came knocking at its door.

Other than the road connection, and the banana-leaf purdah on house-fronts, I couldn't spot any difference between Sheikhpara and Khejurdaha. There were the same hyacinth-clogged ditches, poultry skittering about puddled lanes, the same peeling mud walls and foetid air hanging over the cottages like a mosquito net. But Sheikhpara had more humans teeming in lesser space, fewer community spaces, and more half-naked children. At one end of the village, a large, shady bamboo grove housed the dead: it was the burial ground. There was a mosque – a plain limewashed structure with a loudspeaker tied to a bamboo pole. It was battery-operated, because Sheikhpara had no electricity. Neither had Khejurdaha. In fact, the two villages had a lot in common: no electricity, very few pucca houses with toilets, very few landholders, and a large illiterate workforce engaged in the informal sector. In the scale of human development, perhaps Khejurdaha was better placed, though it had more enlisted below poverty line (BPL) families. But then Sheikhpara could boast of a few large, new concrete houses, with dish antennas on roofs, a handful of motorcycles, and a video cassette rental store: blinding flashes of prosperity in the middle of blinded poverty.

The narrow dirt lane that took us into the heart of the village forked around an enormous neem tree. An arm grew scales of brick paving, the other groped its way into a shaded mango grove. The giant old trees with orchid-lined trunks shimmered in the green light reflected off a pond. We walked fifty metres down the brick-lined path and came to a grocer's store: a tile-roofed hut with a yellow public telephone service cut into the mud wall. A piece of slate, scrawled with chalk, said – LOCAL CALL RE. 1. Cardplayers sat on a grass mat under the shop's awning. An old man with a skullcap and grey beard basked in the pale sun. He was watching the card game with half-shut eyes and taking drags from a handheld hookah.

Ananda asked him the way to Rafiqul's house.

'Father's name?' The old man had a rasping voice.

Ananda thought for a moment. 'He studies in the school at Khejurdaha. He'll sit for Madhyamik this year.'

'That's Uchiar Ali's son,' said a player, without raising his eyes from his cards.

Following the directions they gave us, we came to a huddle of low huts around a courtyard. In the middle of the courtyard, on a dug-out oven, an amber liquid was bubbling on a large, rectangular tin tray. It was khejur gur, the date-palm syrup. A thin, bare-chested man, a faded gamchha tied around his head, was stirring the liquid with a long-handled ladle. A plump woman and a minor girl fed dried fronds to the many-holed oven. A boy was laying out thin-necked terracotta pitchers on a leaf mat. He had large, beautiful eyes, and a mop of curly hair on his head. They were so absorbed in their work that none of them saw us coming.

'Why aren't you coming to school, Rafiqul?' Ananda's icy voice broke the silence.

The boy spun around and saw us standing in their courtyard. The sight stunned him. He glanced around like a cornered rabbit, as if to find a hole to bolt into, and finally sidled up towards us.

'I was suffering from fever, sir,' the boy, Rafiqul, stuttered. He fixed his large eyes to the ground.

'For five weeks? But you don't look that ill!' Ananda teased.

'No sir, I ... I...'

The boy scratched his head and cast imploring glances at the man by the oven. The man put the ladle across the steaming tray and stepped forward.

'I'll tell you. As you can see, Master-babu, I'm making gur this season. Rafiqul is assisting me.'

Set on a thin, prematurely creased face, he had Rafiqul's large, limpid eyes. This was Uchiar Ali.

'You are Ananda Sir, taina?' His face now broke into a warm smile. 'Rafiqul speaks a lot about you.'

The woman, who until now was following the conversation intently, sprinted inside the hut. She returned in no time, her head veiled now, and unfurled an embroidered rug on the porch.

'Come, babu, do take a seat,' Uchiar Ali said, his fingers joined across his chest in a gesture of supplication.

Being an illiterate farm labourer, Rafiqul's father knew how important formal education was. He also knew, he confessed, that the boy should never miss school. No one of his age group in Sheikhpara went to school. The pull to drop out was strong.

'But what to do, Master-babu? I work in other people's fields because I don't own any land. You know this area well. Who'll give me work throughout the year? So I do this and that during the lull seasons. I make gur during the winter months. This season I've taken twenty-two trees on lease. But the cost of firewood is high, and the work requires labour that I cannot afford to hire. So my wife and children assist me. Please excuse Rafiqul for another week, let the shonkranti festival be over. The trees are already giving out.'

Uchiar Ali spoke in a voice thick with despair. Suddenly, he sprang forward and clasped Ananda's hand.

'Don't get me wrong!' Ananda extricated his hand. 'The school authority hasn't asked me to come here. I can talk to the headmaster regarding his attendance. But that's not the point. What I'm really worried about is that the Madhyamik exam is less than two months away and classes are on in full swing. Tell me, how will he cover the syllabus? How will he manage?' Ananda took a pause and glanced at Rafiqul. 'Or is this the end of his studies, like the rest of the boys in the village?'

Uchiar Ali sat on his heels upon the bare ground, his arms hanging over his knees, a pained smile pasted on his lips. He didn't have the answer. Rafiqul, all ears, had slipped into his father's place at the oven. He was turning the ladle in the golden liquid, allowing the sweet vapour to envelop him like a purdah. He, too, didn't have the answer.

As the question hung in the air of a balmy winter afternoon, folding into the yeasty scent of date-palm syrup, Rafiqul's little sister brought for us a quantity of the amber-coloured liquid in two steel plates. Their mother put on the rug a small cane basket full of muri (puffed rice) and spoons.

We protested. 'We haven't come here for this,' Ananda said.

Uchiar Ali bit his tongue and pinched his earlobes with his thumb and forefinger, one after the other. 'It's by the grace of Allah that men like you have set foot in our house. But we are poor people, what can we offer you? And we are also *Mohammedan*.'

We didn't know how to respond to this. The four pairs of expectant eyes watched us. It was as if their lives hinged on our next move. Ananda glanced at me and picked up a plate. I picked up the other. It was warm.

Uchiar Ali smiled and asked us to sprinkle muri on the gur and fold it with the spoon. We accepted his suggestion, and it was delicious: the crunchy rice set off the smoky flavour of the date-palm syrup.

Rafiqul's mother spoke from behind the mud wall. 'We feel so happy that Ananda Sir has come to our house. Rafi tells me everything. He says – Ammu, Ananda Sir will only look at our faces, and he'll know. He will call us after the primary sections have returned to their classes—'

'Don't mention it, please!' Ananda mumbled and cast a furtive look at Rafiqul. His face glowed with embarrassment.

~

The brief winter's day was bleeding to death in the western sky when we returned to the PMGSY road. A skimmed layer of smog hung over the stubble fields. We followed a winding path, past a farmer and his wife harvesting steel-blue cabbages, watched over by a smiling scarecrow with a missing arm, and climbed to the ribbon of silken asphalt twenty feet above the fields. The road curved across fields and channels until it ended on the mist-hazed bank of the river Damodar.

'A Trekker taxi service has started recently,' Ananda said, 'from the river ferry to the state highway. But the service isn't regular – only two vehicles ply on this stretch.'

Signs of hope marked the roadside: piles of raised earth and spaces staked out with bamboo poles for the shops that would come up. Already, at a bend, there was a tea shop built with tar-painted tin. A score of village women had gathered there. Most of them were middle-aged, barefoot, and they wore saris around their bare torsos. From a distance, it appeared as if they had left whatever they'd been doing at home and rushed to this empty stretch of road on some urgent summons.

It was disquieting. Was there dire news? Ananda's eyes squinted with suspicion. The scene was hauntingly familiar. Were they waiting for somebody, something, to turn up, and then to burst into a chorus of lamentation? A few women, I noticed, already had their sari's anchal pressed over their lips.

We came closer and found, to our relief, that they were chatting among themselves. Then we saw a dozen boys in the crook of the road, sitting across from the tea shop. They looked to be between fifty and twenty, all dressed in clean, ironed shirts and trousers, and each had a travel bag with him. The silent boys sat on a bamboo machan, ignoring the women on the other side of the road. From time to time, they seemed to be looking for something in the distance where the road melted into the horizon. They appeared tense.

All the boys were going to Mumbai, we learnt, to work in goldsmiths' workshops. They were waiting here for a Trekker taxi that would ferry them to the highway where they'd catch a bus to the Howrah railway terminus. The women gathered here to see them off were their mothers and sisters.

Except for one tall, young man, all were leaving home for the first time in their lives. This boy, with an ear stud and a chunky digital watch on his wrist, looked to be the leader. He was standing a few feet away from his group and chatting self-assuredly with two girls. The youngest in the group, a boy of around fourteen, would join his uncle's meat shop in Mahim. He sat alone upon a culvert, his back turned to the assembled women, and scanned the darkening horizon for that elusive Trekker taxi.

But it failed to show up. The boys arranged with a three-wheeled pickup, a blue Piaggio Apé, that was leaving the village after a delivery of materials to an embroidery workshop. They climbed into the vehicle's tiny cargo deck and huddled with their knees pressed to their chests. The women stepped forward and gathered around the vehicle. None of the boys would return home before at least a year, we learnt. But there was no display of emotion, no anxious reminders, no tears. The mood was sombre, and they spoke little. The youngest of them sat clutching the side rail, his eyes transfixed on the hooded face of a woman. As the pickup's engine spluttered, the woman pushed back her veil and whispered: 'Bhalo kori khaba!' Eat well.

The women lingered on the empty road until the Piaggio had become a speck of red taillight in the dim horizon. Then they climbed down into the field where a layer of fog hung low like a marquee.

~

En route to his home in Khejurdaha, where I was to spend the night, Ananda took me to the spot where the river Damodar emptied into the Hooghly.

'It's a full moon today,' he said. 'Let's go and see it rise over the river.'

Dusk had now settled, a flock of squawking cormorants flew overhead. We left the road and took a dirt lane into a fishermen's settlement. Wick lamps burned inside the huts, casting feeble light on nets hanging from thatches and boats upturned in courtyards. An 'aatchala' Shiva temple stood at the end of the village, its eight-roofed structure ruined and choked with weeds. The moss-lined terracotta panels on the walls depicted a history of maritime trade and prosperity in this region. The path led to the raised bank of the Damodar, which was almost dry in this season. Stagnant pools framed in hyacinths glinted in the darkness like shards of glass.

'There's a debate,' Ananda said, 'about whether *this* is the actual course of the Damodar. Many believe that this is one of its distributaries. I've been hearing this debate since I was a child. I consulted the works of James Rennell, who made an extensive survey of Bengal rivers in the eighteenth century, also the old gazetteers. I have even talked to a few experts. All agree that this *is* the Damodar's main course.'

A narrow depression of land, lined with parallel rows of trees, suggested the river's course. The bones of a great river glimmered like an old man's foggy mind. Later in the evening, I would hear Ananda's ninety-one-year-old grandfather dig into his memories and talk about this river. He'd talk as if the Damodar was an ancient person, a little older than him, but a contemporary.

The Hooghly was broad and appeared full on a high tide. On the opposite bank, beyond the black line of vegetation, lay the subdivisional town of Uluberia. The entire stretch was in pitch darkness; there was a power cut. Here too, it was dark, except for the twinkling lights on a few fishing boats moored on the bank. There was a mild nip in the air, but near the water, the river exhaled a warm dampness. We sat on cold grass, facing the east, waiting for the moon to rise.

'What was it Rafiqul's mother was saying? About how you'd look at their faces and know?' I asked. 'Know what?'

'That's nothing!' Ananda whisked his hand. He remained silent for a minute, and then picked up a clod and threw it into the water. The river returned a plopping sound.

'Some of our high-school boys come to school without having breakfast or lunch. But the midday meal is for the primary section only. So we try to serve them the food left over after the little ones have eaten. But we have to be discreet, the boys have great self-respect. Ask them if they've eaten at home and they'll lie. You need to study their faces to know the truth.'

We sat side by side, gazing at the eastern sky, above the dark, seamless line of trees. The moon was about to rise, but the sky appeared to have grown darker. It was as if an inky wall stretched across the horizon under a murky sky. Before us was the waterway along which ships of the East India Company had sailed into this part of the subcontinent, bringing their guns and god, their language and their ways of seeing.

Ananda spun around. 'Did you know this? Job Charnock, the founder of Kolkata, had first struck anchor over there at Uluberia!' He spoke in an animated voice. It was as if he had remembered an incident that had happened the other day.

'Really?' I asked.

'Yes. He was planning to set up his base right here. This was a most suitable spot. The Hooghly was wide, and the Damodar was not dead yet. But the fearsome mosquitoes of the swamps drove him away. Charnock spent a sleepless night and sailed upstream to Kolkata the very next morning. Sometimes I try to imagine what this place would have been like if he had stayed back.'

I peered at the black rim of the horizon and tried to evoke in my mind the gleaming lights of a magnificent city. I could not. The grey river stretched under the inky sky and the dark vegetation lining its banks weren't much different from what they had been three centuries before, when this assiduous agent of the East India Company had set his eyes on them.

What if Charnock had stayed back? It was difficult to imagine it. No less difficult was it to imagine what Kolkata would have been like if he had. But it was incredibly more difficult to know if a boy had eaten by studying his face.

STORY OF A COMMUNITY

Every community has a story. It is a story that it constantly tells itself and the world, a story it cherishes like an heirloom and passes on to future generations. Often, however, the story a community wants to be its own and the one through which the world knows it are not the same.

Apu's story is the story of Bengalis. It has tragedy in large measure; a melancholy note runs through it from beginning to end. In fact, this is part of its excruciating beauty and popularity. But it is also a happy story. That is because, here, the story that a community has been telling itself happens to be the same story through which the world has known the community. Until recently, that is.

The person who best narrates this story is Apu himself, in the film *Apur Sansar* (The World of Apu), the third in the trilogy made by Satyajit Ray.

By now our hero has grown up into a fine young man, out of college and looking for a job. He is living in a rented attic room in a dingy part of Kolkata and nursing a dream to become a writer. His college friend Pulu has tracked him down. We see the two men walking down a railway track late at night. They have spent the evening well – a play at a theatre house followed by dinner at a restaurant. Thanks to his well-heeled friend, Apu has had good food after a long time, in a city where he has been struggling to survive without a steady job. Now there is a devil-may-care smile on his face and a cigarette between his fingers.

'Have you been writing anything?' Pulu asks. 'Poetry or anything?'

'A fantastic novel,' Apu declares.

'Really? Tell me about it!'

'It's the story of a boy. A village boy, poor but sensitive. His father is a priest. He dies. The boy comes to the city. But he doesn't want to be a priest like his father. He wants to study. He's ambitious. So he enrols in a college – and we find that through education, through struggle, he gets over all the superstitions and orthodoxy. He is not prepared to accept anything without a debate. But he has imagination, he has sensitivity, little things move him, give him joy. Perhaps he has the ability to do great things. He has the potential—'

Here, Pulu interjects: 'But where's the novel? Come on, this is an autobiography!'

'Of course this is an autobiography!' Apu protests. 'But—'

And thus he goes on.

The two friends amble down a railway track, chattering and arguing, until they melt into the darkness of the city night.

What Apu narrates to his friend is, in fact, a summary of the autobiography, not just of himself, but of the entire Bengali bhadralok class. One can also read it as a fantastic novel that a community began to write a century before Apu himself was born. 'A fact not sufficiently emphasized,' writes Oxford historian Tapan Raychaudhuri in his book *Europe Reconsidered*, 'in the literature on the East–West encounter in modern times is that the Bengali intelligentsia was the first Asian social group of any size whose mental world was transformed through its interactions with the West.' This was also known as the Bengal Renaissance, a social phenomenon that has produced a galaxy of thinkers, writers, social reformers, scientists, Nobel Prize winners and internationally renowned film-makers. Apu's story reflects this 'mental world', its aspiration and transformation, most succinctly.

∼

This story had an early beginning. Because of its geopolitical location, people from different parts of the country and the world, speaking a variety of languages, have been coming to Bengal since the Middle Ages. They have been coming here for two things: wealth and power. During the Delhi Sultanate and later during the Mughal rule, a knowledge of Arabic and Persian languages could give a person both. But after the British established their supremacy, proficiency in the English language became the key to upward mobility. One of the early Bengalis who rose from a humble background and made immense wealth in the eighteenth century was Raja Nabakrishna Deb. He could speak fluent English – in fact, he was a polyglot – and he acted as an interpreter for Robert Clive, the commander of the East India Company. Deb was richly rewarded for this job, and his palatial mansions still stand in Kolkata. Never had the acquisition of a language been so closely aligned with wealth and power.

The East India Company came to this region up the river Hooghly, outplayed other European companies in the race to grab the riches of the Bengal Delta, and became its ruler after the Battle of Plassey in 1757. To establish its rule over a vast stretch of land populated with millions speaking alien tongues, the Company needed trained go-betweens drafted from the native population. So it gave them education, a type of education which would produce – to quote Thomas Babington Macaulay, who had penned the 'Minute on Education' in 1835 – 'a class of persons, Indian in blood and colour, but English in taste, in opinions, in morals, and in intellect'.

Two years before, in 1833, the British Parliament had passed the Slavery Abolition Act. Paradoxically enough, the Company's new policy of liberal education in India was framed not to liberate, but to create a native Indian sub-class, moulded from the inside, trained as intellectual galley slaves for the British imperial ship.

The ground was being prepared for some time. In 1823, Raja Rammohun Roy, a polyglot clerk and a social reformer, was writing to the viceroy Lord Amherst about the necessity of a Western mode of learning for the uplift of his fellow countrymen. In fact, he had drawn up a plan for liberal education that included physics, algebra, chemistry, anatomy – in sum, all the fields of Western knowledge that had been expanding rapidly during this time. Several institutions were also being set up in Calcutta. They included a college in Fort William, the administrative centre of the Company, printing presses at Serampore, a Danish settlement thirty kilometres upriver, and a string of schools run by Catholic and Anglican missionaries. Hindu College, which would later be renamed the Presidency College, came up in 1817.

Around this time, one could witness a strange scene on the streets of Calcutta, something Sivanath Sastri described in his book *Ramtonu Lahiri O Tatkalin Bangosamaj*. A knot of boys would wait in an alley in the city's north, where a Scottish watchmaker lived. As soon as the palanquin carrying the sahib would emerge from his house, the boys would run behind it, chanting a litany.

But they were not hungry beggar boys. They were from middle-class families newly settled in the city, and they'd chant in broken English: '*Me poor boy! Have pity! Me take in your school, sir!*'

The watchmaker, who was also a philanthropist, had set up several schools around Calcutta to give native boys a sound English education. His name was David Hare. The boys would run after Hare Sahib's palanquin to plead with him to admit them to his school.

This was a historic run; equally historic was this hunger, which would persist through the coming centuries. An English education would fetch an office job, which would mean a stable income, social respectability, and power. The material possibilities were plain as daylight. But there was also a most interesting, and rather unintended, side effect. Exposure to the Western sciences, philosophy and literature triggered a new intellectual awakening among a section of the Bengali middle classes. It set them off on a journey down an exciting new road.

~

In the film *Aparajito*, the second part of Satyajit Ray's *Apu Trilogy*, young Apu returns from Benares, after his father's death, to a village in Bengal with his mother. Life here is the same as before – the same poverty and uncertainty, and charity from better-off neighbours. The only difference is the young boy now works as a priest and performs puja in local households. This is how he earns the chal-kola, the rice-and-plantain staple for the two of them. One evening, Apu snuggles up to his mother, Sarbajaya.

'Ma,' he whispers, 'I want to go to school.'

Sarbajaya is surprised. 'But who'll perform puja if you go to school?'

Apu assures her he will manage: he can do the duties of a village priest during the morning and go to school later in the day.

The mother, still anxious, asks, 'But won't it cost money? And where will it come from, pray tell?'

Apu swings his head and looks at his mother's face.

'Ma,' he asks, piercing her with his innocence, 'don't you have the money? Don't you?'

The camera zooms into the newly widowed mother's face as a range of complex emotions – from dejection to selfless love and resolve – play on it. Then it cuts to a sequence of shots inside a school building. It is the day the school inspector is on an official visit. The headmaster is taking the burly officer along on a tour of the school. They enter a classroom, and we find Apu sitting on a front bench. The inspector checks the primer the teacher is using and asks a boy in the front row the meaning of a word. When he cannot give the correct answer, he asks Apu, who is sitting next to that boy. Apu gives the correct answer and reads aloud from a poem.

The inspector and the headmaster are visibly impressed. This incident turns out to be serendipitous for our young hero. A door opens for Apu, leading to a cherished road. The road will eventually take him to the city of opportunities.

Apu is poor, but a Brahmin scholar's son. His family has a standing in the village society despite their economic condition. Apu's wrenching question to Sarbajaya – 'Ma, don't you have the money?' – is addressed.

But what about the question Rafiqul's teacher asked his father?

'Is this the end of his studies,' Ananda had asked on that grey winter afternoon in Sheikhpara, 'like the rest of the boys in the village?'

∼

Rafiqul never appeared for the Madhyamik examination. I learnt this from a letter Ananda wrote me. I also learnt that the boys who had gone to work in jewellery workshops in Mumbai had returned. This too wasn't unexpected. In fact, this was a periodic phenomenon. When the global economic meltdown struck in 2008, it had affected the small export-based industries, particularly the informal sector. Whenever there was communal tension in some part of the country – a terrorist attack in Kashmir, a crime committed by a suspected outsider in a distant city, a crackdown on a camp of labourers whom the city administration picked up as illegal immigrants – or a lockdown during a pandemic, it was always these men who'd be the first to return. But the village economy found it hard to absorb them. 'Who will give them work here?' Ananda wrote. 'There is practically no return on investment in farming. Whatever little parcels of land people have, they use their own labour to grow food and vegetables. Those with larger plots have leased them out to matchstick companies who plant fast-growing trees for timber. Some even sell off the soil to brickmakers. The panchayat gives work under different government schemes to loyal followers of the Party.

In this situation, the return of these men has jolted the power structure in the villages.'

Restless hands, young hearts – a fertile ground for seeds of discontent. A river dies, a river springs to life, carrying the toxic sludge upstream. A power structure, hollowed out from inside by woodworms of corruption and nepotism, crumbles suddenly, unexpectedly, sooner than anyone can imagine.

Meanwhile, other changes were taking place. They renovated a dilapidated madrasa in Sheikhpara, Ananda wrote, and no boy from that village came to the school any more. The aatchala Shiva temple I had seen that evening on the Damodar's silted bank had been restored. The old terracotta panels on it had been covered over with polished granite. The jungles had been cleared, stainless-steel fencing set up around the premises, and there was also electric lighting. 'I forgot to mention that electricity has finally come to Khejurdaha,' he wrote. 'It has come to Sheikhpara too. Now we can hear the call of azan coming from across the fields. We also wake up at dawn hearing recorded bhajans and the Hanuman Chalisa playing in the temple. Men with orange tilaks on their foreheads come to distribute prasad on auspicious occasions. They greet each other with "*Jai Shri Ram*".' Many women in Sheikhpara now wear burqas, and boys have begun to wear skullcaps. And you'll be happy to learn that we have installed an electric pump in our courtyard well. Now we have twenty-four-hour piped water in the bathrooms, and ceiling fans in the bedrooms. It will be less arduous for you the next time you visit us. When will that be? My grandfather asks after you.'

~

I had met Ananda's grandfather on the night I spent in their house. The nonagenarian man spoke about the Damodar as if the sick bedridden river were an old friend. He was among the men who built the school in Khejurdaha. He reminisced about those times and, with his permission, I recorded his words on a voice recorder.

'When Independence came, we thought our circumstances would change. We had much faith in Gandhi-ji, but then suddenly, he was no more. We were the low-caste Koibarto. The bhadralok who replaced the sahibs never consulted us. The upper castes in the village wouldn't allow us to set foot in their neighbourhood, except to build a cottage or dig a pond. How would our circumstances change unless we ourselves did something about it? None among the Koibartos could read or write; we'd never been to a school. The only school in a circle of five villages belonged to the zamindar. It was for the children of the bhadralok who worked in his estate. But now we were in a new country, a country that was put down on paper in the form of a big, fat book by a low-caste man like us. We realized that our children, who'd live a full life in this new country, should be able to read and write, should get some education. So we went about collecting subscriptions to build our own school. People from five villages, including those from Sheikhpara, contributed. We raised the building with our labour. But a school would need teachers. So we went about the district searching for teachers. But who'd come to a poor village to teach low-caste children? We couldn't pay them a regular salary, but we could build them a new hut, and feed them fresh vegetables and sweet-water fish from our rivers. Fortunately for us, there were educated young men from East Bengal who had lost everything during Partition. So the school began with one teacher and eighteen pupils. At first, we built a structure with bamboo and straw. After more and more villagers began to send their children, we replaced it with a pucca structure. We burned the bricks ourselves with clay from the Damodar's bank. We knew how to do all this, and men from Sheikhpara were expert masons. We were equally poor, the Mussalmans from Sheikhpara and we the Koibartos, and equally shunned by the landed folk. We toiled with our hands and lived by drenching our feet with the sweat of our brow. We were children of this soil, children of the same mother, only we suckled from different breasts. So, following Partition, when families from Sheikhpara were preparing to go to East Pakistan, we asked them to stay back. We had once been the feared musclemen of local zamindars. I could take on four men as long as no one had a gun. Nobody could raise a finger at anyone as long as we were here. The country was now free, and we were nobody's slaves. So we thought. And so, they stayed back. Later, some of them shifted to the districts of Malda and Murshidabad, to live among their kin. But we have let nothing happen here. Not when someone stole prophet Mohammed's hair in Kashmir, or when reports of the Khulna riots reached us, or when that man – what's his name? – came on a ship along the Damodar…'

Here, his sense of timescales overlapped. As I listen to the recording now, the verve in his voice surprises me. I try to remember his face, swaddled in grey woollen wrappers and a monkey cap, under the flickering light of a kerosene lamp. I cannot. I can only remember the smell of wood smoke and sesame oil in his room, and his feet – tough, cracked farmer's feet – peeping out of his lungi. When I attempt to recall his eyes, the dim pools of water on the Damodar's bed come to my mind.

I cannot even recall Rafiqul's face. Whenever I try, the face of the boy who had gone to join his uncle in the meat shop leaps into my memory. I can remember the fading winter light, the bend in the shining black road, where the boys packed themselves like cattle into the blue Piaggio Apé. The small, toy-like vehicle brought work to Sheikhpara and took away the workers, shuttling between the two sides of an informal sector. I recall the boy's keen eyes fixed on a hooded face. I imagine him inside a dark cubicle behind a meat shop spattered with blood, pulling innards off a warm carcass hanging from a hook. After all these years, surely his eyes have lost their limpid quality, the muscles on his jawbones have tightened, and there's hair sprouting on his chin, his cheeks, his upper lip. Perhaps he wears a skullcap these days. By now, he must have picked up the rudiments of two languages and figured out the innards of a big, strange city. And yet, every night, when he goes to sleep inside that cubicle in the company of animals he'll halal the next morning, he still remembers the hooded face of a prematurely aged woman. He remembers how she clutched the sari over her mouth and, as the engine revved, how she drew it aside and whispered: 'Bhalo kori khaba!'

This much and nothing more. After weeks of preparation and packing, and endless reminders of dos and don'ts on a journey to a distant, unknown city, all that had remained to be said was this: Eat well.

THE CALL OF HOME

The writer Bibhutibhushan Bandyopadhyay was born in a village named Chalki-Barrackpur by the river Ichhamati, now near the Bangladesh border. After Partition was declared, for a few days, the village slipped to the eastern side of the Radcliffe line until it was restored back to India. Chalki-Barrackpur is a typical sleepy hamlet in south Bengal, surrounded by lush fields, bamboo groves and orchards. It sits by the trickling headwaters of the Ichhamati.

The house where the novelist was born and had spent most of his life still stands. For generations of Bibhutibhushan's devoted readers, it is a place of pilgrimage. But except for the old house, there is hardly anything worth seeing in Chalki-Barrackpur, nothing that can remind his fans of his many novels and short stories that were set here. Realizing this, the local panchayat has erected a giant concrete statue of the writer on the riverbank.

On a sunny afternoon in April, the grey human figure, made of reinforced concrete, was reclining on a concrete chair, its legs crossed and head turned to the east. A field of yellow mustard blazed across the river. The statue appeared to be looking into the distant past, when the river was in good health and murmured countless stories. Now the narrow, weed-choked stream was curled up near the giant concrete feet like a scruffy village dog. A while ago, a boat had drawn a narrow channel across its weed bed. Bright red petals now drifted slowly along it. In the distance, a flaming red gulmohar leaned over the stream, shedding its petals. A kingfisher sat on a fishing net's bamboo frame. On the opposite bank, a thin farmer wearing a reed hat was ploughing his plot with a pair of thinner oxen. The hoots and grunts of the labouring man and his animals fanned out over the river. They were breaking clods, preparing the field for summer vegetables.

A small garden ringed the writer's plain single-storeyed house. From the riverbank, a trodden path wound through a bamboo grove to reach its rear entrance. An old widow, a distant cousin of Bibhutibhushan's wife, took care of the premises. She was keen to take the rare visitor on a tour around the building, to show the spot on the veranda where her jamai-babu, her brother-in-law, liked to place his writing table.

'And here on this terrace, he'd absorb the morning sun, massage himself with a quarter pint of mustard oil and then go for a swim. Do you remember the bokul tree that features in so many of his stories? It's over there. It still blooms during autumn and fills the neighbourhood with its sweet fragrance. There was also an ashoka tree, the one his mother had planted. Pious village women would eat the orange blossoms on Ashok Shoshti, the sixth day of the lunar month in spring. But the tree died last year, after the flood. Perhaps its roots had rotted away.'

'The flood?' I was curious.

'Oh yes. It occurs every two or three years. The village remains waterlogged for a week. But last year it was terrible; floodwater had entered the house.'

She showed the mould visible on the wall under a coat of limewash. A collection of old books, most of them signed copies gifted by the writer's friends, was damaged.

'After the flood receded, it took me three days to clear the silt,' she said and, pointing a finger at my feet, continued coolly, 'And then I discovered a king cobra over there, its hood flared, right on the spot where you are standing.'

It took an effort of the imagination to visualize this wasted stream metamorphose into a raging river, overflow its banks and flood village after village. But then, one would also need to imagine all the stories inscribed on this landscape, which the writer set on paper under the roof of this very house, on this veranda, this room, this garden. It was these stories that had transformed Chalki-Barrackpur, by all means a nondescript village, into Apu's childhood world.

Apu's family lived in this setting for many generations. This was their bhitay. For Apu, bhitay connotes more than the broken house they lived in, or the homestead land. It includes the village, the fields, the river, the image of Goddess Bishalakshi glowing in the bushes, the piquant breath of unknown plants at sunset, the bamboo shoots reaching out to the skies like a lyre bird's tail: a wondrous habitat. Throughout his life, wherever he would go, Apu would feel a deep attachment to this place, an indescribable yearning that is deeper than nostalgia. In Bangla, we call it 'bhitayer taan', the call of home. The phrase sums up a universe of feelings.

Apu inherited this call from his father. It is the same yearning that had brought Harihar back to the village after his wanderings around the country, to settle with his wife in their ancestral house. When he set out again on an extended trip, leaving behind his wife and two little children, his plan was to return quickly after making some money, so he could repair the dilapidated house and lead a settled life. But that was not to be. *Pather Panchali* ends with Apu leaving the village with his parents. In the last scene, the three of them are sitting under the canopy of a bullock cart, their sad, worried faces turned to the receding village.

In Apu's story, the god of the road is Janus-faced. On the one hand he eggs the hero forward, on the other there is this irresistible longing for home. Many a time during his exiles in Kolkata and Benares, Apu recalls in extraordinary detail the quotidian rhythm of life in his native village. It is an unremitting force that runs across generations, a visceral pull that predates Apu's Western education, that binds a community to a land despite all the hardships, an integral part of a living culture packed in two words – bhitayer taan.

IN APU'S LAND

For a few years, Bibhutibhushan taught in Haripada Institution, a high school in Gopalnagar, five kilometres from Chalki-Barrackpur. He was an indefatigable walker; every day he would walk the distance to school and back. The school now stands on a busy state highway lined with sawmills, plywood plants, fertilizer shops and big residential properties. Like a river, the road has created its own floodplains, but the silt of time has buried the vestiges of a past. I fail to locate anything that can remind me of the novelist who had walked this ground seventy years ago. There is only a marble bust of him inside the school premises, and a framed photograph in the teachers' room. That is all. None among the teachers and other staff have any personal memory of Bibhutibhushan Bandyopadhyay. He has slipped away, leaving behind a void, like a trace fossil.

But forty kilometres from Gopalnagar, in a village right on the Bangladesh border, I find him alive in the memory of an eighty-two-year-old man.

～

This is Apu's land. Ula, Mamjoan, Manasapota, Aranghata, Nischindipur, Ranaghat ... place names that mapped the story of his early life. The rivers Jalangi and Churni wash this land and connect the Hooghly and the Padma, the two arterial rivers of the Delta. Centuries ago, these rivers and creeks had built exceptionally fertile lowlands. In *The Imperial Gazetteer of India*, published in 1881, W.W. Hunter writes: 'The rivers have now ceased their work of land making and are beginning to silt up. The general aspect is that of a vast level alluvial plain, dotted with villages and clusters of trees, and intersected by numerous rivers, backwaters, minor streams and swamps.'

The maharajas of Krishnanagar were great patrons of art and scholarship. Nabadwip flourished as the seat of Sanskrit learning during their time. The British called this land the 'Oxford of Bengal', and Christian missionaries, Catholics as well as Protestants, set up here in the early nineteenth century.

Apu's land has welcomed them all. It has a deep tradition of numerous social and religious movements, the most well-known of them being Sri Chaitanya's Bhakti movement, which brought within its folds people of all faiths, particularly the lower-caste groups. The region has also seen the growth of several minor religious cults. It is a land of vibrant culture, built on the bedrock of robust agriculture, whose magic lies in the fertile alluvium the rivers have deposited. At the turn of the twenty-first century, the same rivers had breached their banks.

~

But a year after the big flood, one had to look carefully to find traces of the havoc. Monsoon had ended, and the jute crop had been cut and processed. From the window of a moving bus, I could see the blonde tresses hanging on bamboo frames and bundles of jute stalks standing like tepees. The asphalt road was in surprisingly good condition.

'That's because of the BSF outposts,' Utpal told me. 'We'll go almost to the edge of the Border.'

Utpal Basak was my companion on this trip. He had passed BA with English honours from the government college in Krishnanagar. When the flood hit his village, Utpal had climbed a banyan tree and spent three days there. But he had also returned to college within a month. Many of his classmates had a similar story. Their stories showed the economic resilience of this region, because an entire generation had dropped out of schools and colleges after the historic floods of 1978.

Signs of prosperity were visible on the road. Tall, brightly painted buildings reared up from among clusters of hutments, tractors under sheds, motorcycle showrooms, household-appliances shops, advertisements of multinational brands, dish antennas atop tin roofs, STD-PCO booths, chow mein and soft-drink kiosks, online lottery shops: they flitted past as the service bus tooted and honked its way through a string of dusty, crowded ganjes, neither town nor village, sitting in the middle of the countryside.

'Many of the men you see on the road are Border crossers,' Utpal remarked. 'They work here as wage labourers or carriers of smuggled goods. Some of them will slip away to the other side by evening.'

This area was famous for two cash crops: jute and contraband goods. Earlier, there had been a smuggling racket that ferried electronic items manufactured in Hong Kong and South Korea. It had ceased when the Indian market opened up in the early 1990s. But bicycles, cows and various food items were still smuggled out.

Utpal's family had nothing to do with these cash crops. For many generations, the Basaks had practised the craft of handloom weaving. Utpal was the first member from his family to go to a college. His father and two elder brothers still worked at the loom. His grandfather had been part of a group of weavers who migrated from the Tangail district of East Bengal during Partition, bringing with them a unique style of weaving. The landed Hindus who had patronized their craft had shifted to this region when things heated up. The weaver communities had been forced to follow in their footsteps.

'Most of our kin settled further inland,' Utpal said. 'But my grandfather decided to stay close to the Border. He had hoped that things would again become normal and he'd be able to return home one day. That day never came, and he died a heartbroken man.'

Every time the bus stopped, the suffocating smell of jute stalks retting in canals and waterbodies hit the nostrils. But when it got moving again, the lush countryside bathed in the opalescent light of an autumn afternoon rolled out as far as the eye could see. Shades of green, from the palest seafoam to a deep granite, shimmered as a breeze ruffled the vegetation. The waterbodies were full, their surfaces mirroring the sky. Sometimes we spotted a lone farmer paddling a dug-out canoe over them, like a bird about to take flight into masses of cumuli glowing orange and pink. When had I last seen such a glorious sunset?

After three hours, when we finally reached Sthirpara, the evening had settled. A silken blue light had seeped into the landscape. It was that rare light which lingered during this time of the year, long after the sunset, gilding everything with a silver film. A tribal settlement – a clot of low mud huts with tiled roofs – stood near the bus stop. Young women were sitting out in the open in small groups, their shoulders propped against one another's, and hams pressed on grass. Freshly bathed, their oil-slicked hair spread out to dry, they were chatting in their own tongue. It was their hour of rest, a precious commodity earned after a day of hard labour that they would savour until household chores sucked them back into those huts.

Sometimes, a moment unfolds with such unexpected beauty that it makes us forget how fragile life is. We tend to forget that this might be the season when vector-borne germs stalk the countryside. I looked at a baby, dark as polished granite, in the arms of an old woman, its glasslike eyes reflecting the evening sky. My mind immediately flew forward to an imagined future, when all the adults gathered under the skies would no longer be around, and this evening would return to the dim memory of the child, then a grown-up, in an inexplicable spurt of joy. It never occurred to me that a bout of dysentery or malaria, a ruptured vein inside its tiny brain, could easily pluck that future unripened.

∼

'We had him as our teacher for a brief period. I was in Class 5 or 6. We didn't know what a great writer he was; that was only natural. Someone had lent me a copy of *Pather Panchali*, I remember, but I was too young to appreciate its greatness. I found it to be an ordinary book about the ordinary things of our village life. Where was the story, I had wondered. In those days, the tales of pirates and hunters captivated me. I was also fond of kobir lorai and kothokota, you know, the verbal duels between village poets and oration from the epics. There was a rich tradition of these folk forms in our district. Anyway, I didn't find Master-moshai any different from our other teachers. He rarely came to our class. We'd see him walk down the corridor or find him seated in the teachers' room with his legs resting upon the table, reading a book. Master-moshai was a thickset man with a slowness about him. But he could walk really fast. Every day, he'd walk barefoot across the fields and all the way from his home in Chalki-Barrackpur. We'd see Durwan-ji, our gateman, draw water from a well in the compound for Master-moshai to wash his feet. Then he'd put on a palm-leaf sandal that he kept in Durwan-ji's room. He always appeared to be lost in his thoughts and had tiny burn marks on his kurta from the beedis he smoked all the time.

'One day, Master-moshai was teaching us a prose piece, and he was deeply immersed in the lines that he was reading out loud. It was late in the afternoon, the last period. We were beside ourselves with pangs of hunger. None of us could focus on the book, our ears were pricked to hear the bell ring. We were getting restless and frantic, just as children always are towards the end of the last period. Teachers would usually tell funny stories and crack jokes to distract them until the last bell. But that day, Master-moshai was under some spell. He was reading aloud a long passage, perhaps from an essay by Jagadish Chandra Bose, the great botanist.

'Suddenly, we noticed his glasses misting over. Tears rolled down his cheeks and glinted on his stubbled chin. We couldn't make out what was happening. We were completely at a loss. There was nothing tragic in the essay he was reading from, we could understand that. There was no grief involved here. And that was when I dimly realized, for the first time in my life, that tears could also come from an appreciation of beauty. There was something, some extraordinary literary beauty, in the prose he was reading from, in its style, which we were too young to appreciate. But I have not forgotten that incident.

'We didn't have him at our school for long. I, too, left Haripada Institution after Class 8. I returned to Sthirpara, to our village home. My father closed down his businesses at Gopalnagar and devoted himself to farming.'

This was Satyacharan Ghosal, a retired schoolteacher, reminiscing about his own teacher, Bibhutibhushan Bandyopadhyay. His son Surith was Utpal's friend and an advocate in the local subdivisional court. They had arranged my stay at their house.

'Those were turbulent times,' Satyacharan continued. It seemed as if he was hearing his own voice after a long time and was savouring it. 'India was about to gain independence. We heard a rumour that our village would go to Pakistan. The well-off families here bought land further west, across the Hooghly. My father, too, went looking for a suitable place to shift our residence. Independence came on the fifteenth of August. Two days later, they broadcast Radcliffe sahib's award. This region had been gifted to Pakistan, we discovered to our shock. And then there were rallies, fasting and arondhon, no cooking in Hindu homes as a mark of protest, no lighting of lamps. The Congress leaders hurriedly met Lord Mountbatten, and on the eighteenth, a radio announcement corrected the mistake.

Independence came to this part of Bengal three days after it did to the rest of India.'

We were on the open terrace of Satyacharan's sprawling bungalow-type house. Sitting cross-legged, a red checked gamchha wrapped around his waist, he was slapping mustard oil on his hairy torso. His solemn voice fanned out into the torpid afternoon. A crow sat on a clothesline, its shadow quivering on a tub of bathwater warming in the sun. Somewhere in the garden, a coucal was calling 'koob-koob' in a steady rhythm. Dry, brown leaves shed by old fruit trees carpeted the garden floor. A yellow cat padded over them, possibly after the scent of a prey. Beyond the garden fences, there was a dirt track, a grassy plot, and beyond it a pond. A washerwoman was beating clothes on a stone. I could see her diminutive figure in the distance, between the dark tree trunks. There was a split-second hiatus between wet cloth slapping the stone and its sound reaching up here. The coucal, invisible, filled it with two precise koobs.

For two days this land was in another nation. I don't know if in that other nation a stealthy cat's feet released the warm scent of crushed leaves, or if a coucal filled the gap between a sight and a sound. Does this land, this territory now known as West Bengal, know? Does the West, like the stump of a severed limb, feel an itch on its missing East?

RADICAL ASPIRATION

Sthirpara was an old settlement of mostly Hindu farmers on the bank of the river Jalangi. Across it was Palashi, Plassey, where the East India Company had fought the army of the Nawab of Bengal. Satyacharan Ghoshal's large house was, in more ways than one, at the centre of the village. The nameplate on the door, of three men from two generations, bore the qualifications of the three most influential professionals in a village society: a teacher, a doctor and an advocate. Satyacharan's doctor son worked in the district hospital at Krishnanagar, where he lived with his family. Their photographs covered the walls of the old man's spartan living room. His wife had died eight years ago, and loneliness had puffed up bags of skin under his eyes. The family owned a few acres of land. Satyacharan looked after the farm, a flower garden around the house, read two newspapers, but never watched television. It was the long evening hours that he found the most difficult to bear. The house would remain empty and silent because his younger son, Surith, would spend the evening in the company of his friends.

They usually assembled at a computer kiosk inside the tiny village bazaar. An adda was settling when Utpal took me there. I met Arnab and Diptiman, co-owners of the establishment, the latter busy composing on PageMaker an invoice for a local fish stockist.

Unlike Utpal, his two friends didn't remain in town after they got a degree from college. They took training in computers and started their own business on the premises owned by Arnab's father. So far, the business had been slow.

'But things are catching up, sir,' Diptiman told me.

'This year we've made enough profits to pay my father rent for this premises.' Arnab beamed a smile.

'We've also applied for an IRCTC licence. Once we get it, we'll do railway ticket bookings.'

I was curious about the broadband internet speed in a place so close to the international border.

'So-so,' Arnab replied. 'It's the power situation that's really—'

And before he could finish the sentence, the room plunged into darkness. Curses, despondent laughter, and anxious beeps from a UPS greeted the power cut. A thin, young man with angular features drifted into the CRT monitor's astral glow. His hands were full with paper bags and tiny earthen bowls.

'Here comes Tapa!' Arnab announced.

'Here we are!' Tapa declared in a piping voice. 'Muri, khuri, phuluri and singara.'

Tapa, Surith's assistant in the court, had brought for us puffed rice, earthen cups of tea, chickpea fritters and samosas. His high-pitched voice reminded me of Nabadwip Halder, a Bangla film comedian from the black-and-white era.

They rustled up a nice tiffin: a mound of puffed rice encircled with hot fritters and green chillies on a newspaper spread over the floor. We came to sit cross-legged around it, while Tapa poured tea from a thermos into the teacups.

'I met your uncle at the snack shop,' Tapa turned to Diptiman and sputtered between mouthfuls of puffed rice. 'He bought two samosas. Is he planning to marry again?'

'What have samosas got to do with marriage?' Surith asked.

'Don't you know?' Tapa feigned surprise. 'Since his wife eloped, I mean went on that pilgrimage, the old man has been saving to buy himself another bride. To cut costs, he has stopped keeping a maid or a cook. These days he buys a pair of samosas in the evening, eats the outer covering with tea, and stores the filling to eat with the two rotis that he buys for a rupee.'

Everyone began to laugh, except Diptiman. He worked up a peeved expression on his face and snorted, '*What rubbish!*'

'*Rubbish?*' Tapa protested. 'Anyone can go and check for himself. Some days he buys fifty paisa's worth of sugar syrup from Ashu Moyra's sweetshop. One roti he eats dipped in the syrup, the other one he eats with the samosa filling. On these days he buys one samosa only.'

This time Tapa chuckled at his own banter. Diptiman also joined in.

I asked Surith about the cases he handled in the court.

'Mostly divorce cases,' he said promptly.

This was news for me. 'Are divorce cases on the rise in rural areas?'

'Earlier, women could never muster up the will to go to court. Now they do. Now they are aware of their rights.'

They debated over the causes of divorce, the erosion of family values, and the changing face of the village society. From this topic, the adda drifted to a phenomenon rampant in this region: suicide, particularly among women.

'Not a day passes in the district hospital without at least one case of attempted suicide. Most are women, and below thirty,' Surith told me. 'I know this because my brother is a doctor there.'

'I can't say if the number has gone up, but earlier we didn't hear of them so often. Taina?' Diptiman said and turned to others. They nodded in agreement.

'Most of the times the causes are inconsequential,' said Arnab. 'A tiff with the husband, a quarrel over a new dress, a poor performance in an exam – and that acts as a trigger, to reach out for the can of pesticide. They stock it in most houses here.'

'Sometimes they'll also eat a mouthful of sugar to quicken death.'

Utpal turned to me and said in a reassuring voice, 'Tomorrow, when you'll be visiting the schools, I will take you along around a locality where there has been a suicide in every single house.'

'Are you talking about Mahashaypara?' Surith asked.

Utpal nodded. Surith turned to me.

'There was a time when all the wealthy people in our village lived in Mahashaypara. They owned most of the land here. But now their fortunes have declined.'

'And they have twisted minds!' Tapa added. 'They boycotted the last election because a polling booth was shifted away from the neighbourhood.'

None of them, however, could shed light on the spate of suicides in a particular locality within the village.

'You'll be going there tomorrow,' Diptiman said. 'You'll see for yourself.'

'Every family there owns a plot of land, and pesticides are stocked in every house. That may be a reason.'

'Here we call pesticide "oshudh" – medicine,' Arnab observed. 'Isn't that funny?'

'The companies recommend antidotes on their labels, but who can read them? By the time they take the victim to a health centre, she's dead.'

'I think they should offer free antidotes along with the pesticides,' Tapa commented.

'Else we all should turn to organic farming. What do you say?' Diptiman asked him.

'Last winter, my uncle grew cabbages as big as elephant heads,' Tapa declared. He stretched out his hands to indicate the size. 'And he did it with his own manure only.'

'His *own* manure!' Surith exclaimed.

Tapa hastened to correct himself. 'I mean his farm manure.'

'But you didn't say that. You said his own manure.'

'His own manure for that big plot? Was it sufficient or did you also contribute?' Diptiman chuckled.

Tapa, unfazed by the chaffing and peals of laughter, polished off the last of the fritters and wiped the oil around his fingers against the newspaper spread on the floor.

~

That evening, after dinner, I learnt more about Mahashaypara from Satyacharan Ghoshal.

'Mahashays were the landed bhadralok who had a steady prosperity since the time of the East India Company. After the Permanent Settlement of Bengal, they brought Bhatiya Mussalmans – the tide country Muslims – from the southern parts of the Delta to reclaim new mudflats. These Bhatiya Mussalmans were experts at this job. For a long time, almost all the high-fertile lands by the river had belonged to the Mahashays. But they lost much of it during Partition, when most of these Bhatiya Mussalmans went to East Pakistan, or crossed the river and went to settle in the Murshidabad district, where they were a majority. Then the Left Front introduced the Land Ceiling Act and the Mahashays were forced to surrender all the excess and benami land. And then, there were the refugees who migrated from the east with nothing but the clothes they wore. They worked really hard and established themselves. Mahashaypara's decline continued. Whether we should call this the cycle of fortune or the turning of history, I have no idea.'

We were sitting on the veranda adjoining the large dining room. Nylon netting covered the grilles to keep out the insects. A portion of the large paved courtyard, a hut-shaped haystack, and a cowshed were dimly visible through the netting. The two servants and a cook who ran the household had retired. Despite the many trappings of comfort, the pretty bungalow had a solitary, all-male feel about it.

'But it's not that suicides are limited to that single locality only,' Surith joined the conversation. 'It's happening everywhere. Suicide, divorce, drug addiction – even the villages are changing fast. And life is also very fragile in these Border regions. Here today, gone tomorrow.'

Satyacharan shook his head slowly. He didn't seem to agree with his son. Stretched on a deckchair, arms folded behind his head, he gazed out at the courtyard. A swarm of insects glinted around a lighted bulb on a solitary post. Crickets rattled interminably.

'Partition hit this region badly,' Satyacharan spoke after a long silence. A distant tone had crept into his voice. 'It was as if a meat cleaver was whacked through a living body. All the jute farming you've seen on the way here is but a shadow of what it used to be when Bengal was in one piece. They grew the best jute in the eastern districts and ferried them to the mills along the Hooghly. This region was famous for the mango orchards that extended to Palashi, where Clive had fought the battle with the Nawab. After Partition, the Hindu jute farmers migrated here, cut down the orchards and completely changed the landscape. When the jute industry went under, many switched to paddy farming round the year, drawing water with submersible pumps. Earlier, we'd dig ten feet to reach the aquifers, now it's thirty feet or more. Even then, nobody knows how much arsenic there is in the water. The soil character has changed. It used to have a rich brown texture, like fresh jaggery. Now it's clayey and dull. Who knows how long the earth will *sustain*? Of late, there's been a fresh wave of border crossers. They squat on whatever piece of land they can find – the wayside ditches, the swamps, the sandbanks. But I must confess one thing. They know how to get the most from the land. A family of four can easily subsist on a meagre six-decimal plot of land. First, they dig a small fishpond, plant coconut palms around it and use the dug-up mud to build a pair of huts. Then they plant betel palms on the rest of the land, grow ginger and turmeric under their shades, and raise gourd creepers on scaffolds resting on the palm trunks. That's classic multi-cropping! They have introduced a variety of spices and oilseeds that we never knew could grow on this soil. But such a multitude of people, such limited resources. How long will it all hold out? That's a question I ask myself these days. I won't be there to see that day. But what will happen to this land? I have spent all my life asking questions in the classrooms. But who'll answer my question? Had Master-moshai been around, I could have asked him. He had written about this land with such passion!'

~

'What is your name?'

'Mampi Rani Das.'

'What is the name of this school?'

'Iswar Chandra Vidyasagar Memorial Free Primary School.'

'Which class are you in?'

'I am in Class 3.'

'Do you have a brother or a sister?'

'Yes, I have a younger brother.'

'Does he go to school?'

'Yes, he is in Class 1.'

'Does he come to school with you?'

'No, my brother goes to another school. Little Bud, English medium.'

At this point, the questioner lost the thread of the interview. But the respondent was cool. She was waiting eagerly for the next question. Her round forehead glistened under oil-slicked hair coiled into a pair of tiny tails with red ribbons knotted in the shape of butterflies. She was wearing a smoke-grey frock that the government sometimes distributed among the girl students. It had a navy-blue necktie sewn between the lapels. Mampi sat on the bare classroom floor with her mates. Most of them were girls.

Perhaps, like Mampi, they, too, had brothers who went to private English-medium schools. From the way they waited patiently for their turn, it was obvious that they were enjoying this break from daily routine.

But the questioner didn't have the heart to go on. In fact, he himself was skewered by a question: if by some magic Iswar Chandra Vidyasagar, the great nineteenth-century social reformer who dedicated his life to the uplift of women, could appear here now, in this very school named after him, where there were more girls than boys, would he be happy?

The teachers were not. In fact, they were worried. The cause for their concern presented itself as I was given a tour of the classrooms. The class size grew steadily as we moved from Class 1 to 4. There were more children in the higher classes, despite the fact that a percentage of them dropped out before they were promoted. The writing on the wall was clear: enrolment was dwindling with each passing year.

'They did away with English teaching at the primary level and allowed private English-medium schools to proliferate like mushrooms. This is the net result,' pronounced Nityananda Khan, the headmaster, as he moved his hand in a half-circle.

'But English has returned in the curriculum, no?' I asked.

'Yes, but after a gap of twenty years. By that time the damage had been done.'

The other teachers agreed. Except one of them – a young man who commuted from the town.

'Most of our students are children of farmworkers,' he pointed out. 'The Bangla they speak at home is a little different from the standard bhadralok Bangla in which books are written. Teaching them English in the lower classes means giving these young minds the burden of two languages.'

But none of his colleagues shared this view. A lady teacher complained: 'Not just English, they even abolished the pass–fail system. The private schools have both. Why would the parents who can afford them send their children here?'

'But the private schools don't serve midday meals,' I reminded her.

'No, that they don't,' Mr Khan agreed.

'But, you know, many children here don't eat the midday meal except when egg is on the menu,' she persisted. 'They bring their lunch from home.'

This I had already noticed: steel lunchboxes were peeping from schoolbags. Was it a new form of class division within the classroom? Was it connected with other less visible divisions that girls like Mampi faced? What was the gender ratio among the midday-mealers and lunchboxers? Knotty questions, naughty too. I refrained from asking them.

'Things have changed a lot,' Mr Khan said. 'In earlier times, if you gave a large family feast, all the villagers would come after the guests had eaten. Not any more. Now you have to invite them properly, else they won't come.'

Nityananda Khan joined this school in the mid-1980s and settled here in Sthirpara. That was when the land reforms programme was in full swing. Since then, things had changed. I saw signs of change on my way here. Hero Honda, Samsung and Safed detergent competed for billboard space with Little Bud Nursery School, Holy Child 'Kindergarden' and St Jackson Academy. I never knew there was a saint by that name; or was he Michael Jackson the rock star?

Nobel laureate Amartya Sen's Pratichi Trust conducted in-depth studies of the elementary education system in West Bengal. Of all the findings in 'The Pratichi Education Report', published in 2002, the most revealing was that, contrary to popular bhadralok perception, poor people in Bengal were *not* reluctant to send their children to school. In fact, many working-class parents spent a large chunk of their income on their children's education, including private tuition. Noting this, Professor Sen had made a pointed observation in his introduction to the first of a series of reports: 'We were struck by the reflective and mature nature of these radical aspirations.'

Christian missionaries came to Apu's land early and made possible his story. It was the English liberal education that had transformed the mental world of a poor Brahmin's son. But here were the neo-liberal missionaries of the free market courting the 'radical aspirations' of a village society. I saw hencoop cycle-vans crammed with toddlers clattering down rutted village paths.

Some of these vans wound their way to Little Bud Nursery School, where Mampi's brother went. Advertised as an 'English medium' school, the teachers here gave instruction in Bangla. There were eleven of them, for two hundred and thirty-two students in four classes (eighty-one girls, one hundred and fifty-one boys). The teachers were all young, unmarried women, all intermediate and college dropouts. Their salaries ranged from eight hundred to one thousand rupees a month, less than what a young female farm labourer earned. The school was run from a rented two-storeyed building with a small compound. It had separate toilets for boys and girls, and swings and a seesaw in the compound. The classrooms, partitioned with bamboo screens, had ceiling fans and wooden benches. The pupils wore smart uniforms – red checked shirts and black shorts for boys and skirts for girls – with shoes and real neckties.

Outside the locked iron gate (a rarity in government-run rural primary schools), on the shaded terrace of a temple, a group of mothers had assembled. They were waiting to receive their children. They were neatly dressed and carried umbrellas; their husbands were in service or had small businesses. The children had private tutors, many of them teachers at the same school.

~

After a hectic day, I was returning to Sthirpara bus stand to catch a bus back to town. Utpal walked me along an old part of the village.

'Do you remember what we told you about Mahashaypara?' he whispered into my ear. 'Here it is.'

In the fading light of dusk, all I could see was a neighbourhood of pucca houses that had seen better times. Thick moss stained the buildings like permanent cloud-shadow, elaborate stucco work was crumbling, weeds ran riot in the gardens around the houses. Other than these, there wasn't any obvious sign of destitution. Or tragedy. There'd been a suicide in every single house, I reminded myself. But I didn't know where to seek for the signs of desperation which would prompt a hand to reach out for a length of rope or a bottle of *oshudh* to cure the incurable. Did the light of dusk have a different shade here? The acrid smell of burning cow dung hung in the air. Through a door left ajar, I glimpsed a mud-plastered courtyard, and a stack of ploughs and wooden cartwheels in a corner. Inside a thatched shed, two veiled women were pedalling a wooden mortar. It produced a sound like muffled heartbeats. A bare-chested man was pushing a muddied bicycle heaped with freshly harvested radishes. A banana grove from whose green depths darkness spilled like oil. A tiny pond under the shade of a mango tree, with a flight of broken steps leading into black water. A thin girl in a faded frock was calling back a flock of ducks – '*Choi choi! Choi choi!*' A buxom woman, a metal tub pressed between her bared thighs, was massaging a skeletal cow's udder, preparing it for milking. The animal licked its dead offspring's coat wrapped around a straw effigy. An old man with a milk can in his hand was inspecting the scene with rheumy eyes. Pigeons were flapping back to roost in the latticed ceiling of an upper-floor balcony. Three girls dressed in salwar-kameez cycled past, their dupattas flying behind their shoulders like wings.

IN-BETWEEN PLACES

Like a river in spate, villages would flood the town with 'radical aspirations'. Every morning, busloads of people would pour in from the outlying areas. They would flock to district courts, hospitals, wholesale markets, government offices, cinema halls, liquor bars, and other centres of business and pleasure. Krishnanagar, the once-famous town named after a maharaja – with its royal palaces, art-deco villas, churches and sprawling Civil Lines – was slowly being mofussilized. Fine heritage mansions stood decrepit or were being pulled down. The town's old elite had left; their seats were being taken over by the village parvenu and moneyed migrants from across the border. Krishnanagar was a mess of dwindled civic amenities, collapsing power supply, encroached footpaths and homicidal roads. Every two hours, a suburban train would excrete its load, turning the narrow Station Road into a congealed effluence of motorbikes, buses, cycle-rickshaws, cars and trucks crammed with office babus and drifters, pilgrims visiting Nabadwip and Hare-Krishna monks from the ISKCON temple, litigants, land brokers, patients and livestock crammed in cycle-vans.

The railway service connected the town with Kolkata. As the packed train would pull into the platform, the coaches would fill up even before they were emptied, preceded by much jostling and fighting at the doors. I watched helplessly as desperate commuters flung themselves inside the compartments to grab a seat. Vintage photographs of Partition trains flashed in my mind. After waiting for a few futile minutes, I finally mustered up the courage, and squeezing myself inside a vendor compartment, secured a foothold between baskets of cauliflower and cottage cheese. I braced myself for a three-hour journey.

Hawkers are an integral part of the suburban railway service here. From pain balms to puffed rice, roasted peanuts to ratsbane, they sell everything. Sometimes, they switch products to stay afloat over the seasonal rise and fall in their demand. Thus, the same salesman would hawk green mango sherbet in summer, oranges in winter and cough lozenges during the rains. But of the hundreds of types of products they sell on train compartments, there is one product that never has an off season. In fact, it is not even a product; it is a radical aspiration. It is the English language.

A dark, middle-aged man with sad eyes and a thickly veined neck rising out of a frayed shirt collar elbowed his way into the packed aisle. He held a sheaf of booklets in his right hand like a Japanese fan. With his left hand cupped and positioned before his lips like a microphone, the man recited: 'Everyone knows what machh is called in English. It's *fish*. But do you know what the fish's kanko are called? What their pakhna or kanta are called in English? What are the different varieties of fish like ilish, magur, bhetki, golda chingri, bagda chingri called in English? Everyone here knows the English word for chokh. It is *eye*. But do you know what the *eyelashes* are? What exactly are the *brows*, the *eyelids*, the *cornea*, the *eyeballs*—'

The train was entering the city. Outside the window, sad, moss-lined suburbs collapsed into psychedelic images of Kolkata's metropolitan sprawl. A faint crimson still lingered in the sky, but street lights were on and skyscrapers glinted beyond a shantytown.

Out of nowhere, Mampi Rani Das's face ambushed me: I recalled her expectant eyes, her round oil-slicked forehead, and her ponytails that touched her thin shoulders.

Mampi's brother went to a private English-medium school. By sending Mampi and her brother to two different schools, their parents were making a compromise between affordability and radical aspiration. I was shocked when I learnt this, but Mampi was unfazed. She waited for my next question, impatiently twirling in her finger the false necktie sewn into her frock. Did she ever dream of going to her brother's school, wearing a smart checked shirt, a knee-length skirt and a real necktie? I didn't ask her this question.

'What do you want to be when you grow up?' I had asked instead.

She had offered me a shy smile. 'I want to be a teacher.'

If Mampi could pass out of high school and push on a little further, to the intermediate level or beyond, she could realize her dream. She could enter her brother's school one day, as a teacher.

~

Utpal Basak was still staying in Krishnanagar when I met him after a gap of six years.

I was on a brief visit to the town. When Utpal learnt this, he came to invite me to his place. He was still staying in town, in a dingy suburb beside a narrow-gauge railway line, where he shared a narrow tin-roofed room with two old college friends, Matin Islam and Bishu Hembram. Matin and Bishu had passed BA with Sanskrit and Philosophy honours, respectively. Matin was from Utpal's village, and Bishu's father worked in a colliery in Asansol.

At one level, this was an exciting new social revolution: two young men, a Muslim and a Santhal, opting to study two traditionally Brahminical subjects. But the not-so-exciting fact was that the choice was possibly thrust on them. In the colleges in West Bengal, Sanskrit and Philosophy were among the least sought-after courses and seats were usually available for low-scoring candidates. These were also on the list of subjects recognized by the School Service Commission (SSC), the government body that appointed schoolteachers in the state.

Utpal, Bishu and Matin had already appeared in selection tests conducted by the SSC a few times. Now they were approaching the upper age limit. Recruitments were not regular, and with every passing year, the competition was getting stiffer. A few weeks earlier, there had been a test for the selection of primary schoolteachers. Forty-five lakh applicants had competed for three thousand posts. Bishu and Matin took turns to describe to me how the examinees had crammed the buses, trucks and trains, even climbed the trains' roofs, to travel to distant examination centres.

As I listened, the photographs of Partition trains flashed again in my mind. That wrenching event had not ended. It went on and on, and sprang up in unexpected places.

A grim humour animated their narration.

'Why don't you look for other jobs?' I asked.

'Other jobs?' A despondent smile curled Utpal's lips. 'Last December, the Public Service Commission had advertised for four thousand government jobs. All group-D posts – peon, orderly, watchman, etc. Anyone who had passed Class 8 was eligible to apply. Can you guess the number of applicants?'

I shook my head.

'Eleven lakh!'

'Tell him how many engineers had applied,' Bishu quipped.

'And how many PhDs!' Matin added.

They laughed together, a dry hacking laugh. Evening shadows were gathering inside the room, and I could barely see their faces. Three rough wooden cots heaped with newspapers and magazines had taken up almost the entire space. Rolled-up mosquito nets, strung across the walls like hammocks, served as wardrobes. Beedi ash coated the floor.

Evening had settled when I stepped out. Heaps of raw coal were burning in the Coolie Lines, tongues of blue-orange flames varnished the surface of a scummy ditch. Utpal was taking me to the bus stand, where I was to catch a bus or a Trekker taxi to the railway station. He halted and glanced at his wristwatch.

'Would you like to go to the railway station on a train?'

To the railway station on a train? I was puzzled.

'A narrow-gauge train returns from Nabadwip Ghat around this time. It goes to the junction station. It will be an interesting journey. I am sure you'll like it.'

I had noticed the narrow railway track winding around the neighbourhood. But I didn't know that a train service was still operating on this line. We walked a short distance to a tiny halt station, a low, redbrick structure with a peaked tin roof. Despite signs of decay, the station still had a picture-postcard charm about it. The stationmaster's cubicle doubled as the ticket counter, a hole punctured into a wall. Nothing was visible in the darkness inside, but a hand dutifully took the five-rupee coin and slipped out a punched ticket. A wooden board painted yellow told the name of the station: AMGHATA. An old mulberry tree stood on the low, deserted platform. A madwoman, naked and with a head full of matted shoulder-length hair, had set up her residence under the platform shed. Except for me, there was no other passenger.

Soon, a toy-like train, comprising a miniature diesel engine and two bottle-green wooden carriages, rolled into the platform. Inside the dimly lit coach, a kirtaniya, a devotional music band, was travelling with their drums and clappers. Elderly widows with sandalwood paste drawn on their foreheads in horizontal stripes were the band members. Their leader was a gaunt man dressed in a yellow faux-silk kurta and sporting a shock of burgundy hair which unfurled like a halo around his head.

Utpal noticed my excitement and smiled.

But the smile couldn't lighten the shadow that seemed to have stained his face permanently. I searched in it the lively eyes of the first-year English honours student I had known. Earlier in the afternoon, I had enquired after his family. I gathered that he scarcely visited Sthirpara these days. He hung around in town, gave tuition to a group of schoolkids and wrote endless job applications. Sthirpara had nothing to offer him.

The train began to pull out of the platform with a jerk. I stretched my arm out of the window and touched Utpal's shoulder.

'Shouldn't you better leave this place and return home?' I asked.

'What would I do there, sir? If I go back, I'll have no alternative but to sit at the loom. I can't do that now.'

Utpal walked a few paces alongside the coach and stopped. As the train picked up speed, I turned my head and saw him standing under the mulberry tree.

After Partition, Utpal's grandfather had migrated from East Bengal. He had brought with him a style of weaving unique to the district of Tangail. His father and two brothers had kept the tradition alive. They let Utpal go to a college in town and prepare for the career of a bhadralok. Three years of college education hadn't taught him any skill that could get him a job. He still lived in that rented tenement and scraped out a living by giving tuition to kids. That was one option left to a shikkhito bekar, an educated unemployed, in Bengal.

For Utpal, and also for Bishu and Matin, it had been a one-way road out of the village. Small towns harboured starry-eyed drifters like them. In the village, life was a stagnant pool, a quagmire. It somehow flowed in a town. Here, a shikkhito bekar could live in a perpetual state of hope, drifting from excitement to excitement, from tea shop to liquor den, from adda to political rallies, always waiting for that windfall, for that letter or phone call, for that opening at a bend, until aspirations turned to ashes and prospects rotted into a web of lies.

By the time, if ever, the job situation took a turn, Utpal would be too old to catch the bus. And yet, in a system where seven out of ten boys and girls dropped out before they completed school, Utpal had come far. It was the failure of the system that it couldn't live up to the radical aspirations of a weaver's son. As his teacher, it was my failure that I couldn't teach him anything that could have helped him get a better grip on his destiny. If Utpal could write a proper loan application, if he could read and understand the fine print of various government schemes, negotiate with finance agencies, perhaps he could have saved his ailing family profession. If he could trawl the internet and glean new weaving technologies and designs, if he could connect with export agencies, perhaps he could have become an entrepreneur and created jobs. He could have become a success story, the stuff of a fantastic novel, of a village boy, poor but ambitious, who came to town to study…

But we didn't give him anything. Rather, we robbed him of the unique craft his grandfather had brought from across the border.

WHAT THE RIVER SAYS

Nakul Sardar's sun-baked body and grey kinky hair reminded me of burnt wood dusted with ash. He had aged since I last met him. His eyes were dull, and there was a muddled expression on his face. On a late April afternoon, Nakul was setting a net across a narrow canal on the Hooghly. He finished the work and accompanied us to the opposite bank on a ferryboat.

The river was at a low tide.

'The fish will swim into the canal on the high tide.' Nihar-da sounded like an expert and turned to Nakul for confirmation. But he was wrong.

'They always swim against the current, babu. During high tide, the fish in the canal will rush to the river's mouth,' Nakul explained with a smile, exposing a pair of front teeth crossed like tentative fingers. Then he added: 'But where are they? That paper mill over there has fucked up the river thoroughly – it has turned her into a barren cunt!'

He pointed to a row of tin sheds on the distant bank and a chimney spewing black smoke in the still afternoon air.

Nakul Sardar's way with words hadn't left him, but time had taken a toll on his health. In the light reflected off the river, his eyes resembled a pair of dull eggs set in a bird's nest. He looked happy to see me back, but now he gazed indifferently at the rippling waters.

Minutes ago, he had been in chest-deep water, fixing the long, narrow net on the canal. A piece of cloth tied around his loins like a thong and a beedi pressed between his lips, he had the same indifferent expression on his face. An entire day's work would hardly fetch him fifty rupees worth of fish, not enough to feed three hungry stomachs at home. Did the look on his face stem from the futility of it all? Nakul's idea of work, and his expectations from it, were beyond me. The canal had fish, and he had a net, and the knowledge of where and when to cast it, and also about the ways of fish; perhaps that was enough for him.

The Hooghly looked barren indeed. It meandered across a wide sand bed, a deep channel flanked by stagnant pools of water. In the distance, a line of sand trucks was crawling like termites out of the river's desiccated heart. Beyond it, upon a steep embankment, rows of tents and reed shacks etched a sharp corrugated line against the fiery sky. For the last two years, this has been Nakul Sardar's village. The original settlement lay behind the bund, submerged in a fen from where the water hadn't drained.

When I had met him in the school-turned-into-a-relief-camp, Nakul had invited me to visit his village, Srikrishnapur. It was on a char, one of the many inhabited mudflats on the Hooghly. I had promised I would come, but now I was late. In the meantime, there had been another flood. I had wished to see with my own eyes the char home of a fisherman–farmer, but now it seemed as if I had entered Anil Kaka's nightmare.

This time, Nihar-da was with me.

'I'm happy to see that you have remembered me,' Nakul said. 'But what's there to see now? If you had come during the winter, I could've shown you the birds.'

'Birds?' Nihar-da was curious.

'Yes, in the marshes behind the bund. Lots of birds, all *foreign*.'

Nihar-da rued the missed opportunity for a bit of wildlife photography.

At low tide, the Hooghly wasn't more than a furlong wide. The boatman had only to plunge a bamboo pole into the water a few times to steer his boat across it. He deposited us on a flat stretch of brown sand. Humans, goats, cycles and a pair of motorbikes moved in a single file over a foot track snaking across the dunes. Ragged children were fishing in knee-deep puddles. Their long, matted hair glowed like a halo in the reflected light. Carcasses of boats lay half buried in the sand.

Nakul walked with us for some distance towards the settlement on top of the bund. 'You go right up on top and wait there for me,' he said. 'I'll catch up with you after I check the nets here.'

Steps were cut against the mud embankment, across cactus bushes, to the flat crest of the ridge. We climbed them and gained a first proper view of the disaster. On our left lay the waning river, on the right stretched an expanse of stagnant water over what had once been habitations. The embankment tapered into it like a tongue. It appeared to be the site of a lost riverine civilization: half-submerged brick buildings, grid-like pathways, electric poles without wiring, and dead trees.

Barking dogs, and the saccharine voice of a female radio jockey at a paan–beedi shop, greeted us at the camp settlement. 'And if you wish your favourite song to be played for your sweetheart, then do call us at…'

The shop was empty. Its owner appeared from the bushes below with a plastic water jug; he was wearing a lungi folded above the knees. We bought a packet of Navy Cut.

'So this is now Srikrishnapur, isn't it?' I tried to strike up a conversation.

'Yes, you can call it that,' the middle-aged man replied curtly and proceeded to chop dried tobacco leaves on a cutter.

'But you can also call it Khayramari, and Bijney, and Habibpur…' he said as an afterthought, his eyes fixed on the sharp steel blade biting into a thick batch of brown, velvety leaves.

'What do you mean by that?' Nihar-da demanded.

'What do I mean?' The man stopped the cutter and turned to look at us. 'I mean that people from all these villages have been relocated here.'

But it was impossible to tell the villages from the rows of identical black tarpaulin tents. Fifty-odd families from three villages had been staying here for more than a year. Each tent stood upon a bamboo frame propped on stilts, the living space above, and below it the goats, poultry and household items salvaged from the jaws of the flood. I noticed door frames, treadle mortars, furniture, faggots, farm gear and even household gods. It was a relief camp overstaying its allotted time. Gourd creepers climbed the plastic roofing, tulsi plants thrived on clay altars, and there were even cages with birds in them. Everything, everyone, appeared languid and sun-bleached.

Children were playing with old, paint-peeled toys on the dusty lane between rows of tents. Their rough-skinned mothers were cooking lunch under the skies. A long-haired woman was kneeling over a dug-out oven and, her cheek almost touching the ground, was blowing on live cinders. She squinted at us through a screen of smoke. Her alert posture and suspicious eyes had something feral about them. Flung out in the open, without privacy, without the security of a home, the camp dwellers seemed to have adopted the ways of a primitive hunter-gatherer group. I couldn't believe that these people had once been settled farmers. Most able-bodied men had migrated to seek work as labourers; only the children, the elderly and the women were staying here.

And the ones who thrived on a disaster. We ran into such a specimen; he was a stocky young man dressed in a lungi and a red T-shirt with Che's face stencilled on it. The camera on Nihar-da's neck had drawn his attention.

'Who do you want to meet here? Where are you from?' the young man demanded, blocking our path.

'Are we supposed to answer that? Who are *you*?' Nihar-da snapped.

'I'm a member of the Camp Committee. Anyone who is a bohiragoto will have to report at the camp office first. That's the rule.'

Bohiragoto – outsider. The word took on political overtones when the Left Front's iron grip in the rural areas of the state loosened. More than a quarter-century of winning elections and running a government had seen the emergence of a party society where a single political party controlled all civil democratic institutions. Consequently, when that party society began to crack, it was men from the outside who came and organized the disgruntled people. Since then, the word bohiragoto had grown bristles around it.

It now put Nihar-da on a short fuse. He thundered: 'And who has made this rule, may I know please? Isn't this place inside the territory of India? I am a citizen of India, and I can go wherever I wish. *That* is the rule!'

Arms akimbo and eyes rolled up in a theatrical display of ill humour, Nihar-da suddenly lowered his voice and asked conspiratorially, 'CPM or Trinamool? Which party are you from, haan? Where's your desh?'

The man, visibly taken aback, replied stiffly, 'Bijney.'

'Ah, but that's a village. I'm asking where are you really from? Bangladesh, or East Pakistan? Bangladesh, taina? That means you and your family migrated here after 1971. Had you come earlier, you'd have said Pakistan. And if you said East Bengal, then it would mean you migrated before Partition. Like yours truly,' Nihar-da blurted out and tapped his own chest.

It set the Camp Committee member at ease. He stroked his chin and mumbled, 'Well, if you talk of original inhabitants...'

'Original inhabitants my foot!' Nihar-da barked. 'Nothing like that here, my friend. This land is young, this entire Bengal Delta is. A few thousand years ago, this was all sea, do you understand? All sea. The sea receded, the mudflats rose, and then you and I appeared on the scene. That's it. Now the rivers will swell and shrink, the land will form and wash away. That's the rule, nature's rule. Do you understand? We all are bohiragoto. All!'

The young man turned to me and flashed a sheepish smile.

'The way *uncle* is speaking, it's as if all this happened yesterday. But this is *heesteeree*!'

～

The Committee ran its operations from a large tent, larger than the rest. Thick straw carpeted the floor and there were plastic tables, chairs and a battery-operated television set. A large red flag, with the hammer-and-sickle printed on it in gold, draped a wall.

They stored relief materials here, Bapi Mondal informed us. They had also set up a paid telephone service, so that the workers living in other states could be in touch with their families. It worked both ways; the Committee could also keep a tab on the people in the camp.

'We also run a free clinic. A government doctor attends it every week. We are trying to open an anganwadi centre,' Bapi said, and then asked bluntly, 'I hope you are not NGO people?'

'What if we are?' I asked.

'We aren't allowing them here. Also, no Maoists please.' Bapi smiled affably and turned to Nihar-da: 'Would you like to have tea, *uncle*? Come this way.'

A string of shops stood behind the Committee tent. There was a grocer's store, a potter's, a cycle repair shop, and a VCD rental shop. A tea stall made with bamboo screens stood on the broken tail of the bund. It looked like a toad about to leap into the water. Right behind it, there was a massive landslip: a thirty-foot-high guard wall had crumbled into the river. Water stretched in three directions: clear, brown, black, stagnant and flowing. Abandoned boats with watery, moss-lined floors, each reflecting the sun: a cluster of green eyes.

Nakul Sardar was waiting for us here. He sat on a bamboo machan, a leg folded up to his chest, his chin resting on the knee. He failed to recognize us, though we had met only an hour earlier.

'When will the tide turn?' I asked, seating myself by his side.

He was alerted by my voice.

'Oh, it's you! I don't see well in this weak light.'

Nakul complained of black spots in his line of vision that danced when daylight faded.

'That's a price fishermen pay for their vigil under the sun,' Bapi observed. 'Light bounces off the waters and hits the eyes.'

'Did you see a doctor?' I asked.

'The Committee organized an eye camp last summer,' Nakul replied. 'The doctor-babu said I have cataracts. But he couldn't promise that an operation would cure it. The sap inside my eyeballs has dried.'

I scrutinized his eyes under the mellowed light of the setting sun. There was a yellowish pallor to both the eyeballs; the corneas, too, had a bleached look.

'The irrigation department is repairing the broken bund. Would you like to take a look?' Bapi offered.

We finished tea and climbed down the broken slope leading into the river. Nakul followed us grudgingly. He had grown aloof on seeing Bapi with us. The Hooghly was exhaling the cool breath of dusk. Behind us, along the crest of the bund, stretched the rows of dust-coated tents, with the large Committee tent, a red Party flag fluttering atop, in the foreground. Under a sepia sky, the scene appeared like a battle camp in a Company painting.

A battle *was* on – between man and a river. The trucks snaked along the contours of sandbars like armoured vehicles. Many years ago, dykes were built on floodplains to claim villages and farmlands. Insurgent waters had bombarded the battlements. Now they were being built again to push out the enemy water. But everyone knew that it was a lost battle, nobody could win against the unrelenting power of water. The trucks crawled, dragging their long shadows, to dump boulders quarried from a distant hill and to take away the sand to the city.

'Both the work contracts were given out to the same firm,' Bapi said. 'But we in the Camp Committee have no hand in this. These things are fixed at the highest levels.'

Nakul flopped down on his hams and leaned against the ravaged guard wall. He turned his glazed eyes on the rushing stream and muttered in a low, almost inaudible voice: 'In the past, the river ran gently. Now it frets like a chained dog. A flood would bring a gift of silt, soft and fine like fresh yoghurt. Not any more. These days it brings only sand.'

On our way here, we had seen a farmer turning up a layer of sand on his plot. He was probably doing it in the hope that another flood would carry silt and give him back his land.

'Yes, that's in the nature of a river.' Nakul nodded. 'One flood will bury the land under a carpet of sand, the next one will carry silt and bring it alive. Look over here.'

He rose to his feet and moved his hand across the landslip's vertical gash, the striated layers of beige earth and white sand, the archive of decades of periodic flooding.

Here was the story of a young land, an amorphous scape, not the ruins of an ancient civilization. Even if there had been one, countless floods had washed it away. As they would this civilization too, wipe it clean with the rushing waters. Successive changes would cast newer layers of beige earth and white sand, with the skeletons of missing men embedded in them.

A change in regime, a new political upheaval, and there'd be a new harvest of skeletons – 2011, 2007, 1979, 1971, 1968, 1964, 1950, 1947... and from older times, buried deep in the striated history of Bengal.

The Great Calcutta Killings of 1946?

Yes, why not.

And what about the ones, uncremated, tossed into the Hooghly during the Bengal Famine of 1943, the last of a series during the British rule?

Them too.

Could we separate them from the first great one in 1770, after the East India Company's rule began in this region?

Surely not, they are all here.

And what about the plagues, the famines, the wars and the killings in between?

Oh yes, definitely. The entire Bengal Delta rests on a scaffolding of human bones.

'These days you cannot say anything from your heart,' Nakul said in a tired voice, pulling me back from the reverie. 'You never know if your words are true. All the words our parents have passed on to us have come to nothing. I cast my net in the marshes over there for fish. With so many birds coming to roost, I think I'll have a good catch. Do you know what it yields?'

'What?' I asked.

'Plastic. Only plastic.' Nakul turned his dull eyes on Nihar-da. 'Babu, do the *foreign* birds eat plastic?'

'Are these migratory birds?' I asked Bapi.

'Some of them are, yes. Until last year, we were hunting them for the meat. Then the forest babus came and threatened us. Someone wrote something in a newspaper. A police picket was posted. Just think – so many families living out in the open, and here were policemen to guard birds from another country! Now we hear that they'll convert the marshes into a bird sanctuary. A tourist resort will be built here. We are against any such plan. But if the waters are here to stay forever, what's the point of getting back our land? A tourist resort might give us jobs. Taina?'

I tried to imagine it: neat, air-conditioned cottages with white walls and red-tiled roofs dotting the embankments, motorboats cruising down the marshes, tourists wearing sunglasses and beach hats. Bapi, dressed in a resort uniform, would be guiding a group over the submerged settlement. 'Look over there, that's a Siberian crane,' he would point out, handing over a binocular to a fat man, 'and that one on the broken electric pole is a leaf warbler. Can you see the flock of spoonbills perched on the mound of bricks? That mound used to be a village school, that was a playground, and out there was the mashan, where villagers cremated their dead…'

Nakul's monologue brought me back to the present.

'Sometimes I see will-o'-the-wisps dance on the marshes. On a night of high lunar tide, I set up the nets and stay awake. I stretch myself on a sandbar and listen to the river nibbling away at the earth.'

'The river nibbling away at the earth?' I repeated.

Nakul caught the hint of disbelief in my voice. 'Yes, babu, this bitch has a big appetite! Would you like to listen? Come over here.'

Following him, I knelt down and pressed an ear against the vertical landslip. The earth felt warm and moist against my head, like living flesh. It emanated a piquant scent. It encircled me and awakened buds of strange sensations in the folds of my brain. But I couldn't hear anything except the wind in my other ear.

'The sand is slipping away. Can't you hear?' Nakul whispered.

He and I were kneeling on powdery soil, facing each other, our ears pressed against the compressed wall of sand and silt. Under the pink light of dusk, Nakul's face resembled a terracotta mask.

I closed my eyes and tried hard to concentrate on a thread of sound that seemed to be spiralling out from the depths, the noise of waters nibbling away at the earth with a billion rodent teeth, hollowing it out from under, invisible from above, waiting for that fell moment when it would suck entire settlements with their houses and trees. And now I thought I could hear cottage poles snapping, wattle walls coming apart, the lowing of terrified cattle and the squeal of a thousand human infants – a bawling chorus that churned and thickened and folded in all around us.

Suddenly, I sensed that the noise wasn't coming from the earth below, but from the sky above us. I raised my head and saw an enormous flock of large-winged birds wheeling overhead, calling each other in voices that mimicked squealing babies.

It was an extraordinary sight. What we had mistaken for the dried foliage on dead trees standing in the marshes were actually birds, hundreds of them, from a large colony of grey pelicans. Now they took flight all at once, as if on a cue, making the branches bloom briefly with the white feathers under their wings. They lifted themselves clumsily over the marshes and then rose up and looped the sky in small groups. Some returned to the bare branches, shredding the stillness of dusk with raucous cries, while others winged their way off to the rim of the horizon.

Nihar-da cheered and, brandishing his camera, scrambled to the top of the bund. Nakul remained kneeling, his face raised, his hands resting on his thighs. Bird shadows flitted across his face.

Could he separate the moving specks in the sky from his retinal floaters? I wasn't sure.

II

AYODHYA HILL

GOING BENGAL

Many years ago, three of us college friends went on a camping trip to the western district of Purulia during the autumn vacation. It was early October, the low, forested hills of the dry region wore a resplendent green after the monsoon season. A stream meandered around the foot of an elephant-shaped hill named Gajaburu, and went to meet the river Subarnarekha across a deciduous forest. We had planned to camp below the hill, and for this we had hired a four-man tent from a trek agency. We reached the district town, also called Purulia, on an overnight train, collected provisions, and boarded a bus that dropped us at Baghmundi.

Baghmundi was a tiny ganj set in a wooded plateau. It had a clutch of thatched huts, a forest beat office, a police chowki and a government pharmacy. Stout tribal women wearing striped knee-length saris sold bundles of firewood in a clearing. We asked around a bit until we found a local guide, a swarthy man dressed in a forest guard's hand-me-down khaki uniform, who promised to take us below Gajaburu Hill. He was drunk.

'Yes, I will take you to a beautiful spot inside the jungle,' the man said, rolling his tongue. 'There is a spring nearby where deer come to graze. A nice spot, no one to disturb you there. I'll also carry all your luggage. But it's a long trek and I need something to eat before we set out.'

We gave him some money as advance, urging him to consume something solid, and walked to a mud-and-thatch eatery to fill ourselves. A dozen men, most of them Bengalis, were partaking of lunch served on round, green lotus leaves. Among them were the staff of the government pharmacy and an elderly schoolteacher. They shook their heads when they learnt about our plan.

'Not a good idea,' one of the pharmacy men said. 'Crops have ripened in the fields and elephants are entering the villages every day. They have now moved to this side of the forest.'

'That's not all. Look,' said the schoolteacher and pointed to a bank of slate-grey clouds behind the hill, 'it will rain in a day or two. The stream where you are planning to pitch your tent is notorious for harpa baan.'

'Harpa baan?' We had never heard these words before.

'Yes, flash floods,' the pharmacist explained, in between sucking a fishbone. 'Huge volumes of water suddenly rushing down the hill, without warning. They sweep away everything in their path, even the cowherds and their animals.'

'Elephants and the harpa baan, both equally dangerous,' said the teacher. 'And both unpredictable during this time of the year. I'd suggest you try to get a room in the bungalow over there.'

This time he pointed to a square, nondescript building painted bile green and set in a patch of dusty ground. It was an inspection bungalow of the Public Health Engineering Department.

But surely we hadn't lugged the tent and other equipment all the way from Calcutta only to put up in a dusty sarkari bungalow where babus on duty would leave behind cigarette stubs in toilet bowls and paan-spittle on walls. We mulled over the matter until we found a middle ground between our hunger for the wilds and native wisdom, in a patch of forest about five hundred metres off the road to Ayodhya Hill, a well-known tourist spot, and set up camp. The guide promised to bring us fresh mohua liquor in the evening. We never saw his face again.

But that didn't matter because we had our own stock, and also songs and poetry and the potent madness of early youth. The undulating plains, the moonlight, the racket of birds at dawn, the scent of verdant wood and the nocturnal sounds of the jungle left a deep impression on our minds. We cooked our food, bathed in a spring sheltered among rocks, scavenged dead wood to make a bonfire, studied the fungi and lichens on the forest floor, and chased geckos for two days. Time seemed to have slowed down.

On the third day, we returned from our morning ablutions to discover that our tent had been burgled. All our belongings – a bulky Zenit camera, purses with cash in them, a Sony Walkman, cassettes, wristwatches, torches and a guitar – were intact. The only thing missing was a ten-litre jerrycan half full of kerosene.

We couldn't make sense of this strange theft. Who would take the trouble to come all the way inside the forest to steal only a few litres of kerosene? And why would they leave the other valuables, including cash, untouched? We pondered hard, until we realized that during the two days that we had been here wandering about the jungle, we hadn't seen dried leaves or twigs on the forest floor. We had seen goats grazing on a grassy patch near the pool. Once, in the perfect silence of the afternoon, we had heard a strange noise that had seemed to be the laboured breathing of an animal. But when we had followed the sound to its source, we could see nothing except semi-circular scratch marks of brooms on bare, hard earth and human footprints stamped over them. We had heard the roll of drums at night and the call of roosters at dawn. These signals had been reaching our senses all the time but had failed to register in our minds.

Now, everything fell into place: there was a settlement inside the forest. A shadowy community was leading an inscrutable life here.

We packed up and left the place that morning, humbled and rattled to the core.

~

I returned here after twenty years. A friend had set up his base on top of Ayodhya Hill. He was running a non-formal school for dropout tribal children. He had invited me to visit the school.

A service bus now plied every day between Purulia town and the hilltop. Taxis, too, were available at the railway station. But I chose the longer route, the one that went via Baghmundi. The memory of that camping trip had not faded, and I felt that strange yearning which sometimes prompts a criminal to return to a scene of crime.

The road to Baghmundi was smoother and wider than I remembered it. But the settlements on the roadside were as desolate and ramshackle as before. After Balarampur, a small subdivisional town, the road entered a thin – thinned – forest. There were more vehicles, I noticed: public buses and battered three-wheeled taxis with dusty passengers clinging to them like ants to a lump of sugar. I also spotted several luxury sedans and SUVs.

When I finally got down from the bus at Baghmundi, my memory of the place deserted me. I couldn't recognize the ganj I had known. I walked to a wayside tea stall, my head fogged, and ordered a cup of tea. The stall owner was a jolly Hindi-speaking young man with a cropped haircut.

'The service jeep to the project site has just left, but you can try to get a lift on a government vehicle,' he said, noting the confusion on my face.

'Project site?' I asked distractedly.

Then I remembered it. I had read about it in the papers. Ayodhya Hill was about to get a sophisticated power generation unit, a pump-storage project, the first of its kind in the country and being built by Japanese engineers. So that explained the sedans and the SUVs on the road.

'I'm not going to the project site,' I said quickly. 'I'm going to the top of the hill.'

'Oh? Don't mind, sir-ji. Anyone who comes here dressed in a shirt and trousers heads directly to the site,' the tea seller said with a grin. Then he screwed up his eyes: 'But how will you go to the hilltop up this way? No vehicle runs on this route now.'

Briefly, awkwardly searching for words, I told him about the nostalgia that had drawn me here.

'*Woh sab kal ki baat puraani, abhi yahaan shuru hui hai nai kahaani!*' he sang out and handed me a squat glass of hot, laterite-coloured tea. 'Then you are in for a shock, sir-ji.'

That I could see with my own eyes. The sleepy Baghmundi of my memory, with its low, thatched shacks and the scattering of public buildings, had vanished. Stationery shops, chemists, haircutting salons, food stalls, paan-beedi stalls, a telephone booth and an automobile repair garage now lined the road. I couldn't find the clearing where tribal women sold firewood. Most people I saw now appeared to be outsiders. A block of garish buildings covered with glass and ceramic tiles had come up. A film of ochre dust covered everything. Only the two-thousand-three-hundred-foot-high Ayodhya Hill loomed reassuringly in the distance. But it was browner than before.

A short, grey-haired man in a frayed khaki shirt and baggy pyjamas had been sizing me up for some time from a grocer's shop across the road. As soon as I made eye contact with him, he walked up and offered a greeting. He had come from Dumurdi Vidyashram to receive me, I learnt. His name was Nabin Machhoari.

Nabin peered about me and asked, 'Where did you park your vehicle?'

'I don't have a vehicle with me,' I replied. 'I was thinking of trekking all the way up to the hill.'

'You want to trek? Now? That will take a long time and the road isn't good either,' Nabin expressed alarm. But I also caught a glint of excitement in his eyes.

It was early March, the weather was still mild. The air was redolent with the mysteriously bracing scent characteristic of this land of red earth and sal blossoms. But at one o'clock in the afternoon, the sun was on top of the sky and strong.

'If we take the vehicle road, it will get dark before we can reach Dumurdi. But I know shortcuts that cattle grazers use,' Nabin said. 'We can set off after I buy a few things for the ashram. Did you have your lunch?'

Twenty years ago, there was the eatery that served hot rice-and-curry lunch on lotus leaves. A pucca structure with Formica-topped tables and steel washbasins had replaced it. Greasy puri-sabji and dark gulab jamuns swimming in stale syrup were available there.

The first two kilometres of the road to the hill were straight and across flat ground. The jungles had receded, and huge tin sheds had taken over both sides of the road. Soon we entered a warzone. A battle was being waged, by man against nature, and we seemed to have trespassed into the arsenal of a marching army. Giant earth movers, payloaders and eighteen-wheeled trucks loaded with heavy machinery rumbled towards the hill, along flattened earth, churning up little cyclones of hot grit. Through a brown haze, I saw workmen's tents, giant pipes, girders, and other strange equipment. In no time, a paste of sweat and red earth had caked our skin.

'It's been like this for a long time now,' Nabin shouted through the din.

He pranced along with a heavy gunny bag slung across his back. I lost my breath trying to keep pace.

'When shall we take the grazers' track?' I demanded, tasting laterite in my mouth.

As if on cue, Nabin hit a trail that peeled away from the road and wound across a low shrub forest. After about half a kilometre, the trail began to climb the side of a hill. We reached a settlement of a dozen thatched huts. Not a soul was around, not even a stray dog.

'It's a village of farmworkers,' Nabin said. 'The families here go Bangal-chola during the paddy season.'

Bangal-chola – going to Bengal. I asked Nabin the origin of this phrase.

'I've been hearing it since my childhood. Most tribal people in our area go Bangal-chola at least once a year. It's seasonal work.'

But I noticed that the thatched roofs on the huts had rotted and the gourd creepers on them had died many seasons ago. The settlement had the bleached appearance of a permanently abandoned village.

We continued to follow the trail around enormous basalt boulders, sometimes losing it among the thickets, until we entered a grove of ancient palash trees. The trees were yet to bloom into the flame of the forest, their English name, but they had already shed all the leaves in preparation. It gave the jungle a dry, browned look. We gained height as the trail steadily climbed the flank of the hill. Slanting rays of the sun were teasing out a warm scent from the forest floor carpeted with newly fallen leaves, which evoked a delicate melancholy. But the distant rumble of metal shredded it. The forest was birdless and silent.

After an hour's climb, we got to the metalled road. A murmuring stream trickled down a crack between the stones. It formed a tiny pool on a crook of the road and slithered into the thick undergrowth below. We washed the dirt off our limbs and stepped on an overhang that faced the valley floor.

A theatre of devastation lay below us. A swathe of land, stripped of forest cover, was red and raw, like skinned flesh. Yellow earth movers scurried about on it; from this height, they appeared like tiny maggots. A natural stream had been dammed, and a wide reservoir was being built around it. A sprout of tall, matchbox-like buildings rose on its rim. Concrete guard walls lined the hillside.

'You see this?' Nabin said, showing me the trickling water under our feet. 'There are hundreds of little nullahs like this that drain into the stream below. Now look over there.' He pointed to a dry gully that emerged out of the project site and rolled away to the misty horizon. 'My village lies out there.'

Nabin remained silent for a few seconds and said, 'We used to have two crops a year with water drawn from that stream. Twenty villages depended on it. But since the work began, the flow has stopped. There is no water, and nothing grows in the fields now. Even those who have their own parcels of land now go Bangal-chola during the season.'

Earlier in the day, at the Purulia railway station, I had seen the passenger train that goes every day to Bardhaman, a district known as the paddy bowl of West Bengal. The smoke-blue carriages of the train, packed to capacity with farmhands, reminded me of the Nazi death-camp trains I'd seen in World War movies. But this one was carrying the ragged men and women to their livelihood.

'Weren't the villagers informed? Don't they know what is happening here?' I asked Nabin.

'All we know is that electricity will come all the way from Kolkata, pull water from the dam to the top of the hill, and then it will be transferred back to the city,' he said, adding with a snigger, 'It's a silly contraption the Japanese are building here, sir.'

I turned to look into his face, to measure the depth of bitterness there. The sun had dipped behind the hill now and the shadow had fallen over his eyes. A mild chill was rising from the wet red stones.

'But can you tell me something?' Nabin spun around and faced me. 'Why take the trouble to bring electricity this far if they'll carry it back again?'

In a way, he was right. This project was different from other existing power plants because it would not *produce* electricity. It would recycle it, literally.

The mechanism was simple. There would be a large water storage dam at the foot of the hill and another one on top. Electric power would lift water to the upper dam. During periods of peak demand, water released from the upper dam would rotate turbines to generate power. A considerable amount of energy would be lost in the operation, and the power thus produced would be very costly. So it didn't make much economic sense, especially now that the country had a central power grid, integrating all regional grids, and could buy and sell power according to the law of demand and supply. In fact, this was an out-of-date project that had been in the pipeline for a very long time, gathering sarkari dust, and had taken wings only when the winds of the free-market economy began to blow.

I didn't know what to tell Nabin. Perhaps I could try to explain the mechanism of a pump storage project and tell him whatever I knew about peaking power and load factor in electricity. But it seemed so pointless, standing in a place that would return to the primaeval night in about an hour, as it always had since the beginning of time. I moved my gaze away from the darkening valley to the concrete buttresses of the upper dam. Under the crimson glow of dusk, they appeared like a mad king's castle in a fairy tale.

DUMURDI VIDYASHRAM

Dumurdi was a tribal village nestled in Ayodhya Hill. Thirty families, all Mundas, lived there. They collected minor forest produce, reared livestock, and did some farming on rocky soil around the village. Most able-bodied men and women went to work as labourers in faraway places.

Dumurdi Vidyashram, the non-formal school for young dropouts, stood on the edge of the village in a forest clearing. It comprised four mud-plastered wattle huts and two sheds open on three sides. These were set around a mantle of granite that resembled molten shellac dropped from the sky, with a big neem tree spreading its branches over it. Beautiful murals, made with pot shards and charcoal, lined the cottage walls. There was no fencing around the premises, nothing that set it apart from the general ambience of the village, except a pucca latrine and a plastic water tank sitting on top of a wooden scaffolding. A kerosene pump lifted water from a well. At the entrance to the premises, on a free-standing mud wall, the name and address of the Vidyashram were painted in the English alphabet.

'Why English?'

This was the first question I asked Amitava, pointing to the lettering, as he rushed out to receive me with his arms opened like the wings of a happy bird.

'Why not?' he shot back and guffawed, clasping my shoulders. 'Our children's mother tongue is not Bangla, mind you, and their language doesn't have a proper script.'

Amitava hadn't changed in all these years. The same musical voice, the delicate frame, the same amused expression on his thin lips, and quick eyes set on a soft, lightly bearded face. Only his fair skin had gained a deep tan, and the beard had flecks of grey. He gripped my elbow and proceeded to show me around the premises. On a wide stoop of the cottage near the entrance was a dispensary. A doctor from Balarampur town visited it once a week. Two long, thatched sheds served as classrooms. A third shed, with bamboo fencing around it, served as a crèche for little children. Behind it was the storeroom, where they processed amla and lac collected from the forest.

'When we started this project four years ago, I had no idea how elementary education is linked with a tangle of other issues,' Amitava said. So, what started as a non-formal coaching centre for tribal children who'd dropped out of school had now grown to include a dispensary, a crèche, and a collection centre for minor forest produce.

'I'm sure you know that the sex ratio among the tribal population in our state is significantly better than the overall picture in the country. This means that a girl child is not as unwelcome in a tribal family as she is elsewhere.'

I nodded. I'd seen tribal women work alongside their men in fields and construction sites as equal partners. No doubt they enjoyed a better status in their society than their caste Hindu counterparts.

'Hmm. But if you look at the female literacy rate, it is very low among the tribes. And the dropout rate is also very high.'

'That,' I said, 'is mostly because all adult members of the family go out to work, and it is the girl who runs the household and even looks after her younger siblings.'

'*Exactly!*' Amitava exclaimed. 'And there's no anganwadi centre to take care of the small kids. In this region, most parents remain away from home during the entire paddy season. That's why we set up the day boarding for kids.'

The other big menace, he said, was malaria. It had been stalking the villages here since work on the power plant and the large-scale felling of trees began. Occasionally a fever would turn fatal, but more often it caught its victims in a mild and relentless grip. A child would remain down for one or two weeks, and when she'd return to school, she wouldn't be able to catch up. There would be no literate adult at home to assist her, no facility for remedial coaching in school. On top of that, there'd be insult and punishment from teachers who were usually high-caste Hindus. The result: dropouts.

'A few chloroquine tablets and a little awareness can alter this picture. But the anganwadi centre, even if it's there, won't stock them, and the awareness campaign is a joke. They paint health-centre walls with dos-and-don'ts about malaria, written in Bangla. Not that English or any other language would have made any difference.'

'Okay, so that explains the crèche and the dispensary. But tell me, why are you collecting forest produce from the villagers?' I asked.

Amitava looked into my face and flashed an impish smile. 'Come,' he said, 'let me show you.'

Inside the tin-roofed store, three village women were bottling pieces of dried amla. Pellets of lac were heaped on palm-leaf mats.

'Do you know the concept of opportunity cost?' he asked me and, before I could respond, explained it. 'Even if you make education completely free, there are hidden costs that poor parents have to bear when they send a child to school. Take, for instance, the money a girl can earn for her family if she's sent to town to work as a domestic help. Here we are trying to meet a part of the opportunity cost in our own small way.'

They collected the minor forest produce only from those villagers who sent their children to the Vidyashram. Processed and bottled, the products were marketed through a cooperative society based in

Purulia town. Nabin was in charge of that department. There were also other workers who managed the crèche and ran a kitchen. With three teachers, including Amitava, there were twelve staff members. Seven of them were local village women.

I met them in the evening. Inside an open shed, we sat in a circle around a kerosene lamp on a huge palm-leaf mat. An informal meeting, accompanied by hot tea and muri, was held daily at this hour to take stock of the day's work, update account books, discuss the routine problems and their solutions. This evening, they talked about the low yield and poor quality of the lac. Since stone-crushing had started at the plant site, dust particles were precipitating around the trunks that had lac deposited on them. This had adversely affected production. It was the same story with honey: air and noise pollution were driving away the honeybee colonies from the forests. They went on talking as the chorus of cicadas rose in the surrounding forest.

I tried to follow the drift of their conversation, but the tough uphill trek I had undertaken earlier in the day was turning my limbs heavy as wood. A haze was slowly spreading over my mind. As the darkness thickened and the cicadas grew shriller, I watched the circle of animated faces around the wick lamp beginning to disintegrate. They soon melted away in ones and twos down the forest paths leading into the villages. Only Amitava, Nabin, the cook, and a tall, sturdy woman with a pockmarked face remained. She served us dinner.

'Her name is Savitri Munda,' Amitava whispered to me. 'I'll tell you her story.'

Savitri, it seemed, was walking on padded feet. She never spoke a word.

∼

In the evening's meeting, everyone had looked worried about the vanishing honeybee population. But the next morning, Dumurdi

Vidyashram itself turned into a buzzing beehive. It was a wondrous sight. The dazzling March sun banded the carpet of brown and yellow leaves around the ashram premises. A maze of trails ran across it like lines on a palm. The children came along these trails in orderly beelines, clutching jute bags with books and steel plates in them. Quite a few of them were also holding the hands of their little siblings. The older girls carried the kids in their arms.

The school began at ten. A chorus of young voices reciting tables and poems fanned out into the village, to merge with other natural sounds. During lunch hour, the clanging of steel plates on the stone platform startled the parakeets in the neem tree. The children played under its shade in the afternoon, until it was time to pack the bags and return home. This time they ran across the paths like seeds of an exploding fruit, crunching dry leaves under their tiny feet. With their exit, a sudden silence descended on the ashram premises. Then it was time again for the day-end meeting, and refreshments of tea, muri, and beguni or eggplant fritters, a special item in honour of the guest.

An immaculate rhythm, full of beauty and meaning, had been carrying on for four years in an obscure corner of one of the most backward districts in the country. Most of the boys and girls who came here were school dropouts, but there were also freshers. All were first-generation learners. Here they were taught mostly in their mother tongue, which was Mundari. The children picked up Bangla when they grew up a little, and also Hindi. That is because the Jharkhand border was close and sometimes their parents went to work there. After a year or two of non-formal coaching, the children went to a nearby state-run primary school.

Sometimes, a boy or a girl would come back here, but the Vidyashram did not have the resources to become an alternative to the state-run school system. That was not its aim. A portion of the funds came from the Child in Need Institute. The sale of forest produce and tribal handicrafts also generated some revenue.

~

Savitri Munda was a thirty-something woman, a widow. In the daytime she took care of the kids in the crèche, in the evening she helped in the kitchen. I never heard her speak. A stony silence sheathed her tightly all the time, like her hair combed back behind her round face and braided into a long, thin rope. How such a reticent woman could manage a dozen toddlers was a mystery. I saw her make the little ones sit in a circle around her and feed them balls of rice. Did she tell them a tale or a rhyme during that hour? I had only watched the scene from a distance.

Savitri had lost her husband and her two children when a mysterious disease – possibly cerebral malaria – visited her village. A salishi sabha, village council, had sat in judgement and decided that Savitri had a hand in the plague. They declared her a witch and asked her to pay a hefty fine of two lakh rupees and arrange a feast for the entire village. Her husband owned two acres of land that were now legally hers. But, perhaps, Savitri had also committed another crime. When the census people came to her village, they had enlisted her as literate. So here was a woman who could read and write, who owned a plot of land, and who, according to the salishi sabha, had killed her husband and children. As a witch, Savitri had three options: to pay up, be killed, or flee. She chose the third option. She drifted about for a year until she turned up at Dumurdi Vidyashram's door.

'Savitri's story is extraordinary, but perhaps not so extraordinary after all,' Amitava told me. 'In most tribal societies, a woman faces less oppression in some areas. But, you know, there are other areas where it is very much there.'

I couldn't agree more. I had lived a few years in a hill station and had seen how, even in a loosely matriarchal society, the workload of a woman at home and outdoors added up unjustly and, most of the times, invisibly. It usually took a toll on their health.

'*Exactly!*' Amitava said. 'And have you ever given it a thought? I mean, why are these deprivations so invisible?'

I stared at him and shook my head.

'That's because,' he went on, 'they are linked with other deprivations. A spot of grey in a pervasive shade of greyness. The communists in our country were so obsessed with inequalities of class that they often overlooked other inequalities that are related to caste and gender. We'd also been taught to look that way since our college days, remember? But these inequalities always feed on and also issue out of one another.'

Most of the women working in Dumurdi Vidyashram had their own stories. They were not as stark or as tragic as Savitri's, but were symptomatic. They remained outside the ambit of bhadralok concern. Rarely, because of the efforts of an organization like Amitava's, the stories took a turn for the better.

But Amitava was clear-sighted about the scope of its work.

'No, this isn't a revolution we are scripting here. Nothing big really. These are just some minor adjustments. To really do something that would have a long-term impact, you also need to break a lot of things, a lot of baggage from an old social order. Make and break. That's what Shankar Guha Niyogi did in Chhattisgarh. *Sangharsh aur nirmaan* – fight and construct.'

I wasn't sure if Amitava was referring to the ideas that used to swirl around in our heads during our college days, when some of us hung posters of Che on hostel-room walls, mouthed dialogues from Brecht and sported Castro beards.

'But do you know what the biggest challenge I'm facing here is?' he continued. 'In a society that has remained stagnant and marginalized for ages, where almost no public goods and services have trickled down, it takes a very long time for change to be visible.

Particularly in a field like primary education. But the donor agencies aren't willing to give us that time. Sometimes the funding stops before a project begins to show results, and we are forced to drop it midway. Sometimes, when you are working with a new idea hands-on, you discover loopholes. You improvise as you push on. You learn. Sometimes that is the only gain.'

Amitava lit a cigarette. 'I don't know if the children are learning anything here,' he muttered. 'But *I am.*'

The night was dark, and I couldn't see his face. With each puff, his glasses glowed. We were sitting on the raised stoop of his cottage, facing each other, our shoulders resting against rough wooden columns. The night was pleasantly cool. The ashram lamps had been put out, and the surrounding jungle had made this place a part of itself. A distant metallic noise pierced the silence of the night. A bluish light glimmered intermittently over the silhouettes of trees.

'Is that from the plant site?' I asked.

'Yes, work goes on there throughout the night.'

I told him what I had seen on my way up here.

'What a waste,' Amitava sighed. 'The power that will be used just to run that plant could light at least one electric bulb in every household in every village in this district which goes dark in the evening. That could have given the children more study hours and could have checked the dropping out.'

~

Of all my old friends, it was Amitava who had remained in the business of learning the longest. After a Master's in Economics, he had spent another two years in a graduate programme in Social Welfare, and then done a PhD. After a stint in the gilded wilderness of the corporate world, when I had lost touch with him, he returned. For this he had to pay dearly. His wife had left him, his son was growing up in his in-laws' place. But Amitava was back on course – learning.

This learning differed from the one Apu craved, the one that brought him to the city, the one that came to this land from across the seas. Amitava's learning could only take place in obscure places like this.

Distant sounds permeated the wattle walls. The forest was mysteriously alive. I tossed on the narrow cot and, to coax sleep, focused my mind on the welter of sounds. I could identify wheels crunching loose gravel, an engine idling somewhere, liquid concrete churning in barrels and the intermittent squeal of steel. The sounds got refracted in the haze of my insomnia into pattering hoofs, beastly growls and other aural images that kept me awake through the night. Before dawn, a narrow strip of sky visible under the thatch turned a steely grey. Daylight was breaking. Now I heard a strange noise: it was like the laboured breathing of a forest animal.

I had heard this sound before. I got up on my feet and peered outside. Most of the courtyard was visible from where I stood. It had been a breezy night; tiny yellow leaves of the neem tree covered the stone platform. Savitri Munda was sweeping them away with a broom. Nobody was up and about at this hour, not even the birds. The tall woman was bent forward and moving the broom with deep concentration. She had gathered up her thick mass of hair into a topknot and folded the sari over her knees in local fashion. With each movement of her arms and shoulders, a murmuring circle of dried leaves formed around her.

Here was a woman who had been branded a witch because the census men enlisted her as a literate person. During the two days I was here, I had not seen her even once go near anything relating to reading or writing, ever touch a book or assist a child with their studies. I didn't ask her the reason, lest she found out that I knew her story. But when I enquired what it was she was telling the kids when she was feeding them, Savitri had smiled mysteriously. She had stood with downcast eyes and had drawn inscrutable patterns on the ground with her right toe.

After sweeping the courtyard clean, she now plastered it with clay slurry. She supported her hams on her heels and revolved swiftly on each of her toes, one at a time, as on a pivot, plastering the entire courtyard in just a few minutes, drawing a fish-scale pattern on it. After she was done with the raised cottage banks and stoops, Savitri went to the free-standing wall at the entrance. As if for some arcane ritual, she knelt down, her back taut like a strung bow, and with a ball of cloth dipped in lime mixture, she repainted the letters with quick clean strokes of her hand:

DUMURDI VIDYASHRAM

VILLAGE — DUMURDI

AYODHYA HILL

TALUK — BAGHMUNDI

PURULIA

The sun was yet to appear on the crest of the hill. It was early spring, the hour of birdsong, but the forest was silent. A false sunrise tinged the northern sky. The sodium lamps in the plant site were still on. The nocturnal earth movers had gone to sleep.

III

SIMLIPAL

A CHAIN TALE

Never had I watched a movie in such an unusual location. Every time the thick bamboo grove around the broken house darkened the rectangle of light on the limewashed wall, a starry sky and silhouettes of trees under it became visible outside the windows. The call of crickets and other nocturnal sounds of the forest, too, mixed freely into the soundtrack. Never had I watched a movie – and I've watched this one countless times – in the company of children for whom the images moving on the wall were so familiar. They could effortlessly connect with the little brother and his older sister wandering about in the natural world of a village. Never had they imagined that the things that were a part of their everyday life could be the subject of a movie. They watched with fascination the dance of insects on the surface of a pond, and smiled with the ancient woman when she discovered a guava inside an earthen pot, which her grand-niece had stolen for her from a neighbour's garden. They laughed when the crone, in a fit of anger, threw a bundle of cloth right over a kitten, and when the first raindrop landed on the bald pate of a villager fishing in a pond. They flinched when the pundit-grocer caned a boy for playing tic-tac-toe in class.

It was the coming together of two worlds, the real world and the one being projected on a wall, which were almost identical in so many ways. Except that one was rural Bengal, and the other was tribal Odisha, and half a century separated them.

Forty-three boys and girls, all aged between eleven and fifteen, sat huddled inside a classroom watching Satyajit Ray's *Pather Panchali*. Most of them belonged to the Kolho tribe and spoke Ho.

They could not follow the Bangla dialogue or the English subtitles. But the powerful images and the underlying human emotions reached out to them unfailingly across space and time. It seemed as if it was not just the children who were watching the images but, in some mysterious way, the images too were watching them and gaining another layer of meaning.

I stood with my back to the wall and studied the emotions playing on their faces. When I was their age, I too had seen *Pather Panchali* at a screening in my school. That was the second or third time I was watching the film. The memories were now coming back to me.

Together we followed the story of little Apu and his elder sister, Durga. Now they had grown up a little and were fighting over a piece of tinsel. Apu had taken it out of his sister's toy box. Meanwhile, their mother couldn't see their calf and asked Durga to look for it. Apu followed, wearing a crown he had made of the tinsel. The little brother and sister wandered out of the village and into a field of tall kans grass with white flocculent blossoms. Suddenly, there was a burst of light across the wall, the silvery blossoms waved in a breeze, and the light flooded the faces of the children sitting on the bare, concrete floor. I waited to observe their reactions as one of the most famous scenes in world cinema was about to roll. It began with a faint rumble, and Durga was the first to catch it. Then there was a banner of smoke over the white fields. Now the two children were running wildly to see, for the first time in their lives, a speeding train!

But the faces of the young viewers stiffened, I noticed with shock, and their eyes turned dull. A roomful of children appeared unmoved by a scene that had never failed to thrill moviegoers across the world. The magnificent railway scene in *Pather Panchali* couldn't elicit from them any visible sign of excitement or joy. As Apu made it to the railway track – only just, Durga had tripped – and the gigantic carriage wheels hurtled past in extreme close-up, bands of light and shade flitted across forty-three dark, upturned faces inside the classroom. I could see anxiety there, and distress. I could even spot tears glistening in a few pairs of eyes. A young girl who was sitting in a corner sniffled.

I was at a loss.

In *Pather Panchali*, Apu watches for the first time in his life the spectacle of a steam locomotive charging at full speed across the flat plains, trailing plumes of smoke. It evokes in his mind a sense of awe, and also a romantic yearning for distant lands.

But many of these children, I'd soon learn, had parents who went to work in the distant paddy districts during the planting and harvesting seasons. What effect did the railway scene in *Pather Panchali* have on their minds? What feelings were kindled by the speeding, roaring metal beast that separated them from their parents?

I had no access to their mental world.

~

One day in October, I received an email from Dr Prashanta Pattanayak, the president of Deepshikha, a Bhubaneswar-based NGO working in the field of elementary education. It was a proposal. 'Will you be interested in spending a week in the tribal areas of eastern Odisha? We are running a project there, and we are looking for a person who can go and write a report for us. We think you are the right person for the job. Please don't say no. Let me know when you can make yourself available, and we'll take care of everything, including, of course, your travel and stay there.'

I had known Dr Pattanayak for many years. He was the only Odia I knew who could read Bangla but could not speak it. When I had expressed my surprise at this discovery, he had told me that people like him had not been a rarity in Odisha a few decades ago. For a long time, Calcutta was the cultural capital of eastern

India, and the aspiring Odia middle classes, particularly around the Cuttack region, went there for higher studies. After Independence, their focus shifted to Delhi, and the rise of Bhubaneswar as the new state capital coincided with the decay of Cuttack and its distinctive cultural outlook.

Prashanta Pattanayak was a professor of history at Utkal University, and I came to know him closely on an earlier visit to Bhubaneswar. I was researching a book on a small tribal group in western Odisha who were resisting bauxite mining on top of a hill. Without his help, I couldn't possibly have travelled in that remote, trouble-torn region. That was when I came to know Prashanta as a man who could dream big, talk brilliantly, and could even walk the talk. He, too, must have noticed an incurable wanderlust in me. He knew it would be difficult for me to turn down an invitation like this. 'It is a remote and backward area in Mayurbhanj district,' Prashanta wrote, 'but it is also a place of great natural beauty. I am sure you will love the experience.'

In 2009, the Parliament of India passed the Right to Education Act. This was an unprecedented piece of legislation by which the nation had taken upon itself the responsibility of bringing all children, aged between six and fourteen years, to school. Deepshikha was working closely with Odisha's school education department to implement the law at the grassroots level. The organization was recruiting local tribal-language teachers, generating study materials, hosting sensitization camps and helping the villagers to form school management committees. A Scandinavian donor agency was funding the project. Deepshikha had an agreement with the agency that it would get its performance evaluated by an independent expert at the end of a project cycle. Prashanta wanted me to do the job.

For me, however, it was a daunting task. My engagement with elementary education amounted to a research project I could never complete, and a column I used to write for an English daily based on my field experience.

'But surely these don't qualify me as an expert, do they?' I wrote back to him. 'Moreover, my entire experience is centred in West Bengal, the southern part of Bengal to be precise. How can I put together a report based on a week's field trip to an unfamiliar place where people speak an unknown tongue?'

'Not as unknown as you think, Parimal,' Prashanta replied, this time over the phone. 'Don't forget that this region of Odisha had been part of the Bengal Presidency for a very long time. The tribal people who live there, the Kolhos, are the not-so-distant cousins of the Mundas of West Bengal. The terrain, too, is not much different from the forested areas of western Midnapore and Purulia districts of your state. And I'm sure you'll discover a lot more things in common when you go there. All I can say is that this experience will enrich you.'

Prashanta's words, delivered in his quiet voice, conspired with my temerity and, to cut a long story short, one balmy November evening I found myself watching *Pather Panchali* in a school building inside the forest of Simlipal. It was an upper primary school in a village named Dolipada, one of the many small tribal villages scattered around the reserve forest area.

This was my fourth day here. By then, I had already covered around two hundred kilometres on a motorcycle's pillion and had visited a dozen villages spread over three gram panchayats. I had inspected eight schools, and had talked to teachers, students and villagers – the so-called stakeholders of the project. But the more area I had covered, the more difficult my task had seemed, the more precarious my position as an independent observer had become, and the hazier the object of my search was turning out to be. All I had gathered so far was a cache of images: words, sounds, spectacles and smells. They were as ineffable as the scenes flashing past the rear-view mirrors of the motorcycle I'd been riding, which bore the statutory warning – OBJECTS IN THE MIRROR ARE CLOSER THAN THEY APPEAR.

It was in this confused state of mind that I was watching *Pather Panchali*, when the children's strange reactions to the famous railway scene pushed me into deeper unease.

The film was being shown to give them a taste of great cinema. But there was also a more mundane motive: we had timed the screening to keep the kids awake until dinner was ready. They were from five or six schools within a single panchayat area, and all of them were to stay the night inside the school building. It was a two-day winter camp where the children were being trained to draw, paint, sing songs, and compose and enact skits.

I met them the next morning.

~

'Do all the children in your village go to school?' I asked in Hindi. Nirmal Behera, a Bhubaneswar-based photographer who was preparing a visual document of the project, translated my question into Odia. Bindumani Samad, a local project assistant, reframed it in Ho. The children were from the Kolho tribe and most of them, particularly the younger ones, didn't understand Odia. Their responses, too, reached me via the two languages.

'No!' they replied in a chorus. 'Some of them go to the fields and the forests.'

'And what do they bring back home from the fields and the forests?' I asked.

'Firewood – sal leaves – paddy – guava – goats – mushrooms – amla…'

They jumped to their feet from all corners of the room and merrily contributed to the list.

'And what do *you* take back home from school?'

They were stumped. They searched one another's faces for an answer.

'Books!' a boy shouted from the front row, raising a tattered copy over his head. A broad smile glistened on his ebony face.

'But you bring books from home, isn't it?' I asked. 'What else do you carry back? What is it you don't bring from home?'

Again silence, until a thin boy wearing an oversized white shirt rose to his feet and pointed a finger at his belly.

'Tikin mandijom,' he said with confidence.

The classroom exploded in laughter. I was told that tikin mandijom was afternoon food, the midday meal. As the children continued to giggle, one of the older girls, old enough to guess the answers hidden in the questions that adults sometimes ask, spoke up.

'Vidya,' she said. Knowledge.

'But what do you do with vidya?' I persisted. 'Do you burn it like firewood? Do you stitch it like sal leaves to make plates? What do you do with the knowledge that you take back home?'

The moment the words slipped out of my lips, I knew that this was a nasty question, particularly for these young children. So I hastened to supply the answer myself. Education, I explained, was like fruits that one could take back home and share with family members. It could be minor things one learnt every day: matters of hygiene, for example, like 'one must wash hands before eating food', or that 'dirty water contains harmful germs'. Or it could be the knowledge of our country and the people...

As I went on, and listened to my words being rendered into two languages, I could feel how vain and pompous I was sounding. Some of these children would probably stop coming to school from the next session. They'd join their brethren in fields and forests, and return home with bundles of firewood and sal leaves balanced on their heads. A few of them would accompany their parents to distant paddy lands, riding railway trains that would take them to fertile coastal districts. Right now, they were too young for such a journey. In fact, many of them now stayed at home all by themselves, taking care of their younger siblings and household animals, while their parents remained away for months. During the past few days, I had been to villages where there were almost no able-bodied adults. There were only the children and the elderly.

Earlier in the day, I had seen the children working with coloured pencils and crayons on pieces of paper. I'd seen neat rows of ice-cream cone hills with the sun rising behind them, its rays thick and curling out like the stamens of a china rose. I had seen a path winding diagonally across the paper metamorphose into a river, and raindrops falling from the wings of birds flying in formation. In another drawing, it was a city scene with matchbox houses piled on top of one another, as in a slum, each tenement with a dish antenna on the roof, with a peacock perched on one. A convoy of battle tanks was rolling down the road, with smiling families riding them – always parents and children holding hands.

They'd almost always draw humans as stick figures, I had noticed; the figures had circles for heads and lines for hands, and legs sticking out of rectangular chests and bellies. Entire families floating on the white field of the paper, hauntingly spare and minimalist.

The stick figures were telling a tale: of stick legs that took them to distant fields and forests, and stick hands that worked. The food that the hands earned, after feeding the attached box belly, fed another smaller box belly, and sustained another pair of stick hands. Soon, that little pair of hands would grow strong enough to feed another belly and sustain another pair of hands.

This was a chain tale in the authentic Indian folklore style.

What else could it be? In a place where the poverty level was as high as 75 per cent and the literacy as low as 20, where the food people grew in their fields barely sustained them for three months a year, a boy or a girl returning home with a bundle of sal leaves or firewood from the jungle was more real, and held more value, than one returning from a school. In a place where life was lived from moment to moment, from hunger to hunger, vidya was an obscure investment in a hazy future. Here, the only genuine thing a child brought back from school was tikin mandijom – a quantity of food saved at home, that went on to feed another belly.

'Do you know something? Many families here with two children will send one to school and the other to the forest,' Bindumani had told me. 'If it's a girl, they'll keep her at home for household work.'

Twenty-something Bindumani Samad was a local Adivasi girl, a commerce graduate. Since morning, she was busily running around the school premises, the end of her sari wound tightly and tucked away at her waist in gachh-komor, tree-climbing style. She had a lot of responsibility: looking after the children who came from different villages, settling their quarrels, distributing the drawing kits, and supervising in the kitchen. Her own child, a one-year-old boy, was trailing her with unsteady steps and jumping into her lap whenever she could rest her legs. To pacify him, Bindumani thrust a pencil and paper into his hands and made him sit beside the other children.

'How do the parents react when you tell them about the recent education act, which makes it compulsory for every child to go to school?' I asked her.

'They'll say, take one or two of them, but we won't let you take away all our children to school,' Bindumani replied in a tone of despair, and then asked me, 'What more can I say after this?'

I didn't have an answer.

I surveyed the school building. It had received a fresh coat of pink paint, like all the schools here, making them starkly visible from a distance. The square concrete structures were at odds with the rounded architecture of the tiled mud cottages here. Rather, they resembled the police stations and other government buildings.

Each school building had a large painted clock on its front with the hands at 10.30, a painted height scale, and a sign with the school education department's helpline number and email ID. These were according to the rulebook. But mobile signals were mostly non-existent in these parts, as were computers. In fact, there was no electricity. But the teachers had a dress code: sky-blue shirts and navy-blue trousers for men, and blue-bordered pink saris for women.

I had seen none of them since morning and I asked Bindumani about it. Weren't they supposed to take part in the camp?

Before she could reply, her son came running to show her the drawing he had just executed. It wasn't really a drawing, but a dense black tangle of lines and holes pierced into the paper with the tip of the pencil. Bindumani attempted to snatch the paper from his hand and teach him how to draw properly. But the child would not part with it. He protested with his lips curled downwards, raised the piece of paper above his head, looked up and began to swivel on his tiny legs.

A young girl, the one who had sniffled last evening during the railway scene in *Pather Panchali*, had been observing his act with deep interest. She now said something in their language, and Bindumani laughed. It turned out that the girl had understood the little master's creation. Bindumani's son had sketched the night sky, and the holes pierced into the paper were stars.

AT A MAHARAJA'S HUNTING GROUNDS

The L-shaped brick structure stood deep inside a forest clearing. It had two classrooms and a kitchen. The rooms had no doors and windows, no paved floors, not even a blackboard. A lone charpoy sat in a corner in one of the rooms. The other had a dug-up floor, as in a pigsty. Damp cinders in the kitchen suggested that a fire had last been lit many days ago. This was Hudisahi Free Primary School.

'The anganwadi children, too, come here,' Birsa informed me.

I was surprised. 'You mean to say the anganwadi kitchen is also run from here?'

'Oh no!' Birsa protested. 'There's no anganwadi centre in the village. The kids don't receive food or anything. They just come along with their older siblings. They come because they know this is a school.

'There is one teacher, but he doesn't come every day. He commutes from Baleswar, which is seventy kilometres away. But the kids always turn up.'

Birsa Singh was one of the project coordinators in Deepshikha.

'How do you persuade them to come to school? What do you tell them?' I asked him.

'They don't need any persuasion,' Birsa replied without a thought. 'They just come because it's a school.'

So here was a school without a teacher, with neither a regular midday meal, nor any teaching aid. Not even a blackboard on the wall. It sprang up soon after the Right to Education Act was passed and had remained like this ever since. There was no toilet, no regulation boundary wall, and the source of drinking water was half a kilometre away, inside the village.

Yet, the kids were coming to school. Every day. To demonstrate this bizarre fact, Birsa had brought us here. For this, we had had to undertake a rough three-kilometre bike ride along a boulder-strewn path. But we were late. By the time we reached here, daylight had faded. The kids had given themselves over and returned to the village.

We stepped inside the empty cells. They were almost dark: the bare brick walls had soaked up the residual daylight. We stood like silent mourners and peered out through the square openings. An early sunset varnished the spotted trunks of tall mohua trees. A flock of biscuit-grey plovers was churning up a racket. The eyes took a few seconds to adjust to the darkness inside, and I saw mysterious graffiti the children had scrawled on the brick walls.

It was Nirmal who broke the silence.

'You know something?' he said, weighing each word, studying the scrawlings intently. 'I think we have been missing something all along. We have been looking at the problem through the wrong end of the telescope.'

Birsa and I spun around and faced him.

'Rather than keeping our focus entirely on the problem of children dropping out and devising ways to lure them back to school, we should begin from here, this very place,' Nirmal said, pointing his index finger to the floor. 'Why do they come to school at all? That we must find out first. *Why do the children come to school at all?*'

He delivered the last sentence rather theatrically, turning towards us, his arms resting on his hips. Was it a riddle? Was he cracking a joke? Birsa and I looked at him, at his earnest eyes and deep solemn face. Suddenly, without a cue, the two of us began to laugh. Nirmal peered at us, perplexed, and then he, too, joined in. Our laughter echoed in the empty rooms and fluttered out into the darkening forest like a colony of bats.

There is a type of laughter that, rather than easing the mind, tightens around it like a vice. We could feel its weight even after stepping out into the open, into the world of bird calls and the scent of the wood at dusk.

～

But whether the children went to school or not, the big, bad world would reach the settlements deep inside Simlipal's forests, however remote they might be.

Hudisahi was a village of twenty-two Kolho households. Everyone here lived below the poverty line, although many were yet to receive their entitlement cards. The village was, by all standards, in the back of beyond. The land surrounding it was rocky and fallow, and most able-bodied men worked under labour contractors round the year. There was no road connection, and the villagers had to trek considerable distances for essential amenities, including emergency medical aid. The low tile-roofed mud huts nestled at the foot of the Simli Hills, a low basalt ridge that spanned the length of this forest division.

Daylight had faded when we made our way here, after the visit to that empty school building. The groan of a wooden pulley over a well greeted us as we emerged from a grove of old silk-cotton trees. I spotted narrow monoliths erected under the trees, and instantly felt an uneasiness coil up inside: I knew what these stones meant.

'What is the infant mortality rate here?' I asked, keeping my voice befittingly low. This was the first question that came to my mind at a gathering of villagers.

'*Fifty-fifty*,' replied a young man, wagging his outstretched palm like a weighing scale, before Birsa could translate my words into Ho.

The man, Gusey Banara, had worked for two years at the construction site of the Commonwealth Games Village in New Delhi. He had picked up Hindi there.

If I understood Gusey's claim correctly, a child in Hudisahi had a 50 per cent chance of survival. But that was preposterous, because even in the most backward regions in India the average infant mortality rate hovered around seventy per thousand live births. But *fifty-fifty*? This worked out to five hundred deaths per thousand live births. The figure was numbing.

Gusey was a stocky man who looked to be in his early thirties. He had back-brushed hair and a self-assured air. He stood out from among the crowd of villagers gathered under an immense tamarind tree. Every village I had been to had a similar meeting place under a tree. They could accommodate all the villagers. This, I would learn, was their most important community space.

The dozen-odd men assembled under the tree were of Gusey's age or younger. The oldest among them, Sabram Singh Banara, was ancient. Only the trees and stones could count his age, a villager told us with pride. The old man sat a few yards away from the gathering, curled up like a foetus in the stoop of a cottage, a stick resting between his bare, knobby knees. With his opaque, almost white eyeballs and grey cottony hair on his head, Sabram resembled a photographic negative.

Among the men were members of the school management committee. Illiterates all, their role in committee meetings amounted to the thumb impressions they put on the papers the teacher shoved under their noses. Here, too, they remained mostly silent and responded to our queries with nods and grunts. Gusey did most of the talking, in Hindi. The only other person who knew a little Hindi was Amin Singh, a lanky twenty-year-old. Amin had worked outside the state for an entire season, in a brick kiln in Jharkhand. But the contractor hadn't given him a single paisa on that assignment.

'That man is a bhenchod!' Gusey cursed. 'He cheats everyone and has amassed vast wealth. He lives in Bandhasahi, the village of the Mahatos.'

'Why did you let him go so easily?' I asked Amin. 'Weren't you angry?'

'What can one do?' Amin smiled sheepishly, embarrassed at finding himself the centre of our attention. 'Everyone knows the man is a cheat. But still people go with him, in hope. There's no other way.'

At such a young age, Amin had learnt to deal with his misfortune by generalizing it. Perhaps anger was a luxury here, even in youth, and one soon learnt to devise inner strategies to cope with indignity. In many of the villages, we were meeting men like Gusey and Amin, who had been sucked into distant metropolitan centres by the behemoth of development – in road construction, real estate and infrastructure projects – and then cast off. They returned with dashed hopes and a view of the big, bad world out there. On the way, they picked up one or two languages, and perhaps a communicable disease, including AIDS. Ironically, it was these men, grown embittered and cynical, who came forward as spokespersons of their community. They presented the seamy side of India's growth story. But perhaps, at a deeper level, this was also a timeless narrative, of the wretched of the earth used as grist to history's mill.

Hudisahi could offer nothing to hold back men like Amin Singh and Gusey Banara. The soil here was rocky, and water scarce: technically, it was a degraded patch of forest.

Had it always been like this? I wanted the opinion of Sabram Singh Banara, the oldest of them all.

No, the forest had been thicker and wilder, but life had been easier when Sabram was a boy. That was when he had come with his parents from Singhbhum and settled here. In fact, all the Kolhos in this part of Mayurbhanj had migrated from the forests of Singhbhum more than a century ago. That was why Singh was a popular title in the community, I was told.

But Singhbhum was not their original homeland, Sabram asserted. 'We lived many hundred years there, but we are originally from Harappa.'

This was stunning news. And I'd hear this assertion repeated in several villages during the next few days – a collective memory of migration, handed down from generation to generation, and matured into lore. It narrated how, many thousand years ago, a human group had left a decayed civilization by a river valley and drifted to the eastern part of the subcontinent where they had lived in peace until the British had arrived; how they had fought heroically against the colonizers, lost the battles, and had their tongues cut off as punishment; how seven families had migrated to the dense forests of Simlipal and had set up home at a maharaja's hunting grounds.

Sabram's retelling of the lore, particularly the latter part, bore seeds of history. In the early nineteenth century, British colonialism in Chhotanagpur introduced the mahajans between the rulers and local tribal groups. From free landowners, the Mundas and Oraons became serfs. They rose in protest, and it culminated in the Kol Revolt of 1831–32. Brutal suppression followed, and the tribes remained subdued for some time until, towards the end of the century, they began a passive protest movement by emigrating en masse. Some went as far as the Andaman Islands, others went to work in tea gardens, and some of them, like the Kolhos of Mayurbhanj, migrated to the neighbouring provinces of Odisha and Bengal. A century of dispossession could not rob them of that history; it manifested itself in a title like Singh, or a name like Birsa – a tribute to the rebel hero Birsa Munda.

But Sabram Singh Banara's story gained symbolic overtones when he mentioned the cutting off of tongues, of robbing an entire tribe of the power of speech. The old man spoke slowly, in a gritty voice. It seemed as if he were scooping up water drop by drop from the dry bed of a stream. His narration, rendered in Ho, reached me muddied in translation. By now, dusk had thickened, and a flight of green pigeons returned to the outstretched branches overhead. This was the hour when the voices of men grew heavy. Sabram chewed the words with his toothless gums before he released them. Everyone listened in rapt silence. It was a tale they had been hearing since they were born.

I remembered the evening scene in *Pather Panchali*, where old Indir Thakrun narrates a fairy tale to young Apu and Durga. Her head raised up, her deformed shadow cast on the mud wall by a wick lamp, she tells in a rasping voice the tale of an ogress and two young princes. It is as if she herself has morphed into an ogress under the dim quivering flame that is producing more shadow than light. The children huddle over her outstretched legs as the old woman spins out her tale.

Could Sabram Singh Banara cast such a spell with his tale of ancestry? Or did the children of Hudisahi find Gusey and Amin's tales of the big, bad world, peopled with crooks and thugs, more captivating?

IN A COUNTRY NAMED SUKHUAPATTA PAHAR

Tiny villages with around a dozen huts stood in forests of sal, mohua, silk-cotton, karanja, siris, and other tall, mostly evergreen trees whose names I didn't know. Farm plots were cut into the bottom of slopes to receive the run-off. A network of nullahs criss-crossed the forest floor, giving the vegetation a wondrous lushness even in winter. This landscape, too, had once been part of the Bengal Presidency. It had fed the imagination of Bibhutibhushan, in one of whose novels, *Aranyak* (Of the Forest), he had made the spirit of the forest the central character. Tall basalt monoliths stood on sloping grounds like primaeval beasts. A kusum tree with blood-red leaves hugged the flank of a stony outcrop. The ruins of a stone tower stood on top, covered in shrub jungle.

'This was a maharaja's hunting tower,' Birsa announced as we left our motorbikes and ascended the slope. The spot commanded an excellent view. A hundred feet below, a natural pool had formed in the depression. Purple star lotus bloomed there.

'That pool must have been the haunt of animals during the maharaja's time,' I said.

'It still is. See over there.'

Birsa pointed with his finger to hoofmarks on the wet margins.

'The entire forest was the hunting ground of Mayurbhanj kings,' Nirmal declared. 'This had protected Simlipal from loggers and poachers.'

Ten kilometres down the sun-dappled asphalt road, the forest gave way to terraced fields: cropped brown earth interspersed with patches of bright-yellow mustard. A picture-postcard tribal couple, man and wife, were walking briskly with loads of golden paddy on their heads. A jet-black cockerel flashed across the road, expertly dodging the speeding wheels. A tiny hamlet jumped into view: a knot of mud huts, a lotus-bloomed pond, a council of rough wooden benches under an old tamarind tree. I had been seeing such spots in almost every village. Village councils, known here as shonghos, assembled there every week.

'Tell me more about the shongho,' I asked Birsa.

'All adult men and women in a village are its members,' Birsa said, his eyes focused on the road. 'The shongho sits on a fixed day every week. We plan community work and assign duties. Anyone who disobeys has to pay a fine. The work is mostly fun, from weeding farm plots to constructing or repairing someone's cottage. We also harvest our fields together. We cannot hire labour, and everyone needs the community in times of need. And yes, a shongho also sits to settle a dispute or pass a judgement. But that is not part of its regular assignments.'

I could visualize the semicircle of rough wooden benches set under the tamarind tree coming into life. A space handcrafted by the people living here for generations, weaving a way of life that could be the model for future societies and yet marked as backward. We were used to looking from the wrong end of the telescope, Nirmal had said.

Nirmal had stories to share. The project of a photographic database of nearly one thousand five hundred schoolchildren had given him interesting experiences. He regaled us with some of them.

'The biggest challenge was to identify some of these boys and girls,' he said. 'That's because they were enrolled under names they themselves didn't know.'

'Really?'

'Yes, and it's very common in these parts. One day, in a school in Noto panchayat area, I found the name Asman Kisku in the roll of Class 3. But I couldn't locate the boy, neither in school nor in the village. Nobody had ever heard this name before. And then one day, I ran into a boy named Bagun in Class 3. But Bagun's name was not in the register. I had to play Agatha Christie to find out that Asman and Bagun were one and the same boy!' Nirmal turned to me, 'Can you solve the mystery?'

I shook my head.

'The boy had spent his preschool years at his mother's place where they used to call him Bagun. But during the time of admission, his father had given him the name Asman and then had completely forgotten it.'

Birsa and I shared a laugh.

'Then there was this girl who appeared before the camera against two different names from two different classes. Upon enquiry, it turned out that the second name belonged to another girl who had stopped coming to school a long time ago. And since she happened to be this girl's elder sister, the latter innocently appeared as a proxy.'

We laughed again.

Birsa chipped in. 'One day a father, after downing a few glasses of liquor, came tottering to the school and demanded that we change his son's surname in the school register from Tiu to Singh. Why? "Because I don't like to be called Tiu any more," he declared. "From now on we are Singh."'

We had another round of laughter. It rose above the noise of our motorcycles' engines and flew off into the forest like feathers plucked out of a bird.

What's in a name? In a place where a BPL card or a government welfare scheme is as elusive as the moonbeam, there isn't really anything in it. Unique identification numbers or biometric validation systems are for another planet.

'You go to a school here and ask a boy his date of birth – he will not be able to tell you. In fact, very few parents know it. The teachers put arbitrary dates during admission,' Birsa said.

What's in a date? In a place where the chance of a newborn surviving the first year of life is fifty-fifty, where a high percentage of babies are born at home and the neonatal immunization programme is a joke, it means nothing.

It was now harvest season, and entire families were out in the open. The fields and villages hummed with activity – cutting, threshing, and weaving cylindrical grain stores with ropes of straw. The harvest would last them three to four months, after which the men and women would leave home in search of work. But that could never cast a shadow on the little joys of the present. Out of nowhere, a haat had come up on the wayside. It just needed a couple of peddlers with their paltry ware of spices, dried fish and tobacco, which they were selling directly from bicycles' carriers. Most daily necessities here were met by what the people collected from the forest and grew on their tiny farm plots. But no haat would be complete without a woman sitting under a tree with a large aluminium handi. She would dispense handia – rice beer – in leaf cups to men sitting in a circle around her.

All the households here fermented handia. They would carry it to the fields to drink during breaks. We saw families at harvest resting under trees and drinking the soupy white liquor.

'It is nourishing, rice being the main ingredient, and also mildly soporific,' Nirmal said.

'Most of the handia sold in the haat is prepared with rice distributed at ration shops,' Birsa informed. 'The BPL families get it at two rupees a kilo and sell it at two rupees a bowl.'

'And how many bowls can you make out of a kilo of rice?' I asked.

'Hundreds!' Birsa pursed his lips and exhaled. 'But a haat is no haat without the handia handi.'

In fact, one could sniff out a haat inside the forest from a mile away just by following the trail of wayside handia joints. Each joint would be set up at a distance of about thirty footsteps from another.

'The idea is to rip off the last coin from the homebound.' Birsa chuckled. 'A man will stop at every stall on his way home for a quick cup and might end up sleeping away the night on a culvert.'

An air of warm camaraderie swirled in these joints. Men from far-flung villages met up with old friends and made new ones. Near the circle of slurry-tongued tipplers, two of whom were curled up on the ground, a man was frying lentil fritters. We parked our motorbikes under a shady tree. He served us dollops of yellow pea curry on puffed rice in green leaf bowls.

A handsome young man with polished black skin, a piece of red cloth tied around his head, was sitting an arm's length away from the group. A live junglefowl nestled on his lap. The man had well-formed limbs and large doe eyes, which he was turning in our direction from time to time. Whenever our eyes met, he would turn his head away quickly. But the rooster twisted its neck and flicked razor-sharp glances at us. Sunlight streamed in through the leaves and set its red and blue plumes on fire.

'Where did you find it?' Nirmal asked him in Odia, pointing at the creature.

The young man smiled coyly and turned his head away again.

'Tumey Odia kahipara na?' Nirmal insisted. Can't you speak Odia?

A middle-aged man sitting next to him responded. The young man had caught the bird in a trap set under a threshing board, where it had come at dawn to eat leftover grains. Now he had come to the haat to sell it.

His name was Turi Barja, and he was from Pungichua, one of the remotest settlements in this forest region.

'So you live in Pungichua?' Birsa addressed him with sudden interest. 'We'll go to your village tomorrow.'

He turned to me and said, 'Pungichua remains cut off from the rest of the world during the monsoon months. All because of a hill stream. Recently a lower primary school has come up there and we are thinking of appointing a language teacher.'

Turi Barja, a hunter-gatherer, was illiterate like the rest in his village. When he learnt that we would go to his village, his alert eyes widened with disbelief.

Turi was from a world where generations had grown up, grown old and died without ever going to a school. They would venture out of their village when they were old enough to sell their labour or some minor forest produce. Their first contact with the outside world would usually be in the form of a cunning labour contractor or a moneylender who spoke a different tongue. As a result, the myth of the big, bad world out there, waiting to cheat simple tribal people, endured. It made them turn inward and reclusive.

What change could a school bring to such a place?

~

A PMGSY road connected the outside world with Bandhasahi, the village of the Mahatos. The cottages here had tiled roofs upon brick walls and wooden doors with iron hatch bolts on them. Hatch bolts were a rarity in Kolho villages.

'The Mahatos here are OBCs,' Birsa told me, 'and they are into trading. They buy sal-leaf plates from the Kolhos and sell them at a hefty profit in town. Many also indulge in usury.'

The historic migration of Kolhos from Singhbhum could not save them from the middlemen and the mahajans. Their relationship with the Mahatos was based on exploitation, but also mutual dependence that went back nearly a century. The new road had given that relationship a twist. We spotted small pickup trucks standing in the courtyards.

Now we were going deeper into the forest. The trees grew taller, and the forest more shadowy and ancient-looking. A dirt road led to a trickling stream. It flowed along a sandy bed strewn with boulders.

'This is the nullah that cuts off the settlements on the other side during the monsoon months,' Birsa said.

Concrete pillars of a non-existent bridge rose on the stream bed. Nobody could remember when the contractors had begun the work, or when they had abandoned it. The iron reinforcement bars were rusted. We pulled off our shoes, rolled up our trousers and hauled the motorcycles across.

A rocky track wound along a wooded ridge. The locals called this ridge Sukhuapatta Pahar, or Dry-Leaf Hill. An old, unspoilt forest of sal, kusum, siali, crocodile-bark, and other broad-leaved trees and creepers ensured a steady supply that people collected to stitch leaf plates. The work sustained them during the lean months. We passed a hamlet of five households and, following the directions a villager gave us, took a rutted path. Sunlight streamed in through denuded branches of trees, turning a carpet of leaves iridescent yellow, red and brown. The two motorbikes shredded the silence of the forest. A pair of green pigeons took wing from a bush.

'Who'd think we are going to inspect a school?' I mused aloud. 'It feels like we are in a cross-country rally.'

Nirmal, his shoulders stiff and eyes firmly fixed on the front wheel skidding over loose stones, chuckled.

'Imagine what will happen if we have a punctured tyre,' Birsa quipped from behind us.

'Khyama karibey Prabhu Jagannatha!' Nirmal exclaimed in mock horror. Forgive us, Lord Jagannath.

We shared a hopeless laugh. I couldn't recall having seen a single tyre-repairing shop inside the forest.

～

We could not find Turi Barja, the handsome and tongue-tied young man with the red headband. Nobody had seen him in the last two days. He had probably slipped to the other side of the hill where the forest was thicker, to trap birds or other small animals.

But what had drawn us to this remote place was a story. It was the story of two villages, Pungichua and Tendu, both equally remote and divided by a stream that cut them off from each other and the outside world for three months. When the school education department set up a school in Pungichua, the people of Tendu had protested. If Pungichua could get a school, why not Tendu, they had argued. If the sanction was for one school only, then why not set it up at Tendu instead of at Pungichua? The tug of war had continued for some time, but eventually, Pungichua had won. As a mark of protest, the people of Tendu had refused to send their children to the school.

But that was two years ago. We were here to see the latest situation with our own eyes.

As in Hudisahi, the primary school in Pungichua too sat in the middle of a forest, away from the centre of the village. It was as if the sarkari babus had dropped the unplastered brick building from a helicopter and forgotten about it. The nearest source of water, a forest stream, was some distance away. The three-room building, too, was incomplete. Three classes shared one room, another served as the kitchen, and the third one was a store for masonry equipment. A heap of sand, overgrown with creepers, stood in the compound. Nobody had bothered to remove the shuttering planks from the ceiling.

'After two of the construction workers died of cerebral malaria, nobody was willing to come to this place to finish the work,' Kanaicharan Singh, the teacher, complained.

The students sat upon unpaved floor, under the planks that hung over their heads like sleeping bats. The teacher occupied a charpoy and an overturned tin drum acted as his table.

Kanaicharan Singh, a man of late middle age, was from the Bhumij community. He flipped through the registers and gave me the enrolment data: Class 1 – twenty-eight, Class 2 – twelve, and Class 3 – thirty-seven. Altogether seventy-seven enrolled students and forty-one of them were girls!

A mysterious silence had greeted us since we had first spotted the school inside the woods. Around fifty children were packed in a room, attended to by a single teacher, but there was a complete absence of noise. Not a trace of the usual birdcage cacophony that would usually give away a school from a distance. This was the case in almost all the schools we had been visiting here, and this unnatural hush of the children had never ceased to surprise me.

I now watched them inside the shadowy room, sitting listlessly on the floor, struggling to read from soiled books, or copying Odia letters on pieces of slate. School bags made from cement sacks lay around. A half dozen babies, younger siblings of the pupils, were curled up asleep on the bare brick floor. They would wake up when tikin mandijom would be ready.

The room was damp and almost dark, the unplastered brick walls had absorbed the ambient light. A sunny day blazed outside. Birds chirped, trees murmured, damselflies danced on a breeze.

In this forest world, the children were miniature adults; the society here treated them that way. By the age of twelve, a child would be adept at most life-sustaining skills, would gain a sound knowledge of her natural surroundings, and imbibe the community's values. But they'd leave all these acquisitions outside before stepping inside the classroom, like the plastic sandals they sometimes wore. Their cognition, sharpened by a life lived in close harmony with nature, would go to sleep like their younger siblings on the classroom floor.

But Kanaicharan Singh's hands were too full to ponder these matters. The department had sanctioned a handpump a year ago, but the contractor wouldn't transport the equipment until the bridge was ready. He didn't know when the water problem would be solved, probably not during his tenure. The supply of rice grains for the midday meal, too, was erratic.

But there were other, more critical, issues.

'Do you know what gives me the most trouble?' Kanaicharan confessed to me. 'It is on the days we serve them eggs. Many of my pupils come to school with their little siblings, because there's no one at home to look after them. We cook a quantity of rice accordingly; we can somehow manage these extra mouths. But an egg costs three rupees, and we need to ration it strictly per head. But who'll reason this with the kids? They make such a hue and cry when an egg is halved. They always demand a whole egg.'

The way he turned his pleading eyes on me, it was as if he wanted me to convey this problem to the higher authorities. How could you divide an egg without breaking a child's heart? Would there ever be a nationwide debate on this? Would the Parliament hold a special session to discuss the matter? Would the government set up an experts' committee to solve the problem?

As I mulled over it, Nirmal got busy doing some low-light photography inside the classroom – of faces and objects, of the hieroglyphs scrawled on the brick walls, of steel plates peeping from satchels stitched out of Lafarge cement bags, of tiny pot shards, leaves and seeds neatly arranged on a windowsill, possibly the remains of a pretend-and-play cooking game.

The camera teased the children out of their pre-lunch stupor. Looking at them, it was impossible to guess who belonged to which class. Chronic malnutrition, as old as the forests and handed down over generations, seemed to have a skewing effect on their physical growth.

It was not obvious how many of them were from Tendu.

'Boys and girls from Tendu, please raise your arms,' Birsa announced in Ho.

Twenty-two arms rose immediately, and in different corners of the room. The tug-of-war between the two villages was a thing of the past.

As Nirmal aimed his camera to document this heart-warming news, a boy from Pungichua propped up the raised arm of his mate from Tendu. Both had broad winners' smiles on their faces.

'Your name?' Nirmal asked the boy from Tendu.

'Mathai Singh,' the boy replied promptly. He had a thick mop of springy hair on his head and bright, beady eyes.

Mathai was in Class 2. Every morning, he trekked two kilometres to come to school, Kanaicharan told us. On the way, he had to cross a nullah that passed between the two villages.

'What do you do during the rains?' Birsa asked.

'I stuff my school dress into the bag and cross the stream holding it over my head,' Mathai replied with a proud smile on his lips.

'For them it's nothing,' Kanaicharan Singh said. 'If he doesn't come to school, his father will send him to guard their sorghum plot inside the forest. Isn't that so, Mathai?'

Mathai nodded vigorously, the smile still glistening on his face like a newborn leaf.

The primer open before him had on its pages drawings of giraffe, eagle, camel, aeroplane, apple – all labelled in Odia. But Mathai failed to identify most of the objects when Birsa called out their names.

Did anyone in Tendu eat apples? Was this area under the flight path of an aeroplane? What did they call an aeroplane in Ho? Odd questions tapped inside my head.

'Tell me, Mathai, what is the name of our country?' I asked him.

After Birsa had translated the question for him, Mathai Singh's beady eyes grew dim. He remained silent for a long moment and then replied in a low, halting voice:

'The name of our country is Sukhuapatta Pahar.'

∼

If there was a grain of truth in Sabram Singh Banara's claim, Mathai's ancestors had migrated from a highly developed urban civilization to these forest regions many centuries ago. Now, men from these parts ventured out, to work in brickfields and in mines, to far-off towns and cities to build roads, flyovers and even a Commonwealth Games Village. When he would grow up, perhaps Mathai Singh, too, would follow in their footsteps and go to build the edifices of a new nation. Whether he would claim that nation as his own was another matter.

ONE-WAY ROAD

Two years after I visited Ayodhya Hill, violence ravaged the region. The police and paramilitary forces were waging a battle against, as a former prime minister described it, 'India's greatest internal security threat'. Newspapers and television channels were full of images – of troops marching into villages, of minesweeper vehicles and specially trained Cobra commandos combing the forests, of ghost villages deserted before a raid, of roads blocked with tree trunks and embedded with landmines, of CPI(M) offices burning and their cadres lying murdered, of air force helicopters showering leaflets, printed in Bangla and Ol Chiki scripts, urging villagers to stay away from the Maoists, of posters written in red ink pasted on red mud walls.

As the 24×7 news channels beamed the images into our drawing rooms, they got mixed up with footage of America's war against terrorism, of US Marine commandos dressed up like astronauts, entering sun-bleached, mortar-torn villages in central Asia, of columns of refugees fleeing smoking battle zones, of untended cows roaming deserted homesteads, of petrified eyes peering out of holes in bullet-scarred walls.

As the summer of violence peaked, Amitava telephoned from Purulia to inform me that they were closing down Dumurdi Vidyashram. The temperature there was hovering at 50°C and there was an acute water crisis. The springs had been drying up since work on the power plant had started, but this summer the situation was desperate. The Maoists operating in the area had issued a threat: they wanted the Vidyashram to be closed down because it received funds from a foreign aid agency. The villagers didn't want to send their children to the school.

Amitava was planning to return to Kolkata after he settled the affair there. Nabin Machhoari and two other workers had received job offers in the Purulia-based cooperative society. Savitri would stay with a family in Dumurdi until Amitava could relocate her to another project. She could never return to her own village.

For many years, West Bengal had a high percentage of literates without a school-leaving certificate. Among the women, this had been as high as 40 per cent. Noting this, well-known demographic expert Mahendra K. Premi wrote in his book *Population of India in the New Millennium: Census 2001*: 'It is surprising to note that women's education in West Bengal with 40 per cent literates without any education level attained and only 18 per cent having completed secondary education is very low and needs some explanation.'

Savitri Munda was the explanation.

The image of her polishing the courtyard and signage of Dumurdi Vidyashram with clay slurry under the feathery light of dawn was something I'd never forget.

~

By the time Savitri Munda would finish her early morning chores, the sun would rise above the hill. In a distant forest, the birds would begin their orchestra. Adult men and women would already be away at work. Only the very old and the very young would remain in the village.

A Kolho village in Simlipal, unlike the villages of other tribal communities, is a diffuse settlement of cottages set apart from each other in a forest clearing. This arrangement gives the villages a sylvan quietude. On a cool, breezy morning, the sun would shimmer on the green leaves, and the misty Sukhuapatta hills would loom in the distance.

A Pied Piper would choose this hour to visit the village, to call out all the children there. But this piper was a woman. She would come riding a bicycle and, rather than playing on a flute, would go about ringing the cycle's bell. She'd wear a starched blue sari and a watch on her wrist. Sometimes, she would stop by a cottage and call a child by his name, enquire about the girl who hadn't been attending school, the boy who was recovering from a fever, the one who hadn't returned yet from distant paddy lands. She would inform them when the school would distribute new uniforms for girls, or if there'd be egg on the day's tikin mandijom menu. Before the sun had climbed over the Sukhuapatta hills, all the children would step out of their cottages and follow the Pied Piper.

Dolipada was the name of the village, not Hamelin, and its Pied Piper was Bindumani Samad. The Pied Piper of Hamelin had led all the children into a gloomy cave. The Pied Piper of Dolipada led them out of it. They knew her tunes. She spoke their tongue, and told them stories and rhymes in it. Bindumani's clean starched sari, her bicycle and the wristwatch would probably have gone unnoticed elsewhere. But here, where a timeless pattern of subsistence livelihood bound women of her age, she was a picture of change.

Bindumani had a BA degree. Her husband, too, was a graduate, and worked as a social worker in another organization. They spoke Odia at home. Her one-year-old son understood the language and could even speak a few words. They had plans to send him to a good boarding school when he was old enough, preferably in Bhubaneswar. A generation ago, Bindumani and her husband would probably have converted to Christianity. A Baptist mission had been working in the region for decades. But Bindumani was aware of the various government schemes targeted at her community. Her work at Deepshikha had given her the gumption to avail them.

Bindumani Samad was born in 1986, the year the central government declared the National Policy on Education. That was a landmark policy which laid a special emphasis on promoting education among the tribal people, with curricula framed in tribal languages. The initiative never really took off, but Odisha set up many primary schools in this forest region. Bindumani went to one of them. She went to the degree college in Sarat, the subdivisional town, twenty-five kilometres away from her village. She was the first woman in the entire gram panchayat who had ever ventured out of her village for a college degree.

'Those were hard times, because in our village all were out-of-school children,' Bindumani said when I asked her about it.

'Then how did you manage to not become one of them?'

'I just hung on.' She smiled and wiped the sweat off her face with the end of her sari, before coiling it again around her waist in the tree-climbing style.

To hang on. This phrase contained a story of grit and hard work, of never dropping out, of walking long distances to attend high school, of fighting harassment and surviving the indifference of teachers, even mockery, of having no one at home or the village to help with studies, of withstanding pressure to give up and join out-of-school siblings in fields and forests.

Earlier, she had told me about the challenges she faced in her work at Deepshikha, about how parents were reluctant to send their children to school. She had asked me what to say to persuade them.

I didn't have the answer then. Now I did.

'Why should you ask them to send the child to school for tikin mandijom?' I told her. 'You can tell your own story instead. You are a living example of what vidya can give a girl.'

The smile that lit up Bindumani's face told me that she knew it.

~

I went back to Ayodhya Hill after a gap of six years. By then the situation there had become 'normal', though I wasn't sure what exactly the word meant in that setting. Did it still mean going to bed with a hungry stomach? Or going Bangal-chola? Or never going to school?

I wasn't sure whether this was normal or the new normal, but I found out that the paramilitary units had returned to their barracks. And sleep had returned to stricken eyes. And families had returned to ravaged homes. And men had returned to weed-choked fields. And a generation of children had dropped out of school and joined their parents in the fields.

This time I was travelling like a tourist, following the itinerary customized by the state tourism department for the weekend traveller, 'with an appetite for adventure, the pristine Ayodhya Hill, the Turga and Bamni falls, Charidha village famous for Chhau masks and, the crowning glory of the hill, the Purulia Pumped Storage Project'. A tourist would need to have a gargantuan appetite to enjoy the charms of a pristine hill, the ethnic crafts and a hydro-electric power plant rolled into a single tour package.

The 'crowning glory' on top of Ayodhya Hill turned out to be the artificial lake of the upper dam, whose still waters reflected the hill's denuded scalp. I spent a night in the tourist lodge run by the Comprehensive Area Development Corporation, an undertaking running under the public-private partnership model. It was a two-storeyed building, painted lilac and parrot green, with doors and windows fitted with wire mesh to keep out the malarial mosquitoes.

But they let in the distant barking of dogs. It echoed in the hills deep into the night and shredded my sleep. Earlier in the evening, the lodge's staff had been telling me stories of how the jawans of a Naga paramilitary battalion, stationed at Baghmundi below, had been hunting street dogs for meat. The entire dog population of the area had fled to the jungles, they claimed. I had no idea how much of it was true, but as I lay sleepless in bed, strange thoughts haunted me. Had these dogs turned feral? Were they now roaming the hillside in packs? A painted Chhau mask on the wall over my head made hideous faces at my insomnia throughout the night.

The next morning, I went to have a look at what remained of the Dumurdi Vidyashram. The cluster of huts that I had seen buzzing like a beehive, now lay derelict and silent. Termite nests covered the wattle sheds. A dry breeze chased around brown leaves. A gecko leapt away across the granite platform. A spotted dove was cooing on the neem tree.

IV

AJAY

VI

THE LAND OF PLAYING CARDS

'Do you know the name of the first foreign-funded NGO in this part of the country?' Amitava asked me.

I shook my head. A mischievous smile twisted the corners of his lips.

'Let me help you,' he said. 'It also worked in the field of education.'

I still didn't know.

'Okay.' Amitava raised his hand. 'Its CEO inherited the premises from his father. The Nobel Academy of Sweden had funded this NGO.'

We laughed. We were right there – the NGO built by Rabindranath Tagore in Santiniketan.

Amitava was on a two-year teaching contract with the Rural Extension Centre of Visva-Bharati University, and he had invited me to spend the weekend at his place. They had provided him with a nice accommodation inside the leafy campus. It was the middle of April, the end of spring, and nature in these dry ochre plains was in all its vibrant glory.

On the morning of Poila Boishakh, the Bengali New Year, the university authorities organized a programme inside the campus. The day officially marked the beginning of summer season on the Bengali calendar, but at six in the morning, the air was gentle and redolent with the scent of flowers. We walked half a kilometre from Amitava's quarters to the abode of Gurudev – as Tagore is called here – a constellation of pretty buildings set amid well-tended greens. The sun-dappled path stretched under a canopy of old rain trees and led to an exquisite tinted-glass prayer hall. A genteel crowd had already assembled inside and spilled on to the lawns surrounding it. Students of Sangit Bhavana were singing Tagore's songs with practised grace. The atmosphere was charged with passionate devotion; one could almost mistake it for a religious gathering.

The men, turned out in dhoti-panjabi, shuffled about gawkily as they tried to get their unaccustomed legs around the pleats of their starched dhotis. But the women were prim in batik-printed cotton saris. They sat on the steps of the prayer hall, on bare brick parapets, on grass under the trees. Many had their eyes closed, shoulders swaying, and lips silently following the lyrics.

'Here you have a big dollop of the cream of Bengali society,' Amitava whispered.

That I could see. I could spot a few well-known professionals and even a couple of celebrities.

'Many have links with Santiniketan that go back two or three generations,' Amitava added.

As the morning ripened to noon, the crowd moved to a grove of old chhatim trees, where the ashram school's children were hosting a programme, and then, in the evening, to an open-air concert on a wide ground, before a row of buildings that showcased a curious blend of Western and Oriental architectural styles. The same set of men and women, moving from place to place, the same ritual of greetings and small talk, rendered in perfectly accented Bangla. Only the settings and dress changed as the day waned.

I had been to Santiniketan before, but never on an occasion like this, and never as the guest of an insider. Amitava was now part of the university's faculty, though temporarily.

'So, how do you find it?' He glanced sideways at me.

I was blunt. 'It all reminds me of a neoclassical court comedy, or perhaps a Tagore dance drama.'

'Yes, *Tasher Desh*.' Amitava grinned conspiratorially. The Land of Playing Cards. 'Tomorrow I'll take you to another episode of this play.'

~

It was called Khoaier Anyo Haat – the other mart on the khoai. It came up every Saturday in a eucalyptus grove by the side of an irrigation canal on the margin of old Santiniketan. It was early afternoon, and the sun was still strong. But a crowd of men and women had begun to trickle into the ravine-like ground known in these parts as khoai, land eroded by the river Ajay and its many tributary streams. A few local sellers displayed tribal handicrafts, but there were also students of the Kala Bhavana, Santiniketan's school of fine arts, with their more sophisticated work.

'Hi, *Ameethaba*!' a piping female voice called from behind us. We turned around to find a thin, blonde woman waving at Amitava. Dressed in a batik kurti and khaki shorts, she came riding a puttering, paint-peeled Bajaj scooter.

Amitava introduced me to Ruth, a Polish woman who looked to be in her late twenties. The way she joined her palms in greeting and the deep tan on her skin proclaimed that Ruth was a seasoned Santiniketanite. She was from Charles University, Prague, on a fellowship in Sriniketan, Santiniketan's sister town, which housed Visva-Bharati's rural development wing. Ruth parked the scooter under an acacia tree, lit a beedi and unpacked her wares from a canvas sack. These turned out to be curious food items – bottled fruit juice, flavoured yoghurt, garlic butter and a variety of jams. She spread a hand-printed cotton cloth upon the ground and began to lay out the bottles.

'Would you guys like to have some roasted wood-apple sherbet?' she offered.

We refused politely and moved to the centre of the haat. A young tribal girl was selling steaming momos on green banana-leaf plates.

A jeans-clad Baul singer strummed a gupijantra, a musical instrument made of a single string and a gourd shell. A thin scattering of men and women drifted about, checking out the various items. On sale were terracotta figurines, kantha-stitched fabrics, reed baskets, painted pots, and other ethnic bric-a-brac that one normally sees in a bhadralok drawing room rather than in a tribal cottage. A tastefully illustrated banner of the haat committee proclaimed eco-friendly rules and regulations.

But commerce was an insignificant part of the pageant. The haat had the air of an open-air exhibition, a pantomime where everyone was a player and a spectator. It was a rendezvous where the chic and the arty met, for the eleventh time during the day, or the first time since they had last met in a first-world city. They were part of Santiniketan's inner circle. Tourists rarely came during this season. Under the murmuring eucalyptus trees, they appeared like a vision that would soon be swept away by a gust of wind.

Amitava exchanged greetings with a few of them. He introduced me to a retired bureaucrat and his wife, Mr and Mrs Sen. The Sens ran a vocational training centre for poor tribal girls, I was told, in a village ten kilometres away from Santiniketan. It was named Nabo Digonto, the new horizon. Mr Sen, a portly man with thick salt-and-pepper sideburns, had worked in several key government departments. His wife, Anita Devi, was an accomplished Rabindra Sangeet singer and the granddaughter of a well-known disciple of Tagore. She was a tall woman with well-groomed hands, an aquiline nose and grey shoulder-length hair quaintly streaked with golden dye. When Amitava told them about my interest in elementary education and the column I wrote for a newspaper, they immediately warmed to me.

'That's wonderful!' Mr Sen said energetically. 'Two of our old friends who live in the US will visit Nabo Digonto day after tomorrow. Why don't you come along if you are free?'

As Amitava had a busy Monday at the centre, and I'd have nothing in particular to do, I accepted the invitation.

~

Visva-Bharati is one of the first foreign-funded NGOs in the country which Rabindranath Tagore set up with the cash award that came with his Nobel prize. Amartya Sen, Santiniketan's other illustrious son, set up another NGO here after he won the prize eighty-five years later. Known as the Pratichi Trust, it works primarily in the fields of primary education and healthcare.

Sen couldn't have chosen a more appropriate place. Santiniketan sits in the district of Birbhum, which ranks among the lowest in West Bengal in terms of human development. This out-of-placeness had always haunted this world-famous address. But with economic liberalization and a new four-lane expressway to Kolkata, Santiniketan, with its uncluttered rural setting and salubrious climate, had become a weekend getaway for the affluent Bengali middle classes. Tagore's abode of peace had metamorphosed into a cluster of luxury villas, country houses and resorts that had come up in the outlying villages. They gave the careworn city dwellers a taste of farm-fresh nature, packaged to fit the weekends and middling-deep pockets.

Some of these resorts even boasted a profile in social work. They ranged from free homoeopathic clinics to sales counters for handicrafts and pickles made by local village women. The unwritten slogan was: 'Enjoy rural Bengal and do something for the poor people who live here'. These were like spas of the mind, which massaged the conscience of the Bengali bhadralok, chronically left-minded and newly tasting the fruits of economic liberalization. But there were also several dedicated NGOs working around Santiniketan for the uplift of the poor tribal people. That is because a little something could make the most visible impact here. That little something could be a free anti-malaria clinic, an arsenic-free handpump, a smokeless oven, or a concrete latrine cover.

Or a hostel for poor tribal girls. Being a family-run trust, Nabo Digonto could not receive funds from the government agencies. The Sens relied entirely on donations from well-wishers who included a wide circle of their friends. The Guptas, a US-based Bengali couple visiting Santiniketan on a professional assignment, belonged to that circle. On a warm Monday morning, Mr Sen had arranged a guided tour of the trust facilities for them. I slipped into a rear seat of his Toyota Fortuner.

The bulky vehicle took half an hour to untangle itself from Bolpur's traffic before it hit the highway. Now we entered a Tagore watercolour: a red, undulating Martian landscape and groves of toddy palms rising like tongues of fire into a coppery sky.

Mr Sen occupied the seat beside the driver and briefed us about the genesis of Nabo Digonto.

'After giving thirty-five of the best years of my life in the service of the nation, I was fed up. You see so much poverty and backwardness around you, and yet you can't really do anything. Your hands are tied with red tape. I couldn't share this despair with anyone except Anita, my wife. She had spent her youth here in Santiniketan; it's like her second home. Both of us were itching to do something, to give something back to the place that means so much to us. We already had this little farmhouse in Asondanga, which I had bought way back in the 1980s from an artist who went to settle in Paris. After I retired, I invested my entire provident fund and gratuity money and built Nabo Digonto brick by brick. So far, my gratuity is the only government money that has gone into the trust.'

Sen laughed, twisting his head to eye Mrs Gupta. A girdle of fat around the back of his neck quivered like a harmonium's bellows.

The Fortuner left the highway and wobbled along a rutted lane. Endless fields broken here and there with toddy palms and bamboo groves gave way to scenes of a nondescript village. Reddish mud huts with rotten straw thatch; bony cows with philosophical eyes standing in their own filth; women scrubbing pots on a scummy pond; a column of ducks marching along a bamboo fence where dung kebabs were drying; old men with stubbly chins queueing up before a kerosene shop. Asondanga was a far cry from the trim and lavish Santiniketan, and only ten kilometres away. I tried to imagine how its shades and shapes had made their way into the canvas of the painter who had sold off his farmhouse to settle in Paris. Perhaps they never did, perhaps he was an abstract painter.

We entered a tribal neighbourhood at the back of the village and stopped before the tall gates of a walled building. The gates rolled open and let the vehicle in. A pebbled driveway led to a sprawling two-storeyed house set in a vegetable garden. Anita Devi was standing in the portico, her palms joined, a handsome smile fluttering on her lips like a monarch butterfly.

'I hope the journey wasn't very uncomfortable,' she spoke in a mellifluous voice as we stepped out of the air-conditioned vehicle into the rising heat. 'My children are away at school. Let us make use of this quiet and take you around the premises. Come this way, please.'

Anita Devi spoke a Rabindrik Bangla, a literary version of Bangla thickly peppered with Tagorean poeticism, much to the bafflement of Mr and Mrs Gupta.

'You cannot imagine how higgledy-piggledy this place had been when we took possession. Weeds smothered the grounds, there were no boundary walls and – can you imagine! – a village lumpen ran a liquor den inside the compound. The building had a studio on the ground floor and two bedrooms on the first floor – all in a very pitiable condition. It took five years of hard labour, and money, to transform all that into this. We started with three girls, now we have twenty – all purely tribal, all from purely poor families.'

Mrs Sen's insistence on the absoluteness of the girls' poverty was as spotless as the Bangla she spoke.

The building was a piecemeal accretion of rooms and passageways around what had once been a cosy artist's retreat. Signs marked the rooms: RECEPTION HALL, DINING HALL, KITCHEN, LIBRARY, DORMITORY, SEWING ROOM, COMPUTER ROOM and so on. Anita Devi lost her way in the maze of corridors and needed the help of an assistant, a silent tribal woman in a green-bordered white sari. I learnt that the lady stayed in Santiniketan and came here only occasionally, when they fixed visits like this.

We were shown around the empty rooms where the boarders ate, slept and learnt. Rows of wooden cots with bedrolls and mosquito nets, books and slates on wooden shelves, and garments on hangers – all neatly arranged.

A macabre sensation hit me. It felt as if we were on a guided tour through a former prison house or a concentration camp, where the belongings of long-deceased inmates were on display. Perhaps that was because the objects looked old and worn, like in a museum: old, mouldy books; rusted sewing machines; and computers from another era.

Anita Devi explained.

'Of the many things I have learnt from Gurudev's life and work, the most valuable is the virtue of begging. Begging for a cause. When he was setting up Visva-Bharati, he travelled the world with a begging bowl. For all those who want to work for the downtrodden, this is a lesson in humility. And this is very Indian, you know, very Upanishadic. Datta, Dayadhvam, Damyata. We go to people and say – donate whatever you can, whatever you don't need any more, because here we make use of everything. You cannot imagine what smiles of joy even a little gift can bring to our children's faces.'

Anita Devi intoned each word beautifully, with the right mix of passion and inflexion. The Guptas were charmed. But my doubting mind lapsed into a twisted line of thinking. When Tagore had set up Visva-Bharati, there had been no University Grants Commission. Also, now the governments had a host of schemes for the upliftment of poor tribal people. Many of these schemes existed on paper because the money returned unspent. Wasn't begging-bowl philanthropy a little out of place in a welfare state run on taxpayers' money? Also, shouldn't basic rights be a matter of entitlement rather than charity? I dared not broach the subject, because her ex-bureaucrat husband had already declared his aversion to public money. 'Sarkari money is always dirty, like politics,' he had said. The Guptas couldn't have agreed more.

As Mr Sen got busy explaining various modes through which a donor could support the trust, Mrs Sen continued with the guided tour. We were taken to the library, to a room with a few shelves piled with old, discarded novels and a set of *Reader's Digest* magazines. ('Of course they can't read them yet, but how they love the pictures!') We were taken to a room with half a dozen rusty Singer machines and a couple of garment-design charts hanging on the walls. ('A school or college certificate isn't everything. So we are preparing them to earn a living.') We moved to another room that had a few computers, most of them from the pre-Pentium generation. ('And here we are preparing them for the future world.') Finally, we were taken to a large reception hall, to the studio of its former owner. On the walls were photographs of the children performing on stage, in Santiniketan and in Kolkata. Every winter, the girls were ferried to the city to take part in cultural programmes. Patrons and would-be patrons of the trust received the invitations.

'Our girls are so talented,' Anita Devi gushed, and then switched to a tone of horror: 'But you can't imagine their condition when they first turn up here. They have lice in their hair, vermin on their bodies and filth on their tongues. For the lice and vermin, we use carbolic soap and shampoo. And do you know how I scrub out the filth from their tongues and minds?'

She stopped, looked at us quizzically, and then offered the answer herself.

'With Rabindra Sangeet! Yes, Tagore's songs. I personally teach them the songs and ask them to sing and sing, so that their insides are washed clean. For them, it's like a rebirth.'

We saw their photographs. Under the coloured stage lights, dressed up as characters in a Tagore dance drama, or gathered around microphones and singing with upturned faces, the children appeared vivacious and happy.

In contrast, their real-life counterparts were timid and tense. They had been summoned from school to be presented to us, and to present before us a small programme. Altogether eighteen girls, aged between eight and fourteen and wearing school uniforms, all of them from the Santhal and Mahato communities. As they filed into the premises, led by another woman dressed in a green-bordered white sari, the scene reminded me of the ducks I had seen in the village. The girls soon changed into colourful costumes and returned to the reception hall. A few of them now had gulmohar blossoms in their hair. We took our seat on wicker sofas arranged in a corner of the hall as they began a performance of Rabindra Sangeet and dance.

Nothing was impromptu about the show. After the customary welcome song and an address, delivered by a sweet little girl with a tonsured head, a group of older girls with red gulmohar in their hair presented a Tagore song:

Aji jhoro jhoro mukhoro badorodinay
Jani nay, jani nay, kichhutay keno jay mono lagena

This was a popular number that expressed a melancholy mood on a wet monsoon day. Not only did it sound queer on a bright summer's morning, but the delicate ennui that was central to the lyric also seemed to clash with the lively innocence of the girls with flaming red flowers in their hair.

It produced a jarring effect on my mind. I stepped out to the veranda for a smoke.

The sun blazed on a kitchen garden. Patches of pale green marked out the tender shoots of bitter gourds peeping out of cloddy earth. Long ridge gourds hung under a canopy of creepers. Amid these distinct shades of green, strange grey shapes made with concrete and pebbles stuck out here and there. I stepped out to inspect. They were pieces of sculpture mounted on brick pedestals, which the artist had left behind. I studied the abstract forms for long but failed to make out anything. Neither pretty nor resembling any familiar shape, they had a haunting, weather-beaten appearance.

And then I spotted a minor girl. She was standing alone in the middle of a plot of turned-up earth. For a moment, I mistook her for a piece of sculpture. I walked up to her. She was still wearing the school uniform.

'What is your name?' I asked her. 'Why are you standing here under the sun?'

The girl didn't respond but stood there stiffly, her eyes fixed on her feet. Had she committed an offence? Didn't she speak Bangla? Her eyes were dry, but threads of sweat trickled down her cheeks.

I left her to herself and walked down the garden path to an opening cut into the high boundary wall. A portion of the village was visible from here. A woman was chopping straw on a bonti, a brood of chicks skittered around a plate of feed. Life went on out there, following its own rhythm. I turned back and couldn't find the girl. Snatches of a Tagore song were coming from the hall. Now they were singing in chorus, led by Anita Devi herself.

What if the poet could come here now? I tried to imagine him inside the hall, in a deep lounge chair, his face famously framed in the fluff of white hair. I failed. What appeared in my mind was his strangely haunting bust that the great Santiniketan artist Ramkinkar Baij had sculpted in bronze. It was the head of an old man bent in coiled pain, his face imprisoned in its own shadow, his eyes a pair of dark hollows under a translucent forehead.

Perhaps the poet would have preferred to stay outside, here in this garden, in the company of these abstract shapes left behind by the artist who sold off this farmhouse.

AN EMBROIDERED VILLAGE

That visit to Nabo Digonto had left a mild acidic taste in my mouth. To make amends, Amitava invited me again to Santiniketan a few months later, during winter. This time, he assured me, he had lined up a completely different experience.

It was the middle of January and bitterly cold in this dry region. We left Santiniketan one afternoon and travelled forty kilometres to Jaydev Kenduli, a village by the river Ajay. Jaydev Kenduli was the birthplace of the twelfth-century poet Jaydev, and here, folk singers congregated every year on Makar Sankranti, the day that marks the end of the winter solstice. Baul singers from all corners of the Bengal Delta, including Bangladesh, came for a three-day music festival. They performed in night-long recitals in the akharas, pavilions of different gurus, set up on the dry riverbank.

The Bauls, simple rustic men and women placed low in Bengal's caste hierarchy, are followers of an arcane faith system. The men would usually wear saffron or patchwork robes, sport long beards and ankle bells, and play the ektara, a single-stringed instrument. They came to this important festival to offer their new compositions and also to sing from a repertoire that had been passed on across generations.

During our college days, Amitava used to play the guitar and sing Western country songs, the blues, and also Baul and Rabindra Sangeet. He didn't sing any more, but his passion for folk music hadn't died. He was friends with several singers at the fair. We spent an enthralling night out in the open, sitting on tarpaulin laid over the sands and watching them perform in the throes of ganja-induced ecstasy. The men sang standing on their feet, swaying and wheeling to the bursts of music that seemed to coil out from deep inside them. When the early-morning cold began to freeze our limbs, we two left the place to go to a farmer's home across the river to catch some sleep.

At three o'clock, a razor-sharp wind was blowing over the Ajay's dry sand bed. Fatigued, we groped our way across grey dunes that seemed to stretch to the end of the horizon. Smoke from the cannabis the Bauls were smoking in clay pipes had fuddled our brains.

'Look over there, that's Gouranga Bauri's village,' Amitava said, pointing his finger into the distance.

A yellow moon was setting over a distant silhouette of hutments. It cast an ivory light over the endless expanse of sand.

'And who is Gouranga Bauri?' I asked.

'He's a farmer. I first met him when I came to this char village on a field trip with a group of students. Gouranga-da and his family helped us a lot during that time. I've been coming here since then. I love this place.'

Snatches of ektara and a sharp, silken voice fanned out from the pavilions behind us into the stillness of the night. The unforgettable voice of a plump Baul woman with long, matted hair and rudraksha beads around her neck was still buzzing inside my head like a trapped bumblebee:

Ved bidhir por shastro kana
Arek kana mon amar
Eshob dekhi kanar haatbazaar

All the scriptures are blind
My mind, too, is blind
Everything here is a market for the blind

Shuffling our feet over powdery sand under the pale moonlight, around pools of tinfoil water, we made our way into the sleeping village.

~

I woke up late in the morning. A bright sun was sending tendrils of light through the reed walls of a hut. Thumps of wooden mortars were coming from different directions. It was the morning of Makar Sankranti, I remembered. Villagers in Bengal celebrate this day with preparations of pithay, varieties of rice cakes, made with newly harvested rice ground at home.

Gouranga Bauri's family comprised his wife, a son, a brother and his wife. The brother's wife was pregnant and was away at her parents' place; Gouranga-da's ten-year-old son had accompanied her there. By the time we finished our morning cup of tea, I discovered that everyone in the family was brimming with warm hospitality. We had planned to return to Santiniketan in the morning, but they wouldn't let us go.

'How can you go on this auspicious day without tasting our pithay?' Boudi, Gouranga-da's wife, warned Amitava with mock anger. 'I'll never allow you to set foot in our house again if you do that.'

'And isn't this your friend's first visit here?' Gouranga-da smiled, pointing at me. 'You must show him the famous *spots* around our village. People come from faraway places to visit them.'

Amitava relented, and we spent a fine winter's afternoon wandering around the village of Ichhaipur.

Near the village, a rocky outcrop covered with jungle ran parallel to the river. There is an old story that in mythical times, a king named Surath had taken shelter here after the Kols defeated him in a battle. The king had built his fortress in the forest and worshipped Goddess Durga. It wasn't clear how much of it was history, but the ruins of an ancient battlement and a stone temple were still standing inside an acacia forest. The other famous 'spot' here was a fifty-foot-high fine terracotta tower built in the eighteenth century by a local zamindar named Ichhai Ghosh. The village got its name from him.

But Ichhaipur was a recent village on a new almond-shaped char, a sandbar on the river Ajay. The land revenue department called these lands 'payosthi jomi', the water-born land. All the settlers here belonged to backward caste groups. They had migrated from across the border as recently as in the 1980s, claimed the shrub-covered char and started to grow crops on it. Fertile alluvium, freshly minted, with a high content of fine sand allowed water to pass through easily, making the fields suitable for leafy vegetables. Gouranga-da took us around the plots where tomatoes, chillies, peas and potatoes were growing.

'Did you see any pond in the village?' he asked. 'You won't. If we dig a pond to harvest the rainwater, it will seep into the earth before the beginning of winter.'

The river swelled during the rainy seasons, and flood was a regular occurrence. 'But we count on it as a blessing. The water stands on the plots for three to four days and then recedes. It leaves new layers of silt.'

'What about the village? Where do you move when a flood strikes?' I asked.

'We move to higher ground. As you can see, we use reed panels to build our huts. We can take them down at an hour's notice, leaving the bamboo poles standing. It takes only half a day to fix them back again, after the homestead lands rise and dry up. In autumn, new grass grows on the char. We change the panels every two years, before Durga Puja.'

The thatched roofs and walls woven with golden yellow grass had given the settlement a gleaming look. In fact, everything in Ichhaipur had this stamp of newness, even the trees. The guava, papaya, mango, and other fruit trees around the cottages could not have been more than ten or fifteen years old. But what I found most intriguing was that we didn't come across any old person in the village.

When I mentioned this, Gouranga-da laughed. His own father was old, he told me, but he lived in Bangladesh. The old man visited Ichhaipur rarely. Gouranga-da and his brother would visit him more often. That wasn't a problem because they had passports. Every family in the village had ration cards and a proper land deed.

'Here we all belong to the *Red Party*,' Gouranga-da declared.

He offered us tea at the only village tea shop. We sat ourselves on a bamboo platform and sipped red tea from squat glasses. A red banner covered a part of the tea-shop wall. BRIGADE CHOLO, it proclaimed in bold lettering, urging the masses to attend a CPI(M) rally in Kolkata's Brigade Parade Ground. Below the names of prominent speakers was a rising red sun, a red Party flag, and a long procession of men and women with clenched fists raised to the skies. The graphics looked suspiciously familiar. Had it been copied from the now-defunct *Soviet Desh*? Amitava wasn't sure. Perhaps Nihar-da could quell my suspicion.

On one side of the shop, on a piece of bamboo matting mounted on a wooden frame, pages from the CPI(M) mouthpiece *Ganashakti* were pasted. The tea-shop owner kept a copy of the same newspaper for its customers. No other newspaper could be found in the village – *not allowed*, said Gouranga-da. There was an anganwadi centre, but no temple. Instead, there was the Party office – a one-storeyed brick building with a flagpole before it. This was the nerve centre of the village. Invisible threads spread out from it in all directions, as on a spider's web. In fact, before Amitava and I were up and about, two local committee members had met Gouranga-da to enquire about the two bohiragotos who had come to his house early in the morning. His younger brother,

Subal, was a member of the Party's youth wing. We were given his room.

Subal's cottage was at one end of the three-roomed household. It had a rough wooden cot, a dressing mirror and a bamboo clothes hanger fixed on poles; coils of brightly coloured saris hung on them. There was a laminated colour photograph of Subal and his wife, and a poster of a naked, white baby boy draping part of a flimsy partition wall – for decoration, and also perhaps for the sake of decency. A ceiling cloth with beautiful appliqué work hung below the thatched roof. This, and the quilts, pillow covers and a drapery on a mirror, displayed exquisite needlework. We learnt that these were Boudi's handiwork.

She responded to our words of praise with a shy smile. But Gouranga-da complained, 'She has ruined her eyes. Last year, I took her to an eye specialist in town. She'll go blind if she continues with the needlework, the doctor has warned. But will she ever listen to anyone?'

'What to do? I can never let my hands sit idle,' Boudi smiled helplessly. 'And now I must stitch a few quilts. A new member will be arriving soon in our family.'

She turned her head to Subal with a glint of happiness in her eyes. Subal blushed and lowered his face. He hardly spoke when Gouranga-da was around.

Since morning, we had been witnessing what she meant by not being able to let her hands sit idle. It had begun early. She had plastered the courtyard with slurry, powdered rice grain on a mortar, baked an enormous quantity of cakes, prepared fodder for the cows, fed the poultry, and then, in the afternoon, gone to their farm plot to help Subal harvest potatoes.

At dinner, she cooked for us a curry made with the freshly harvested potatoes, pea shoots and fenugreek seeds. Also lentils, and payeshpuli, rice patties swimming in thickened milk. Rice, lentils, wheat, fenugreek, milk, jaggery – all grown in their own fields and prepared for consumption with hands that could never sit idle.

We four men sat on grass mats in the open courtyard, in a half-circle, with Boudi at the centre. She was roasting rotis, one at a time, on a dug-out oven and tossing them on to our plates.

'Now that you have visited the Kenduli fair, you must come to our own fair,' she said to us. That was the Baruni fair at Thakurnagar, about which I had first learnt from Bharati Das. Here, too, the entire village set out on hired trucks. They stayed at the fairground together like one extended family – cooking and eating food from a community kitchen, meeting up with their kin spread across the country, and even matchmaking.

From descriptions of the fair, the talk drifted to stories of going to Party rallies in Kolkata. There, too, the same excitement, the same familial sharing and bonding. There had been one a few weeks before, whose poster we had seen in the tea shop.

'That's almost like going to the Baruni fair,' Boudi said. 'The preparations are the same.'

I was curious.

'We the women of the village don't sleep the night before. We prepare food for the day – hundreds of rotis, potato curry, and boiled eggs. The trucks leave before dawn.'

This time Gouranga-da and Subal went, but Boudi had gone to the rallies on earlier occasions. During those visits to the city, she had been to the Victoria Memorial, the zoo, the museum and other 'spots' there.

'The traffic situation was terrible this time,' Subal told me. 'By the time we reached the toll plaza of the new Hooghly bridge, it was late in the afternoon. The crowds had begun to disperse from the rally ground.'

'Our trucks couldn't even enter the city,' Gouranga-da rued.

I had seen the rallyists so many times, from the window of a bus, a taxi or a tram, standing still on clogged streets, trapped, sharing my irritation with fellow passengers, watching in mute anger the unending tides of humanity – the sun-scorched faces, the hurrying feet, calloused farmers' feet, bare or shod in cheap plastic sandals, hands holding up placards that the eyes couldn't read, streams of bohiragotos descending on my city like a flash flood. And the next day, wide-angle shots of the sea of dark heads would invariably be splashed across the pages of city newspapers, to go with the reports of inconveniences the citizens had to suffer. Never had I imagined that one day I'd be sharing such an intimate hour with some of those bohiragotos.

Intimate and beautiful, under a round moon. Beyond the open courtyard, the lights of the village flickered, and shadowy men and women swaddled in wrappers moved about. The night was growing chilly.

The winter sun had set early, the sandy soil couldn't hold back its heat. Less than fifty years ago, all this had been part of the Ajay's bed. The icy ghost of a river that had once flowed over this very spot was now coiling up from the underland. We huddled close to the embers as the flavour of steaming rotis, of piquant fenugreek seeds, and the sweetness of milk sent waves of heat into our bloodstreams. Less than thirty years ago, jungles covered this spot. It was the habitat of jackals and monitor lizards. Nobody set foot here. And then came a group of humans. They cleared the jungles, turned up the earth and grew food on it. The food was now getting diffused into our metabolic system. The reed cottages, glowing from within, appeared mysterious and floatable, like sky lanterns. A fire whispered on the straw-fed oven, a river wind sighed under the reed thatching, crickets kept up their concert. A universe of sounds. In a few weeks' time, a human baby's cry would join them.

A strange sensation ambushed me. It was euphoric and humbling at the same time. Such a simple efflorescence of life, and yet, I could never hope to fathom its mysterious centre. The words of Lalon Fakir, the mystic Baul who knew no borders, came back to me:

Pandit kana ohonkaray
Matbor kana chugolkhoray
Pandit kana ohonkaray
Sadhu kana onbicharay…
Ved bidhir por shastro kana
Arek kana mon amar
Eshob dekhi kanar haatbazaar

The pundit is blinded by his ego
The leader by his sycophants
The pundit is blinded by his ego
The saint is blinded by wrong judgement…
All the scriptures are blind
My mind, too, is blind
Everything here is a market for the blind

ERASURE

Five years had passed since that magical evening at Ichhaipur. The red sun printed on the 'Brigade Cholo' poster had set in West Bengal. One afternoon, Amitava telephoned me from Santiniketan.

'Have you heard the news?' His voice was grim.

'What news?'

'Gouranga-da is in Kolkata, admitted to the Medical College hospital. His house was attacked.'

A wave of political violence and vendetta was then sweeping across West Bengal, but Ichhaipur was not in the news. Or perhaps it was, and I had missed it.

'The attackers hit him with a machete, almost chopping off his hand from the wrist. They also burned down the cottages. Fortunately, none of his family members was home. Subal and his friends took him to a hospital in Panagarh. From there, they shifted him to Kolkata. Gangrene has set in. The doctors will probably amputate his hand.'

I felt a strange numbing of senses as Amitava recounted the details.

Every time I entered the Medical College hospital through the gate on College Street and looked up to view the facade of the majestic building with its tall Corinthian columns and cornices, every time I saw the crowd of people waiting upon the grand staircase, the unforgettable Odessa steps sequence from Sergei Eisenstein's *Battleship Potemkin* flashed in my mind. The sea of lost, pale faces, riven with anxiety and despair, the sunken eyes, at times covered with folded arms, the chin propped up on a fist, the limbs ranged out on the wide steps in countless postures of resignation and hope, the arms encircling knees, the hands holding sheaves of paper and X-ray plates, water bottles and palm-frond fans, the bodies stretched out on the staircase, waiting, sleeping – every time the images struck me as if they were suspended in stasis, and would cascade any moment, down the wide staircase, like flaming lava. It was as if they were waiting for a cue, for a mysterious signal, and then the armies of death would march down from over the ornate cornices, the entablatures and capitols, with a rattle of boots, the cannons would come alive on the battleship, and the marble lions would wake in three clean shakes from a montage. And then the terror-struck deluge would hurtle down the steps – the orphaned perambulator, the spectacles crushed under hurrying feet, the trampled baby, the blood spouting from a blinded eyeball, and the screams coiling up and sweeping away like a ball of flame towards the Emergency Block, a hundred hysteric ambulances hooting, with stretcher-bearers running in their wake, and a lonely arm raised over the head of the stretcher and holding a saline bottle, with shell bangles jingling on the wrist, audible despite the din like the last tramcar's bell in a midnight city.

They couldn't find a bed for Gouranga-da. He was sitting with his back propped against the wall, the lower part of his body stretched on a blue plastic sheet laid out on the corridor floor. He wore a lungi and vest, and had a week's stubble on his chin. A huge bandage encased his entire right arm. There wasn't any feeling of pain after they had administered the injections, Gouranga-da told me; the arm now felt like a piece of furniture attached to his shoulder. He was also running a temperature.

The real wound lay within: his spirit had been crushed. The figure I saw before me was but a shadow of the farmer I had met five years ago, a man in the centre of a world he had built with his own hands.

All that was gone. The fire had consumed everything, including all the identity documents and land deeds that they had obtained over the years with great persistence. An identity derived from two decades of hard labour on a land reclaimed from the bed of a river had been erased. This loss was greater than the amputation of an arm.

Subal and two of his friends had come with Gouranga-da. Reporters from television news channels had already tracked them down here. Finding Gouranga-da seated on the corridor floor, they had asked him to lie down on his back, and then, mounting their cameras over his head, had taken interviews. They had wanted him to name the party his attackers were from.

'What could I say?' Gouranga-da smiled weakly. 'The same people, the same char between the two banks of a river – kinsmen all. Tell me, how can I make these city babus understand this?'

~

For some time, the air was rife with rumours of an impending gram dokhol, a siege of the village. The men who hadn't switched their party colours with the changing times had fled Ichhaipur. But this was also the time when the paddy was ripening in the fields. Days before the incident, unknown men were seen patrolling the village lanes on motorbikes. Their faces were masked with gamchhas. Sensing trouble, Subal had slipped away to his in-laws' place in the neighbouring district. He later sent his wife's brothers to bring all members of the family.

Gouranga-da sent Boudi and their son with them, but he himself refused to leave the village.

'How could I?' he told me. 'How often can a man leave his bhitay in a lifetime? I have built it all with my own hands. The huts, the fields, the furniture – all. I have planted each of the trees around the cottages. How can I leave it all and go in a wink?'

The rampage began on the afternoon of Doshohora, the tenth day of the waxing moon. Gouranga-da was out in the fields, fixing a trellis over tender cucumber shoots. He rushed home when he heard that they were setting the village on fire. He watched the flames, borne on a gust of wind, racing towards his house. Soon, the sparks flew to their thatched cowshed, and it burst into flames. Gouranga-da saw silhouettes of men against the blaze, their faces covered, carrying machetes and country-made guns. The cow had broken free and was jumping about madly. The flames leapt out to the big, newly woven cottage on the eastern end of the courtyard. Inside it were a bicycle, a few sacks of mustard seeds and a bag of urea. Spotting a tin can in someone's hand, Gouranga-da rushed to the hut and stood before the door, stretching his arms across the bamboo frame. 'Banchoth!' – spat out the man with the tin can and dealt a blow on Gouranga-da's neck, sending him crashing to the ground. As he crawled forward and gripped the door frame with all his strength, Gouranga-da could feel two men grabbing at his waist from behind and trying to drag him away.

'Lay off, you son of a whore!' someone was shouting at the top of his voice.

Gouranga-da recognized the voice: it belonged to Bishu, a neighbour who had been the secretary of the Party's branch committee. Now he was out to make a show of his loyalty to his new party. It was Bishu who dealt the blow with the machete. Gouranga-da saw his fist almost coming off the wrist before he lost consciousness.

When he came to, the night had settled and there was nobody around. Pots and utensils were strewn across the courtyard. A light rain had doused the fire. Smoke was curling up from a heap of burnt quilts. Blood still oozed from the gaping wound on his wrist. Gouranga-da searched in the darkness for a piece of cloth, found a needle and thread, put his wounded hand in a jute bag and slipped away. He fled to the jungle, to the ruins of a castle there built by a vanquished king in mythical times.

Gouranga-da could not recall later how many days and nights he spent there, in the forest of old acacia trees. But he managed to bring himself to stitch his own nearly severed hand back into the wrist, clean the dirt and insect droppings on the wound, and even burn the skin to sterilize it. He bore the pain of a needle piercing the raw flesh, but when the smell of his own burnt skin hit his nostrils, he fainted.

His senses returned intermittently. One day, two days – Gouranga-da couldn't remember how many. There was no feeling of hunger or thirst. Sometimes, it rained in the forest. The patter of raindrops drumming on leaves reached him in sleep. He dreamt that his torn palm was still clinging on to the door frame of the burnt cottage, quivering like a giant moth.

One morning, he woke up from a deathly sleep. He could not feel his hand, his head; he was hollowed out from inside. He untied the rag from around the wound and noticed that the skin had taken on the texture of wild arum roots. He could not remember what had happened, or where he was. The needle still lay before him. At first, he could not recognize it. It was as if he were seeing the object for the first time in his life. He twiddled it for some time, marvelled at its slender form, its pointed tip, its tiny eye. The graceful shape of a needle gave him back his memory.

It was a long needle, one which his wife Saraswati used for embroidery work. But never had he given the object such intense scrutiny. Its shape impressed him deeply. He looked around him with a newborn's eyes. The morning sun now strained through the foliage of tall trees and was warming the damp yellow leaves pasted on the rocks. Birds were calling, a scent of moist earth suffused the air.

The patterns that Saraswati embroidered on the quilts – the miniature trees, boats, oxcarts and flights of egrets – did not belong to the mudflats where they had settled. Those were from the home they had left behind the Border. They left it, were ejected from it, long after Partition. Before that, for over thirty years, they had clung on. They left only when they were uprooted by force. They couldn't take with them the bhitay – the rivers, the fields, the trees, the skies, and all the birds and animals that lived there. But Saraswati had carried them in her memory and had unburdened their forms on fabric with a needle and thread.

I learnt later that a few of those quilts had escaped the fire. They had been used to wrap the valuables when the family had fled Ichhaipur before the attack. They were being put to good use now by the new member in the family. Subal had a daughter.

Gouranga-da's injured hand couldn't be saved; it was amputated from below the elbow.

V

RAIMANGAL, KALINDI

TAKE ME HOME

Dulal Kumar Mondal had done his PhD in pure mathematics from the Indian Statistical Institute (ISI), Kolkata. An associate professor in the West Bengal Education Service, he was posted in one of the prominent colleges in Kolkata and lived in a rented government flat in a respectable neighbourhood in the city.

Was Dulal Kumar Mondal a bhadralok?

A difficult question.

We were working in the same institution for over six years, but I cannot say I knew very him well. Dulal was a reticent person, and he seemed to have mastered the art of remaining inconspicuous – should I say invisible? – in any official gathering. These personality traits hadn't made him popular among his peers and students. But I knew that Dulal was a bright and dedicated teacher, and I suspected he was a very sensitive person. The college we worked in was big, with around a hundred full-time faculty members, and Dulal and I belonged to different departments located in different parts of the large campus. We didn't get to see each other often. But that apart, he appeared to have grown a shell of silence around him, which I found impossible to penetrate. Dulal never failed to address me as 'apni', the respectful form of 'you', in spite of my protests that we were born in the same year.

And yet, despite his studied aloofness, one thing about him intrigued me. Every weekend, come sun or rain, Dulal Kumar Mondal would leave the city to go to his village home, which, although barely eighty kilometres from Kolkata as the crow flies, was practically in another world. I had very little knowledge of this world, that too as a tourist.

It was the Sundarbans. Seshergram, Dulal's village, lay deep in an island on the southern periphery of this world-famous mangrove forest. Seshergram regularly popped up in the news because of tiger attacks. Such news – of a man-eating tiger attacking and taking away a villager – was so remote from our urban consciousness that whenever we spotted such an incident in the papers, my colleagues and I would buttonhole Dulal and demand to know more. He would respond with his trademark reticence, visibly uncomfortable on finding himself the centre of attention. Only once did he remark: 'In our village there are only two houses where there has never been a tiger attack.'

His words, and the casual tone of his voice, stunned us. Someone asked, 'Your house too?' To this Dulal smiled and raised three of his fingers.

He had made the gesture with such chilling matter-of-factness that no one had the heart to prod him any further. And then I remembered that we hardly knew anything about his family, except that Dulal, well into his thirties, was still a bachelor. His deadpan manner, which encrusted his reserve like a tortoiseshell, roused my curiosity hopelessly. All this, I suspect, had got to do with the world where Dulal had his home.

This was when I had been touring different parts of West Bengal on that school education project. One day, as I was poring over the enrolment data of different districts, I came across a puzzle in the *West Bengal Human Development Report 2004* published by the Government of West Bengal. It highlighted an odd statistic: in some areas of the Sundarbans, girls outnumbered boys in schools in a ratio of 2:1. Naturally, this had mystified the researchers because it didn't fit into the general picture of gender ratio in enrolment.

More puzzling was the observation of the local teachers. They had tried to justify the mystery by claiming that 'girls are more serious than boys'.

One day, I took this riddle to Dulal. He heard me out and responded with an enigmatic smile.

'Our college will be closed next Tuesday because it's the University Foundation Day,' he said. 'If we take casual leave on Monday, we can have a long weekend. The weather now is pleasant. Why don't you come along with me to Seshergram? You can view the riddle with your own eyes. You might even solve it yourself.'

∼

Where exactly does the Sundarbans begin? L.S.S. O'Malley writes in *Bengal District Gazetteers: 24-Parganas* (1914) that 'when the East India Company acquired the Diwani or civil administration of Bengal in 1765, the Sundarbans extended much further north than at present. Even in the vicinity of Calcutta the country was largely an uncultivated waste, especially to the east, where the forest approached to within about seven miles of the town.' If we can imagine Kolkata's topography at that time, we can deduce that the eastern and southern peripheries of the town were part of the great mangroves. Perhaps it wouldn't be too difficult to imagine those times. As late as in the early nineteenth century, people scarcely ventured into the Chowringhee area, now the busiest hub of the city, after sundown because of the tigers that prowled there. Entally, another crowded central neighbourhood, got its name from hental, *Phoenix paludosa*, a variety of mangrove date palm that had once covered this area. At Sealdah, the location of the city's most important railway terminus, engineers had excavated peaty remains of an ancient mangrove forest.

Half of the hundred-odd islands on the Indian part of the Sundarbans were reclaimed fully by the early twentieth century, and today, there is no trace of the forests on them, not even a single mangrove species. And yet, they are part of the Sundarbans.

That again takes us back to the question: where exactly does the Sundarbans begin? Is it only the forested islands that are now part of a protected biosphere reserve? Or does it begin from Canning, a bustling town erected on the ruins of a port that the British had planned to build? Or does the Sundarbans extend up to Salt Lake, the reclaimed wetland on the eastern part of Kolkata, which is now a modern township?

Perhaps the Sundarbans is a metaphor: it stands for anything that is sinking, threatened, delicate, fecund, fabled, uncanny, ancient and young – all these and more at the same time and in the same space. It is a constellation of islands that lie on maps like scales on the flared tail of the Bengal Delta. Stories of grit, love, loss, mystery and wonder inscribe it. The story of a magical land. Wise, old men familiar with the ways of this land claim that they can accurately tell where exactly the Sundarbans begins by sniffing the wind and feeling it on their skin.

~

There are two ways to get to Seshergram. The first is by road up to Dhamakhali, eighty kilometres from Kolkata and an entry point to the Sundarbans, followed by a four-hour boat ride along the rivers and creeks to the island on the edge of the forests. The other option is to go to Hasnabad, the railhead on the northern border of the Indian Sundarbans, and hop across a mosaic of inhabited islands by ferry boats and motorized rickshaw-vans.

Dulal always preferred the first option. Accordingly, on a misty morning in March, we caught a bus to Dhamakhali from Kolkata's central bus terminus at Esplanade.

Every time Dulal returned home from the city, he carried with him some essential item. This time, it was a foldable toilet seat for his invalid grandmother. He shoved it under the bus's seats and called me to the right side of the aisle.

'The sun will be on our left for the entire journey,' he explained.

The bus threaded the city's eastern sprawl and soon hit the Eastern Metropolitan Bypass. Rows of giant Saurav Gangulys stared out of billboards, hiding from view hillocks of garbage and endless marshes interspersed with neat rectangles of green. Under a pale morning sun, the last of the cauliflowers were wilting. Men were busy planting summer vegetables, wielding a magic that recycled the city's waste into proteins and vitamins.

These were the East Kolkata Wetlands. Every time I pass by them, a strange feeling of pride mixed with despair hits me. These are the world's largest wetlands linked to a metropolis, and the oldest integrated resource recovery system, recognized by Wetlands International as a designated wetland site protected by UNESCO guidelines. Using wastewater nutrients, the wetlands produce tonnes of fish and vegetables. They also give employment to twenty thousand farmworkers, both men and women. But Kolkata is used to seeing this place as its seamy underbelly, something to be kept hidden behind eye-candy billboards. Or to be turned into prime real estate.

Within half an hour, the tall skyscrapers of new townships receded, and our bus passed nondescript villages – clusters of houses lost in a garbage land. A wide scummy canal ran parallel to the road.

'That's the Kulti Gong,' Dulal said. 'Once upon a time, this was a river. Now it's just a sewage channel, Kolkata's biggest drain.'

We passed sluice gates on the channel, and now, miles upon miles of fishponds came into view.

'This is prawn country. The sluice gates protect the Kulti Gong from saline high tides. Here it is drained into the bheris, the prawn farms that you see over there.'

Endless bheris dotted with thatched watch sheds stretched to the horizon. Flocks of cormorants roosted on treetops. The landscape evoked the mood of a brooding Japanese watercolour.

Dulal punctured the mood. 'A dreaded mafia lord owns some of these bheris and brickfields. Gang wars break out all the time, even in broad daylight. A murder here is as common as rice-and-water. They tie bricks to a victim's leg and dump the body into a pond. It becomes prawn feed.'

The brick kilns with their rows of smokestacks wove the sooty mirage of a colliery town. Prawn and brick: products for urban consumption, dragging in their wake hot money stained with blood.

∼

We reached Dhamakhali at noon. The bus route ended at the ferry ghat on a river named Chhoto Kolagachhia. It was a thin stream running at low tide down the middle of a wide silt bed. Scores of small passenger boats were stuck in wet mud. The tide would turn in an hour, we learnt.

'Here we are,' Dulal announced, inhaling deeply. 'We call our land bhatir desh, the tide country.'

We were finally at the gateway of the Sundarbans. Were we, really? Except for a strong smell of drying fish, I couldn't detect anything in the wind. We ate fish-and-rice lunch at a riverside eatery and found a bhotbhoti, a motorized ferryboat.

The tide was now slapping the boat's hull. The narrow vessel was full, with two dozen passengers, bicycles, plastic drums, sanitary ware and a live cockerel. Dulal and I sat on our haunches upon bare wooden slats near the stern, bracing for the four-hour journey. Across from us sat an old Muslim man dressed in a loose, white kurta-pyjama. His grey beard, white skullcap and thick-lidded eyes gave him the air of a Sufi mystic. A white rooster, cradled in his arms, was sizing up the passengers with ruby eyes. When the boat puttered into life, he tied the end of a rope attached to the bird's leg to a hook embedded in the floor.

Chhoto Kolagachhia meandered for about two kilometres before it lost itself in Raimangal, ashen grey and tame under the noonday sun, and stretching from horizon to horizon. This was one of the two mighty rivers of the Sundarbans, I learnt, the other one being the Matla.

'Now it appears so quiet,' Dulal said fondly, lowering his arm and touching the water with his fingertips. 'But in summer, it will turn choppy and fearsome. It will toss the boat like a banana-flower shell.'

The boat was tracing a zigzag route across the wide waterway to reach out to the settlements on both the banks. This ferry service was the lifeline of the islands that were encircled by tall embankments as protection against the tides. But all we could glimpse behind them were treetops and tiled roofs. Deep flights of concrete steps reached down to the water. Passengers were waiting patiently on top of the bunds. At one island, a newly married couple embarked: the bride was dressed in a parrot-green sari and the groom in a synthetic kurta. A group of village women gathered on the bund ululated and blew conch shells as the boat, and the couple, set out on the next leg of a long journey. The boatmen unloaded sanitary fittings at Kumirmari, a big and well-populated island.

Beyond Kumirmari, the bluish haze of the Marichjhapi island drifted into view. This island had been the site of a bloody atrocity committed by the state against a group of hapless Dalit Bengali settlers. That was in 1979. For three decades, the incident had remained buried in public memory, like a submerged island. Tides of political change had now uncovered it. But from our boat, the distant island appeared indistinguishable from other uninhabited islands.

'Nothing stands there now,' Dulal said, looking in that direction, his fingers shading his eyes. 'Jungles cover the ruins of the settlement.'

I noticed that since the Marichjhapi island had appeared on the distant bank like a wisp of dark memory, the passengers on the boat had fallen silent. We could hear the thrum of the engine and the purl of waters. Some had turned their heads towards the island. Now appeared, on both the banks, the forests that were part of the protected national park. They would continue until the end of the journey.

We were now entering Project Tiger territory.

Forests. Does the word evoke an image of tall, old trees speckled with pencils of sun and echoing with the call of beasts? Forget it here. Here, between man and forest, lie coiling waters, a liquid labyrinth that ebbs and flows every six hours. The high tide opens watery vistas into a world of gaunt, leafy trees – geon, bayen, keora, sundari and other sturdy mangrove species. It briefly allows the narrow boats into the Sundarbans' dark, moist heart. At low tide the waters recede, laying bare spidery stilt roots sunken into soft mud. Mud: supple and translucent as a newborn's flesh, studded with scarlet crabs and nicked with the feet of fish-eating birds. Crocodiles rest on them like bored maharajas, and spotted deer foot the shadows. But the most sought-after species, also the most feared, is a highly elusive animal and its sightings are very rare. The locals call him 'Boro Miyan', Mister Big.

After about three hours on the vast expanse of Raimangal, our boat veered into Korekhali, a narrow channel. This channel connected Raimangal with Kalindi, another major river that marked the boundary between India and Bangladesh.

'Here, we call these channels do-aniya, because the tides flow in and out from both its ends,' Dulal informed me.

Korekhali had sparse human settlements along its left bank. On its right was the forest, with nylon netting strung along the water's edge. The forest department set up these nets to keep the tigers from entering the settlements.

'Aren't the nets too flimsy for the big animal?' I wondered aloud.

'Yes,' Dulal agreed. 'But they normally avoid any kind of obstacle.'

'Unless they become man-eaters,' said the old, bearded Muslim in a low, silken voice.

By now the crowd of passengers had thinned. The white rooster had found a perch on the folded toilet seat we were carrying and was dozing with its free leg tucked under the belly.

The old man continued:

'Boro Miyan is a most patient animal. And clever too. He will search out a gap in the netting and then swim across the river. But he follows etiquette. In the villages here, you'll notice thin latticework around all cottage porches. Boro Miyan can easily push through them if he wants to, but normally, he doesn't.'

I was struck by the respectful tone in which he referred to the dreaded animal. Such an attitude towards a wild, ferocious animal was alien to me. I could vaguely sense that I was entering a world of mystery – not only of physical nature but also of perceptions. I turned to gaze at the monotonous, impenetrable wall of green, barely twenty feet from the boat, to look for a sign of life. Daylight had weakened. Shadows were gathering under the fronds of low hental bushes. Another half an hour into the dwindling Korekhali, and the engine roared and spewed thick diesel fumes in protest. The boatman switched it off and steered the boat forward with a long bamboo pole. Our journey was soon cut short at a place called Kalitala. The river had shrunk here into a muddy stream trickling along a deep silt bed. Seshergram was still four kilometres away.

Kalitala had a panchayat office and a few brick buildings. The handful of passengers on the boat, all men, climbed down and strode off in different directions. The old man transferred the rooster into the arms of a boy who had come to receive him with a water jug. Then he adjusted his skullcap and unrolled a prayer mat upon the flat top of the bund.

'Now we must find a rickshaw-van,' Dulal said. 'But before that, let's have a cup of tea. The last tea stall in this part of the island is over there.'

A pair of village men were sitting on a rickety bench before the tile-roofed tea shop. One of them was reading aloud the morning's newspaper. His listener wore dark spectacles normally used after a cataract surgery. Dulal bought a big packet of buns.

'We don't get these things in our village,' he said with an embarrassed smile. 'Nobody even drinks tea in our home. I am carrying tea leaves with me.'

'But why these buns?' I asked.

'Oh, that's for our tiffin.'

Tea, tiffin. We were carrying with us the rituals of another world.

LAND OF TIGERS

Huddled behind the embankment on the river Kalindi, Dulal's family home comprised three mud cottages thatched with nipa palm, and a large shed that was the dining area. The shed also served as a night shelter for guests during large community gatherings in the village. Thin wooden lattices secured the porches, a reminder of the striped fear lurking in the forests. There was no kitchen. Dulal's mother and sisters-in-law cooked out in the open, or under a lean-to during the rains. At a corner of the wide mud-plastered courtyard stood the grain store – a barrel-shaped receptacle made with bamboo. There was a cowshed, a cote for ducks, a haystack and a pucca latrine in the backyard. Behind it was a vegetable garden that almost fully met the regular household needs, a sweet-water pond, a stretch of paddy fields, a prawn farm, a winding creek and, beyond it, loomed the Sundarban Tiger Reserve.

The layout was similar in other households of Seshergram, except for the pucca latrine. The only other house that boasted one belonged to a Party leader and prawn exporter. His two-storeyed brick house, painted terracotta red, commanded a prominent location in the village.

The only item of luxury I could spot in Dulal's house was a beautiful hammock hanging low on the porch, like a swing. Dulal's father had knitted it himself with coloured jute fibre. Guests were invited to sit on it. Sometimes, one of Dulal's two younger brothers would occupy it briefly, after some household chore, before getting their hands busy again on other tasks, like weaving a mat with coconut fronds, chopping straw for the cows, or mending a fishing net. There was no end of such work around the house.

The two brothers, Gour and Manik, had the gaunt, wiry features of their father. Both were married and had children. Dulal had inherited his clean, slender features from his mother. A tall, thin-boned woman in her early sixties, she had retained a certain handsomeness of youth despite the hard life in a Sundarbans village. An outbreak of measles was sweeping through the island, and Gour's eight-year-old daughter was suffering from it. She lay curled up on a string cot, upon green banana leaves, in the covered porch that she shared with Dulal's grandmother. Infirm and almost blind, the old lady remained coffined in a mosquito net day and night.

I was shown the hut that would be mine for the next three days. Inside the dark, damp room there was a plain wooden cot, a dresser, and tiny images of gods and goddesses jostling upon a low wooden stool. A large print of a late Tagore, framed and faded, stared into the shadows with large, bewildered eyes. Below it sat a big bamboo rice basket plastered with cow dung. This last item was as old as Dulal, his mother told me.

'Ours was the last cottage on this side of the village. The creek then flowed past the garden, and beyond it was the jungle. And what a jungle it was!' she exclaimed, pressing two fingers on her cheek.

'What about the tigers? Weren't you scared?' I asked.

'Do we have a choice? We live in *his* home after all.' She smiled.

They had come to this land of tigers after they were uprooted from their homes across the border. It was during the Khulna riots of 1950. The forests in those days were dense, fearsome and teeming with tigers.

Other animals, too, said Dulal's father. It included a sizeable deer population. Men took trained village dogs to the forest and hunted them for meat.

'But isn't that illegal?' I asked.

'I am talking about a time before Project Tiger started,' Dulal's father said. 'The forester babus never came this far on their rounds. Samshernagar was considered a most remote island in those days. The bhotbhotis weren't there. It took one or two days, depending on the tides, to reach here on a rowboat from the mainland.'

'Father was a big hunter,' Manik said proudly.

'But that was before Manik was born,' said his mother. 'Their father would go to take a dip in the pond, asking me to keep his lunch ready, and would return in no time carrying a big antler on his back.'

A shy smile fluttered on the old man's lips. 'In those days, there was no government facility in Seshergram. We'd travel to the block office in Hingalganj and run from pillar to post to beg the babus for even a handpump. I got so many projects sanctioned with a bribe of deer meat – bund work, cyclone shelter, paved paths, tube wells – you name it.'

He had been a member of the Krishak Sabha, a leftist organization of farmers, and head of the local gram panchayat for two terms.

'But times have changed. Two things have brought a big change here – prawn farming and bhotbhotis. They go hand in hand. A good catch in the interior islands can now be transported to the exporters in Kolkata in half a day.'

'And both depend on the BSF,' added Manik. 'All bhotbotis here run on diesel the BSF men sell us.'

'It's impossible now to imagine how things were twenty years ago,' Dulal said. 'Did you notice the road we came along over the bund? It wasn't paved when I was young. During the rains, it would turn into a slushy slide. We went to school wearing only a gamchha, carrying our dress and books on our heads.'

'Life was hard, but we were used to it,' said his mother, and turned to me. 'For you city people, it's still hard, son. No electricity, no roads, and the water is saline. At least the latrine was built before Suchismita came to our house on a visit.'

I had come prepared to face these hardships, except for the undrinkable drinking water. In earlier times, the rainwater collected in ponds had been the only source of potable water in Seshergram. It was germ-infested, but had a sweet taste. But when the panchayat sank tube wells on the island, a minor miracle occurred. All the handpumps spewed incessant jets of foamy yellow water mixed with a combustible gas. To demonstrate this miracle, Manik held a burning matchstick to a faucet and the bubbles instantly burst into a cold flame.

'It spoils the crop if it's allowed to run off into the fields. Even the cattle won't drink this water. But we have become used to its taste,' he said.

They had cut channels to drain the run-off into the river.

'I had taken samples to a testing lab in Kolkata. They only found a high proportion of methane,' Dulal said reassuringly. 'It poses no health risk.'

Maybe not, but it had a strong brackish taste and could never quench the sensation of thirst during the three days I was there. This was one of the many mysteries that the Sundarbans seemed to throw up at every bend.

~

Sometimes, a mystery presented itself in the form of a statistical puzzle. The abnormal gender ratio in school enrolment, for example.

I witnessed the first part of this puzzle in the upper primary school in Seshergram, the only school in this part of the island. On the day I visited the school, the girls outnumbered the boys, particularly in the higher classes, though not exactly by a ratio of 2:1 as was highlighted in the *Human Development Report*. But I failed to get my hands on more accurate data, because the attendance registers were kept in a locked cupboard. The key was with the headmaster, and he was away on some official work at the circle office on the mainland. The classes were being managed by an assistant teacher.

Half of the hundred and twenty-odd enrolled students were present in the long tin-roofed brick cottage. Bamboo screens divided it into classrooms.

'Normally we have around a hundred children. But many of them are ill; there's a measles outbreak in the village,' explained Ananta Ghoshal, the teacher.

But what was behind the mystery of the missing boys? Where were they?

Ghoshal, who I'd later learn had migrated here during the 1971 Bangladesh war, was forthcoming.

'In the river, where else? Go to the bank of Korekhali and you'll find the brats catching meen with mosquito nets.'

Meen are prawn larvae that swim into the mangroves on the high tide to feed on algae and leaf mould. During the next three days, I'd catch sight of the boys in rivers and creeks hunting the microscopic grub.

'An entire day spent in the water can fetch twenty to thirty rupees. Tell me, why would the parents send them to school?' he remarked bitterly.

In his late fifties, Ananta Ghoshal was a dark, thickset man with sunken cheeks and oil-slicked hair. He was wearing a full-sleeved terylene shirt tucked into his trousers and gold-rimmed glasses. Two ballpoint pens were clipped to his shirt pocket.

The tin-roofed cottage didn't have enough space for all the enrolled children. With less than 50 per cent attendance, a ceaseless din percolated the bamboo screens and swirled inside the brick walls. When the scent of spices thrown in hot oil sizzled in the air, the noise reached a new level of animation.

The school had no toilet facility when Dulal had been a student. The children relieved themselves out in the open, amid a plantain grove behind the school. They used to indicate their needs as chhoto bairay and boro bairay, the 'small outside' and the 'big outside'. Three decades had passed, but there was no toilet facility yet. The school, however, had a kitchen. This was because of the stipulations of the Sarva Shiksha Abhiyan that made cooked midday meals mandatory. Four members of a self-help group did the cooking. They were local village women, lively and hard-working. Every day, they cooked rice, dal and a curry; fish or eggs were on the menu twice a week. As there was no regular market on this remote island, they collected provisions directly from the villagers. The government supplied the rice, and one rupee fifty paisa per student for all the other expenses.

'How far can one rupee fifty paisa go?' one of the cooks confronted me with the question. 'And yet we have to buy pulses, cooking oil, spices, firewood and other ingredients with this amount per head.'

'So how do you manage?' I asked her.

'We manage somehow – we have to,' she replied. 'They are like our own children. Most of the times we manage with vegetables from our own gardens.'

Another woman, her sari coiled around her waist in tree-climbing style, was chopping firewood with an axe. She stepped forward and complained: 'Funds are very irregular. Sometimes the village grocer refuses to give us the supplies on credit. We have to pool our own resources to keep the kitchen running.'

I learnt that, together, they earned three hundred rupees per month.

'Are you going to write all this in the newspaper?' asked the one who had been pushing a ladle in a large kadai full of bubbling yellow dal.

'What if I do?' I asked her.

'Then please write that here we also have an acute scarcity of water.'

In the courtyard stood a concrete water reservoir with a row of taps near the bottom. A marble plaque proclaimed the generosity of the MLA in arranging funds from his local area development scheme. That was four years ago. The solar-powered pump had never materialized. The children drank from a shallow pond; they also washed their plates in it. A few hundred metres away stood a BSF outpost fenced with barbed wire. Inside its compound, on a high wooden scaffolding, sat big water tanks painted regulation olive-and-grey. They got their supply of sweet water from another island, Dulal told me, transported here every day in a tanker boat.

'Hasn't the problem been solved yet?' Dulal asked, surprised. 'I gather that every working day one of the two teachers visits the circle office on official work.'

The women shared a hearty laugh, after making sure they were out of Ghoshal's earshot. They repeated the word 'official' – pronouncing it comically as *opfeechhial* – and continued to giggle.

'Sometimes, both Headmaster-babu and Ghoshal-babu go on *opfeechhial* work.'

'What happens then? A school holiday?' I asked.

'Why? We teach them!' claimed the woman with the cleaver, pushing away loose hair from her forehead with the back of her wrist.

'You? Really?' Dulal exclaimed in amusement.

'There, Shikha does. She's *eight-pass*.'

The woman named Shikha was washing soybean nuggets in a tub of boiling water. An embarrassed smile coloured her face.

'Come on Shikha, tell them what you teach,' coaxed the woman with the cleaver.

Shikha bit her paan-stained tongue and pushed the sari over her forehead to hide her face. They burst into another round of laughter.

The work the four of them did here, cooking food and serving hundred-odd children every day, six days a week, was not commensurate with what they earned for it. But there was something in the nature of their duty that seemed to have instilled in them a sense of purpose. Here, they were doing what they did at home daily – cutting vegetables, grinding spices, chopping firewood, washing rice, cooking dal – but an element of fulfilment was visible. A chore had been elevated to work they were doing out of choice.

When I congratulated them for this, the sweaty faces glowed with pride.

'Please stay back until the food is ready. If you watch the children of Adivasipara eat and how they enjoy each morsel, it will fill your mind with happiness,' said Shikha.

'Come sun or rain, the children from Adivasipara will never miss school,' said the woman with the cleaver.

Adivasipara was a cluster of about twenty households belonging to a Munda community. It was on the southern margin of the island. Most kids from Adivasipara were first-generation learners, so their regular attendance in school was of crucial importance. What the happy labour of these women gave them here was clear as day: a hot meal and much-needed nutrition. What was not so clear was what they received inside the classrooms.

'Where's the time for teaching?' Ghoshal listed his complaints when I confronted him. 'A lot of our time and effort goes into running the midday-meal scheme and keeping accounts. Then, if there's a brief delay in serving them food, the children will bang the steel plates on the floor and raise a racket. Then again, it's so difficult to keep them in class after the meal is over. This is not the right atmosphere for imparting education, as I'm sure you will understand.'

Ananta Ghoshal did his studies in an intermediate college in Khulna. That was when the 1971 war broke out. He snuck into India with only the clothes he wore, with no relative or contact here. He drifted about for some time on the islands, doing odd jobs, until he came to Seshergram. Here, he found shelter in a villager's house and, in exchange for food and lodging, gave tuition to the children of the household. After the government regularized his service, Ananta

Ghoshal got married. After a pay revision, he shifted to Hemnagar, a better-connected place on an adjoining island. He now commuted from there on a local ferry, carrying his daily requirement of drinking water in two plastic bottles. For the last three years, he has been trying to get a transfer nearer his home, or even in a town on the mainland.

Ghoshal took me aside and whispered: 'You are a Brahmin, Bhattacharya-babu. So am I. You'll understand my plight, sir. This isn't a place fit for a bhadralok. All low-caste chhotolok here. You can see that I don't have many years of service left, and I've given this godforsaken place twenty-three years of my life. All useless, sir. Now the only thing I want from the government is a posting in a respectable place before my retirement.'

He then clutched my wrist and extracted from me a promise that I'd convey his plea to the top brass in the school education department in Kolkata. I looked into his imploring eyes, marvelling at his naivete. Even if he assumed that I had the power to lobby top officials, which I didn't, how did he deduce that I'd wield it for him? That was because he and I belonged to the same well-born community: the bhadralok. And it was the sacred duty of a bhadralok to reach out to another bhadralok caught in a chhotolok setting. It was like a code written in the genes, or a protocol shared by highway truck drivers.

~

'After four years in that school, we were sent to an uncle's place on the island of Kumirmari, the one we passed on our way here. Gour was never good at studies. He dropped out before Class 8. Manik, however, was bright. But life at Kumirmari was difficult, more difficult than it was in Seshergram, because here we never went hungry. Uncle had a big family to feed, and he didn't own any land. We had two rice meals a day for only three months a year. For the rest, we'd make do with a watery gruel made with milo grains.'

Dulal interrupted his monologue and turned to look at me.

'Have you ever tasted milo grains?'

I shook my head. I couldn't remember seeing them.

'Well,' he continued, 'we'd eat milo at lunch, mixed with greens and salt, and our tummy would balloon. But it could never beat the hunger for rice. Manik gave up and returned home before he could complete schooling. I also have two sisters. Both live at their in-laws'. They never went to high school. But I have married them off in places where there are good schools. Their children will never miss out for want of opportunity.'

Dulal uttered the last sentence with a deep contentment ringing in his voice.

The family now owned a pump set, a power tiller and a husking mill – all running on diesel. Manik looked after the machinery, hired them out to neighbours, while Gour farmed the family-owned land. Their wives remained busy with household chores throughout the day. They seemed to have mastered the art of invisibility before an outsider, and even before their own menfolk. I couldn't remember having seen their faces under the veils of their saris. They responded to queries from their husbands or in-laws in low, tired voices, looking away into dark corners.

Their day revolved around food, foraging for food and the storage of food. Food and its preparation. Morning, afternoon, evening – three rice meals a day. Rice, coarse and heavy, and watery curries made with small fish and vegetables, ladled on heaps of steaming rice with quick flicks of the wrist. No dal. The two women would lurk behind a bamboo screen in the dining area, waiting for the men to finish the mess on their plates – it seemed as if they were digging earth in a hurry, a mundane chore they were used to – and then they would dart in and serve another helping of rice and another variety of curry. They tasted the same on my tongue thickened by the brackish drinking water.

Dulal's watchful mother oversaw the ritual. She lamented the fact that they couldn't serve me prawn or crab, the two delicacies available in plenty here, because of the measles outbreak. 'When Suchismita came on a visit, there was such a good catch. She had never seen such big crabs,' she told me with a proud smile, turning her eyes on Dulal.

There was something in those eyes I couldn't decipher. I'd learn about it later.

The traditional faith system forbade crustaceans in the kitchen when someone in the family was suffering from measles or chickenpox. It also forbade the treatment of these ailments. That apart, medical facilities were almost non-existent in these remote islands. I saw Gour's wife nursing their sick daughter day and night, in between household chores, applying mud packs to her skin and changing the banana leaves on the rope cot. The girl whimpered throughout the night. Her feeble voice blended with the incessant wheezing of her great-grandmother. The old woman was faintly visible during the daytime inside her mosquito net, lying curled up like a giant lobster. Inside the hut, the air was damp and musty. The doors were low, and the windows were little oblongs cut into thick mud walls. But these spaces were only for sleeping at night, and for the infirm and the sick. One only needed to step out into the courtyard, and it was all air, sunshine, river breeze and open skies.

But that was during the day. As evening settled, the rhythm of life withdrew around the straw-fed oven and kerosene lamps struggling to thin the pitchy darkness of the Sundarbans. Then came the mosquitoes, big and buzzing like drones. Clouds of these long-legged insects curled out of the mangroves and attacked humans and animals with equal ferocity. Even the cows had to be kept under mosquito nets.

Gour's schoolgoing son, Pocha, would sit on the porch with his homework, read aloud from a primer and swing his torso sideways like a clockwork doll, to drill a passage into memory and also to ward off the winged bloodsuckers. Darkness would thicken and smother the lighted wick, the flame gasping audibly. Soon, the boy would put away his books, jump into the open courtyard, do a cartwheel, cuddle the brown household dog named Bhulo, and join the adult men sitting under the skies.

A few village elders would drop in at this hour to meet Dulal, to have certificates signed and documents attested. He was the only gazetted government officer on the island empowered to do these things. He was also the only PhD, I was sure, but that degree had no use here.

Taciturn men: they'd sit upon their haunches on bare, polished earth, knees pressed against their chests and arms resting on them. They would speak only when they needed to, in words bare as bones and shorn of emotion, to exchange information on crops and tides. But if there was a guest from the city, they could be coaxed to talk about tigers.

This was the land of tigers. Every household here had its share of close encounters with the famed beast. Every family had its own story and its own heroes. The stories were not only etched in memory, but also embossed on the very landscape – the paddy fields, ditches, courtyards and cowsheds. Like mysterious relief work, these were visible only to the locals. The last time a tiger had attacked Dulal's house was about five years ago.

It was a winter's night. The day before, their cow had given birth to a calf. Boro Miyan was attempting to crawl into the shed through a gap in the bamboo screen. The household dog was the first to raise an alarm. The dog, actually a bitch, saved the cow and her newborn before it was struck by the claws of the frustrated animal and died. Bhulo was her offspring.

Not that all Sundarbans tigers were compulsive man-eaters, they told me, but all men in these remote forest areas were potential poachers. That was how the forest department liked to see them.

Until a few years ago, hunting a big cat was rice-and-water for the poachers. They had devised an indigenous method. Boro Miyan had a craving for date-palm jaggery, and the wily men would smear pesticide-laced jaggery on tree trunks to put them down. They'd then skin the carcass, plier out the teeth and nails, and bury it in a pit lined with lime. A few months later, they'd return to the spot and dig out the bones.

'Nothing would be wasted,' Manik informed me. 'For those who had direct contacts with overseas customers, a single carcass could fetch anywhere between two to three lakh rupees.'

But these days, because of all the media attention, the forest department was very alert and proactive. Very few men were in this line of business now.

'In earlier times, the relation between man and tiger wasn't this bad,' one of the elderly villagers said. 'It took this turn after the Marichjhapi incident.'

Dulal's father had a different view. 'It started when the central government announced the tiger project and made portions of the forest off limits to the forest dwellers. Before that we used to call it boro bagan. After Marichjhapi, Boro Miyan got the message that the forests belonged to him, only to him. Not us.'

Boro bagan, the big garden, and Boro Miyan, Mister Big, always a male member of the species. Dulal's father spent the nights within breathing distance of both, in a flimsy watch shed on the bund overlooking their prawn farm. He was used to their presence. In fact, the tone of deference in his voice, which I had noticed earlier on the boat, was absent in Manik's view of things.

I wasn't sure how Gour felt, as I hardly heard him speak. He usually crouched in a corner, away from the circle of light cast by the lamp, overshadowed by his two smart brothers. His eyes had the alertness of a solitary animal. He responded to the words directed at him with low grunts. The few words that escaped his lips sounded like sighs. I would never know what it was that lay behind his animal eyes.

After the tiger tales burned away like kerosene in a lamp, the villagers left. We lingered in the courtyard, fighting off the mosquitoes and waiting for dinner to be ready. Above the silhouettes of thatched roofs, the stars glowed. A meteorite traced an arc across a familiar constellation.

Suddenly, Bhulo began to bark at something. We saw light wavering on the bund. A group of men carrying lanterns were coming this way.

'Jagannath-da bari achho? O Jagannath-da!' they called Dulal's father.

A snake had bitten a girl, and they wanted Dulal's father to come immediately. A shaman doctor had arrived, and he needed the help of the old man for haath chala, an occult ritual of letting the hand find the nature and extent of the poison.

'If it's really a viper, shouldn't you take her to a hospital for an antivenin shot?' I blurted out, shocked.

'But that's in Hasnabad, a six-hour journey by boat. And nobody knows if the serum is available there,' said someone in an irritated voice. The welter of shadows cast by the lanterns danced and multiplied on the mud walls.

They left as abruptly as they had come, taking Dulal's father with them. The lights receded along the bund, over the high branches of the trees. The darkness that returned had grown thicker, it seemed, and was full of arcane signs.

'Don't worry, my father has never failed,' Dulal assured me. 'But if you ask me how he does this, I really don't know.'

After dinner, Dulal and I climbed to the top of the bund for a smoke. Bhulo gave us company. A damp breeze was blowing over the broad expanse of the Kalindi. The lights of Bangladesh glimmered along the distant bank. Below us, a pair of boats were tied to a tree bending over the water. They bobbed gently and rubbed against each other, producing a sound like hands clapping. Bhulo chased away the fireflies that swarmed around his tail. Seshergram was asleep.

Manik had returned to Seshergram before completing his school education. He couldn't win the battle against hunger pangs. Dulal had. From this last human settlement in the Sundarbans to the ISI in Kolkata, it had been a long road for him. I could never have known how long it was if I hadn't come here, if I had known Dulal only in the privileged setting of our workplace.

I turned and looked at him. Dulal was gazing at the distance. No, he wasn't planning to tell me the plot of a fantastic novel – that of a village boy, poor but ambitious, who went to the city.

He himself was that novel.

~

When he stood on his feet, Jagannath Mondal had a hunched posture; but when he walked, he had a brisk mincing gait. He was showing me around their prawn-and-paddy farm by the creek. In the shallow water divided by dykes, shrimp and paddy thrived together in ankle-deep water.

'A particular strain of paddy and a particular species of shrimp,' Dulal's father pointed out. 'Here we call it dhainyo chingri.'

He had returned late the night before and come directly to this watch shed. The girl had survived.

The low eight-by-six-foot shed was built with strips of wood; inside, a bamboo machan took up the entire space. Farm implements were stored under it. A thelo-huko, a tobacco pipe on a coconut shell, hung from the rafter.

'Come and sit here,' Jagannath Kaka said, inviting me to another narrow machan outside the hut. It offered a sweeping view of the forest across the creek and a part of the village. A high tide gurgled on a siphon hose. The bright spring morning shimmered on the leathery leaves of the mangrove plants. Not a trace of the dark mystery of the night before.

This island had been different when Jagannath Mondal had first arrived, driven out of his home in East Pakistan during the riots of 1950. Samshernagar was a Muslim settlement that had once belonged to a zamindar named Samsher Ali.

'The first settlers on these deep southern islands were brave men. They were honey collectors and woodcutters. They also cultivated the land. When we first came here, we found abandoned settlements that had belonged to them. So we occupied them.'

'Where did they go?' I asked.

'Many had crossed the Border to the other side; others migrated to the northern districts of Malda and Murshidabad. Partition ruined the trust between the communities. It was like a fissure across a bund, suspicion rushed in like salt water.'

The old man inhaled deeply. 'Those were hard times.'

The district of Khulna, where the Mondals had their home, had turned into a killing field. Looting, rape and murder were as common as rice-and-water. Their own village had a mixed population. Sensing trouble, the Hindus began to leave. But this also made them vulnerable, because refugees on the move were a soft target. Vigilante mobs patrolled the roads and ferry ghats to loot and kill. One evening, a few families around the neighbourhood slipped out clandestinely under the cover of darkness. It included the family of Jagannath Mondal. They left with only the clothes they wore, taking nothing, leaving behind young Jagannath to keep up a ruse. He stayed alone in the emptied neighbourhood for an entire day, took the cows to the fields, lit lamps and blew a conch shell in the evening, to pretend as if everything was perfectly normal. The next morning, when dawn broke, he took a brass pot to the fields, as he had done every day for his morning ablutions. He never returned.

Jagannath Mondal went to the river ghat and stole an empty fishing boat. At Hingalganj, in India, he caught up with his kinsmen. They were waiting on a boat for the high tide, to sail upstream to Hasnabad, a railhead, and from there to catch a train to Calcutta. But everyone was at a loss; nobody had any plan for the next course of action. They didn't know anyone in the big city. They had always spent a sheltered life in a rural setting, and none of them had even set foot in Dhaka, let alone Calcutta. It was Jagannath Mondal, all of nineteen years, who took charge and prevailed upon the group. All the families had lived in the tide country for generations. It was the only home they knew. One lifetime wasn't enough to turn a deaf ear to its call. On young Jagannath's bidding, they steered the boats downstream.

The old man now spoke slowly, haltingly, losing and recovering the threads of his memory. From time to time, he rubbed his palms on his bare knees, as if they were a pair of little drums.

'And then there was the war of 1971,' he said with a hint of vehemence in his voice.

Seshergram was in the line of fire from across the river. It was of great strategic importance to the Indian army. Military tents came up all over the island, fighter jets scrambled overhead. Most of the villagers fled to the mainland, fearing shelling, leaving their houses locked or under the care of old people. They dug trenches inside the huts and hid there during the bombing raids. His own mother, Dulal's grandmother, remained holed up in one for ten days, listening to the drone of jets and the whine of their cows.

After the war ended, the refugees came in waves. Jagannath Mondal couldn't get over a sense of déjà vu.

'Only twenty years had passed. But the people in our village had already forgotten everything. They fleeced the asylum seekers. They snapped up the valuables the hapless people had salvaged from their homes in exchange for food. Even milk for the infants!

I'll chop off your head if you touch anything, I had warned my wife. Three families had taken shelter in our cowshed. One day, she saw them chopping wooden window frames. Seasoned jackfruit-wood, wrenched out of a house they had left behind forever. She gave them firewood and took the frames in exchange. That was the only item we ever collected from the shoronarthis.'

The pucca house, for which Dulal's mother had collected the window frames, was yet to be built. I saw them hanging from the rafters inside the dining shed. They stored utensils upon the shutters.

Dulal's father crawled inside the watch shed and came out with a small brass pot.

'This is the one I had carried to the fields that morning,' he said, his voice brimming over, holding out before me the round pot with a wide rim.

'Now I drink water from it,' he murmured. 'Only from it.'

I took the pot in my hand. It had tiny dents around the base. A relic from a history, not kept as a memento, but a part of daily living. Life here was serious business. There was no space to store up memories as nostalgia.

∼

But sometimes, an event remains buried in the memory of a community, like the peaty remains of ancient trees in the subterranean depths of the earth. The memory of an event, a wreckage of history, even a fantastic novel – unfinished, tossed away.

Partition had uprooted them and sent them far away from the green, fertile country of their homes into the forests of central India. It was called Dandakaranya, a mythical region that featured in the Ramayana. The central government resettled them in refugee camps, officially called Permanent Liability (PL) camps. The land there was barren, and the earth gritty and red, like angry eyes. Many of these settlers died in a few years in the inhospitable terrain.

And then in 1971, another nation was born out of a torn land, another wave of refugees came to join the survivors in the heartless forests of Dandakaranya. But this could never be their homeland. The call of home coursed through their veins.

Around this time, the leftists in West Bengal were strengthening their base by reaching out to the refugees and organizing them. They visited the PL camps in Dandakaranya and invited the homesick settlers to come and set up on an uninhabited island in the Sundarbans. 'Let us come to power in the state, and six crore Bengalis with twelve crore arms will welcome you there,' a party leader had declared. The Left Front came to power in West Bengal in 1977, and the very next year they came – men, women and children in their thousands. They sold off everything they had and took the one-way road out of the forests of central India, to settle on the island of Marichjhapi.

To write a fantastic novel.

To be more precise, to write a fantastic chapter in the ongoing two-hundred-year-old novel of human habitation in the world's largest mangroves. Like the earlier settlers, they too were bold, resourceful and hard-working. And they belonged to the lowest strata of Bengal's caste hierarchy.

But they were a highly organized group. Within a few months, they cleared the jungles on their new island settlement and set up abaad – farms and homesteads. They built bunds, all-weather roads, sewage systems, set up a market, weaving units, a boat-making unit, a bakery, a dispensary, and a school – yes, even a school. All this with their own labour and resources.

The descendants of the early settlers would come on boats from nearby islands to witness how a people's collective was building a well-planned and self-sufficient habitat out of a wild forested island. They'd remember the stories they had heard from their parents and grandparents, about the first settlers in the Sundarbans, about a time when there had been no state, no dole or scheme, no BPL cards and ration cards, no quota for kerosene. They'd also remember, with a twinge of guilt, how times had changed, how the people in the tide country had grown dependent on the state and its governments.

In 1977, the year the CPI(M)-led government came to power in West Bengal, the central government rolled out an ambitious plan: to turn the forests of the Sundarbans into a protected habitat for its alpha species, the Royal Bengal tiger. This entailed clearing an extensive area of human encroachment. Marichjhapi fell within the designated area. Now it became the responsibility of the state government to implement the project.

There was another subplot in this story. After Partition, the communists in West Bengal had aligned themselves with the plight of the refugees, organizing them, helping them demand their basic human rights, forcing the state to bend its laws to accommodate them into the system. In this way, they had strengthened their organizations at the grassroots. It won them the people's mandate, despite an anti-communist government in Delhi. Now the party had taken over the state's governance. Now the Party *was* the Government. But here were a few thousand people, refugees all, who were building their refuge in the wilderness on their own, with no external aid, to shake off the mark of 'Permanent Liability' that the state had foisted on them.

It gave jitters to the Party-that-was-the-Government. It had its own plans of rehabilitation and the creation of a Party society in the state. So the Party-that-was-the-Government ordered the settlers to leave Marichjhapi and go back to Dandakaranya.

Nobody had imagined it wouldn't be easy. Nobody, it seemed, had taken into account that many among the settlers had stayed put in their homeland across the border for a quarter of a century after Partition, surviving discrimination, riots and other atrocities. And then again, they had come back from central India, after surviving great hardship there, all the way to the southern margin of the lowlands. Uprooted repeatedly, tossed about from place to place, the few thousand refugees had their backs against the wall. This was their last chance, their last battle.

A highly motivated group, they now started a movement. They organized protest meetings and public campaigns; they invited journalists from Calcutta to spread their story and influence public opinion. They built resistance, boulder by boulder, to face the onslaught of the state machinery, remaining united, hand in hand, just as the people in the tide country do before storm-tossed waters, forming a human wall before the weakening mud bunds.

But nothing worked. The new government was riding a wave of popular support, particularly of the peasants and workers. A few months earlier, there had been a massive flood, and large parts of southern Bengal were still reeling from its impact. The fantastic novel being scripted by a group of unlettered, low-caste refugees in a remote Sundarbans island failed to reach out to the world.

And then, the state unleashed its forces. That was quite easy: the target was a few thousand people on a small island, away from 'civilization'. First, the state police cordoned off Marichjhapi using motor launches and destroyed the wooden rowboats to cut off the population from the rest of the world. It followed the protocol of medieval siege warfare. This continued for weeks. Starvation lurked; people died for want of medicines; children were born. And then in the fourth week of January 1979, hundreds of state policemen and mercenaries descended on the island under cover of darkness. They picked up men, women and children randomly, and herded them into boats and trucks kept ready on the mainland, to deport them back to Dandakaranya.

In its abruptness and use of brute force, this was an uprooting worse than the one that happened during Partition. In the mayhem, families got separated. Mothers lost their children, husbands lost wives, sons lost their old parents. Those who fled deeper into the forests were shot, and the bodies were tossed into the rivers. After all these years, the figures of the missing and the dead are still unknown.

'In those days, we didn't have these bhotbhotis,' Jagannath Mondal told me. 'There were only a few fishing trawlers in the larger islands. The police took all of them for the job. They carted off the dead and the dying, and ferried them to the mouth of the Raimangal. They became food for the crocodiles. For the next ten days, during high tides, we spotted bloated carcasses drifting into the creeks. That was when Boro Miyan developed a taste for sweet human flesh. Some of those who were wounded and half-dead were swept away with the tides and got caught in the low branches of trees. A few of them even survived. But they could never return to their own people. They became vagabonds and went about begging from island to island. A few of them are still around. The islanders know them, never refuse them food and alms.'

Around us were the breezy March morning, the dazzling sun, the forest greens, the murmur of water, and bees buzzing in mangrove blossoms. But Jagannath Mondal could still see the shadows that lurked under the skin of the day.

The forest department here distributed a type of plastic mask to the honey collectors who ventured deep inside the jungles. The men were supposed to wear these masks on the back of their heads. It was a ruse meant to confuse the tiger, because the animal usually preferred to attack humans from behind. Jagannath Mondal had such a mask on the back of his head, I imagined, as he rowed on the creeks of his memory. The tiger of amnesia could never touch him.

A FOLK TALE

I had heard Dulal's mother mention a girl named Suchismita a number of times. Each time she uttered the name, an ineffable expression would soften the lines on her face.

Who was Suchismita? Dulal became uneasy when I asked him.

'Suchismita Chatterjee,' he said, and paused for a moment. 'She's a friend. Suchismita did her PhD from the ISI, like me. She's now settled in the US. A few years ago, she visited our village and stayed with us for a few days.'

He didn't say anything more. The next day I had scheduled a visit to a high school in Samshernagar. I returned early in the afternoon, when the house was almost empty. The children were in school; Jagannath Kaka was at the bheri as usual, and Dulal's mother had taken his lunch there. Gour was in the fields, and his wife had taken out the goats. There was a rare stillness around the house, surrounded by somnolent sounds. The cow swished its tail at the flies like a clockwork toy, and the grandmother wheezed inside her mosquito net.

'Come, let's take a ride into the jungle,' Dulal offered. He took me to the creek behind the paddy fields on their family boat. Bhulo the dog accompanied us.

Years of living in the city hadn't robbed Dulal of his rowing skills. That became evident when he steered the small boat around the conflicting high tides on the double-mouthed channel and propelled it into a very narrow creek worming through the thickets. The creek was hardly ten feet wide, navigable only at the peak of high tide. Mud-coloured water had swelled above the stilt roots of the thick-leaved trees, inundating the forest floor as far as the eye could see. As Dulal wielded the long pole to glide deeper into the tapering inlet, the tree canopies closed in above our heads and formed a luminous green tunnel. It was filled with a pearly light and a strange silence. Countless patterns shimmered at the slightest shift of vision. Bees swarmed around pale blossoms on some of the trees. They set the forest humming like a cathedral with a thousand green-tinted windows. A gentle shower of petals was caught in the current and, braided with other detritus, drifted slowly with the bees in their wake. An intimate recess had opened before us.

Bhulo sat on the prow, his back tensed, his snout cocked up. Was there a scent of danger? I could only smell the fishy water laced with a thin fragrance of mangrove blossoms.

Here, Dulal began to talk about Suchismita.

Like him, she too was working in the field of pure mathematics. Suchismita was from a middle-class family in north Kolkata, where they had been living for many generations. Her grandfather was a well-known barrister. Suchismita was focused and resourceful, and it was she who had prodded Dulal to apply for a post-doctoral fellowship at the Ohio State University in the US. One of her uncles lived in nearby Cleveland. Everything had been meticulously planned by her. She had decided to move first to the US and, after she made the arrangements, Dulal was to follow. Before leaving the country, she came to Seshergram to meet his family.

But Dulal didn't follow her to the US. He had a change of mind. This was before the era of email and mobile phones, but Suchismita tried to contact him frantically. A teaching assistantship was waiting for him at the university; the paperwork for an immigrant visa, too, had been completed. But Dulal never went.

The explanation he gave me for his inscrutable act from nearly twenty years ago, as we sat facing each other on the boat inside the silent green forest, would later strike me as inadequate.

'An opportunity like that doesn't come every day, I knew it. But I also knew that I couldn't have gone far in the field I was working. If I had moved to the US, it would have been solely for Suchismita's sake.'

Dulal confessed to me a few other things. His sentences were incoherent and interspersed with long silences that seemed to be seeping into him from the forest. I cannot recollect his exact words now. But perhaps what Dulal wanted to express before me, but could not say so in as many words, was this, or something like this: for the life that could have been his had he followed Suchismita to the US, he would have had to forsake the one he had here. From the beginning, he suspected that there was no common ground where these two lives – the one he had and the one that Suchismita had chalked out for him – could converge. That suspicion hardened when she visited Seshergram.

'But that wasn't because there was any lapse on her part,' Dulal hastened to explain. 'She had come during the hot, humid season before Durga Puja, in late September. You can imagine how difficult life can be here during this time. And she was a city-bred girl. But the way she adjusted to village life, the way she reached out to everyone with an easy warmth, charmed every member of my family.'

I could vaguely understand this. It was like the coming together of two different worlds, bound by a common language and also the indefinable roots of a single culture. The charm must have been mutual and genuine.

But Suchismita Chatterjee was a Brahmin's daughter.

Caste has remained an intangible and, at the same time, a rock-solid reality in Bengal, despite the trauma of Partition and three decades of communist rule. It hardly ever raised its ugly head in violent forms, unlike in other parts of the country, and there has never been a political or social churning along caste lines. Caste discrimination has always worked silently, insidiously, and has spread its tentacles along the joints of social institutions. Had Suchismita married via the traditional matchmaking network, her family would surely have posted a matrimonial ad in a Bangla daily, beginning with her Brahmin caste, followed by her gotra or clan, and then her degrees and financial profile. But she was a highly educated, self-driven girl and, one could imagine, the pampered daughter of doting parents. One could assume that, in this case, they might have lowered the bar to let into the family circle a bright low-caste boy from the Sundarbans. But surely that wouldn't have applied to other members of his family.

While Suchismita was in Seshergram, Dulal had noticed something on his mother's face. He mentioned this to me in an oblique way, but I could imagine it. It was the slate-grey shadow that appeared on the skies of the Sundarbans moments before a cyclone, one that stained the faces of the islanders living on the edge of the forest on the Bay of Bengal. Dulal had seen this shadow forming over his mother's face.

A familiar shadow, a familiar story. Many years ago, at Hingalganj, young Jagannath Mondal had turned the direction of a boat and surrendered it to the ebbing tide. The pull continued to run in Dulal's veins.

∼

In Bibhutibhushan's *Aparajito*, a girl enters Apu's life. Her name is Leela, and she is from a rich zamindar household where Apu's mother takes up work as a cook after his father's death. Apu is thirteen when he first meets the girl, two years his junior, and she will have a deep influence on him. In fact, it is Leela who fuels his ambition to break free from the narrow destiny preordained for a poor Brahmin's son. From early on, Apu is conscious of his passion for Leela and her devotion to him, and also the unattainable nature of their longing for each other. It continues for many years until it ends with Leela's untimely death. She commits suicide.

Satyajit Ray left this important chapter in Apu's life out of his film trilogy. He couldn't find a suitable actress to play the role, he had said in an interview. There is no way of knowing how the love story would have affected the structures of the films had Ray kept Leela.

But Dulal was not Apu. Apu's destiny lay on the road; Dulal had a destination at the end. Every week, without fail, he would take the road that led to Seshergram.

Suchismita, too, was not Leela. She married a university professor, a Sri Lankan Tamil, and set up in Seattle. She worked in a software company. Dulal hadn't met her since her visit to Seshergram, but they had kept in touch. Suchismita had a daughter. Dulal never had another woman in his life.

~

On my last afternoon in Seshergram, we went to meet up with Dibash Kotal, Dulal's childhood friend. Dibash belonged to the Munda tribe and he lived in Adivasipara. He and Dulal had studied together up to high school, until he dropped out. On receiving the news that his old friend had come home with a colleague on a long weekend, Dibash had come to meet us. But we were away, visiting another part of the island. So he had left a message, urging Dulal to pay him a visit before we returned to the city.

If Seshergram sat on the southern edge of the map of the Bengal Delta, Adivasipara was on the point of falling off that map. The tiny settlement hugged the south-eastern tip of the island. This was the cartographical point where the pale yellow of human habitation ended. On the east lay the unblemished green flakes set in the pale-blue capillaries of creeks and rivers that joined to form the aquamarine of the Bay of Bengal. On most maps, however, the green tint of the Indian Sundarbans is a shade lighter than its Bangladesh counterpart. But standing on top of the embankment, looking out into the dark, dense uninterrupted walls of mangrove trees choking the horizon, I could see that such colouring made no sense. The narrow river on our right had tapered to a creek, and the jungle on the opposite bank was so close that I could feel its piquant breath on my face. A row of ancient keora trees bent over the water on this side. Small fishing boats were tethered under them. Two men were together knocking a boat's canopy with thin strips of dark red wood. The sound of hammers ricocheted off the forest wall.

The Mundas of Adivasipara were the earliest settlers on this island. The title Kotal, soldier, was conferred on them by the zamindars. It was these zamindars who had brought tribal men from the Chhotanagpur region two centuries ago to fight the Arakanese pirates who once ruled the Sundarbans.

'Every inhabited island here has at least one tribal settlement that has been there since the East India Company's times,' Dulal told me. 'It is these people who had cleared the forests and had built abaad for the zamindars.'

We found Dibash in front of his hut. Sitting on his haunches in the mud-plastered courtyard, he was repairing a bamboo crab trap with deep concentration. A pair of steel-rimmed reading glasses hung over his nose. Seeing us before the wicket gate, he took them off and called out in a cheerful voice: 'Zorina, they have come!'

Of middling stature, Dibash had a thin, boyish face, smooth, dusky skin, and a mop of thick, curly hair on his head. A tall woman, taller than him, stepped out from inside the cottage and unrolled a reed mat on the porch. It was a neat little cottage with rounded mud walls and a riot of flowering gourd creepers on the tiled roof. There was another tin-roofed brick hut at the end of the courtyard. It had no windows.

Every family here had one such hut, I learnt. These were built under a government scheme after a devastating cyclone struck the

Sundarbans six years earlier. The brother of a local Party leader received the contract.

'In government records,' Dulal said, turning to me, 'all the tribal people in Adivasipara live in pucca houses.'

'But not even a cow would stay an hour in that dark airless box.' Dibash smiled without bitterness. They stored fodder and firewood in it.

Dibash wanted to discuss an urgent matter with his friend. He had taught in the local primary school for three years on an ad hoc basis. The district school inspectorate sanctioned a full-time teacher's post, and he lost the job. Dulal had then advised his friend to write to the education department. Several first-generation learners from the tribe studied in this school and Dibash was a suitable candidate; that was how he framed his plea. He also sent a copy to the office of the Scheduled Tribes Commission in Kolkata. The local Party leaders got wind of it and had been badgering Dibash to withdraw the plea. They were accusing him of trying to divide the village community.

'Now where do I go from here?' Dibash asked his friend, clasping his hands together in a gesture of helplessness.

'What rubbish!' Dulal said, angry. 'What was wrong with that letter? It was very much within the provisions of the law. How can it divide the village community?'

'They are telling me that according to the law, the STs have 8 per cent reservation in jobs, and there are three teaching posts in that school. "You know arithmetic, now tell us what is 8 per cent of 3?" That's what they're saying.'

'They have also passed rude remarks, Dada,' Zorina remarked. 'They've called him kulayer po!'

Kulayer po, the son of a tribal. Without turning his eyes towards his wife, Dibash raised his palm to stop her. A pained expression twisted his face.

Unlike the wives of Dulal's two brothers, always silent and veiled, Zorina was affable and self-confident. Her brother worked in the railways in Baruipur, a town near Kolkata. Their elder son was staying at the brother's and studying in a school there. The younger son, yet to go to a school, lived here with his parents.

'My brother wants all of us to shift to Baruipur,' Zorina confessed to Dulal. 'Your friend has an education, won't he find a job in town? So many people are making a living there.'

Dulal looked curiously at his friend. Dibash returned him a helpless look.

'There's nothing for us here,' Zorina went on. 'Next year the younger one will begin to go to school. And now we hear they'll even roll back the midday-meal scheme. I keep telling him – let's go there once and see for ourselves. But will he ever listen to what I say!'

Dibash rubbed his hand over his chin.

'It takes no effort to say, let's go. But is going really that easy?' he spoke in a tired voice. 'You leave the land fallow for a season and the forest will come back to devour it. It requires such hard labour to reclaim it.'

His words seemed to rise from a deep core within his being, deeper and older than Dibash himself, than even the civilization on these mangrove islands. I remembered the words of Sabram Singh Banara in Simlipal. He had told me how the Kolhos and other central Indian tribes had their origins in the Indus Valley.

I shared this strange story with Dibash, but it failed to stir him. Instead, he narrated to me how the East India Company's agents and local zamindars brought his ancestors here from the Chhotanagpur region to clear the forests. The settlers from southern Bengal appeared much later. They built embankments around the islands, farmed the cleared land and soon outnumbered the tribal population. The Shabars and Mundas were pushed to the margins, literally, on the peripheries of the islands.

'I am not claiming that we are the earliest settlers here, but we have been staying in these mangrove islands the longest,' Dibash said. 'There are ruins of ancient civilizations inside the forests here. People say, there were settlements here long before the British arrived. Arakanese pirates had driven them out. I have very little knowledge of history. But it's a fact that nobody could stay long and continuously in the Sundarbans. Even the British had to abandon the port town they were building at Canning because of a cyclone. Only we stayed put. But for how long? That I don't know.'

~

Dusk had settled when we took leave of Dibash and his wife. Shadows oozed from the serrated hental leaves. We climbed up to the sweeping arc of the embankment. Before us was a vast luminous expanse of water where the do-aniya creek surrendered itself into the broad, sinewy Kalindi. It appeared as if a subterranean source of light was glowing in its depths. A hundred feet below us, enclosed by high embankments, sat Adivasipara – the cottages, homestead lands, farm plots and fisheries. Centuries ago, Dibash Kotal's ancestors had migrated here from central India and had cleared the forests, fought off tigers and snakes, and built it all. Dibash could never surrender them back to the jungle, come what may.

Dulal and I walked back to the creek to find our boat standing on wet mud encrusted with tiny red crabs, ten feet away from where the water had been trickling down a deep channel an hour ago. A low tide had begun soon after we had disembarked; Dulal had miscalculated its timing. We now waded into pillowy knee-deep mud and climbed the boat. We began to wait for the tide to turn. Neither of us spoke a word.

The sepia of dusk had thickened, and it was gaining a bluish tint. The forest on the opposite bank had come closer, it seemed.

'Is Zorina a Muslim?' I asked.

'No,' Dulal replied. 'You mean her name? That's a common name given to girls of all communities here. On these islands, you will find Hindus with Muslim names, like Pir. Similarly, there are many Muslim boys with names like Dokkhin or Dokha.'

So far away from the vigilant eyes of the pundits and maulvis, in the teeth of a fierce nature, faith and rituals seemed to have undergone a fabulous blending here. The story of Bon Bibi and Dokkhin Rai – the guardian spirit of the jungle and her arch-enemy who disguises himself as a tiger – lived on in the hearts of the people. Shifting faith, shifting identity, shifting land. The Sundarbans was a metaphor for such fluidities.

I was thinking of Dibash Kotal. Born in a community with an abysmal literacy rate, he had aspired to become a teacher. Could he, too, perhaps have become the hero of a fantastic novel? Dibash didn't hear the call of the larger world. He remained tied to this piece of land his ancestors had claimed from the forest two hundred years ago. Perhaps Dibash was only a protagonist in a folk tale – nothing more, nothing less.

On the opposite bank, there was a small fishing boat moored in a parting in the forest wall. It was the mouth of a branching channel. I noticed the dim outline of a man on the boat. It was dark, and we could hardly see anything. I alerted Dulal and together we looked closely to discover, to our shock, that it was a little boy. He was sitting in a hunched posture, his legs stretched before him, picking something from a fishing net bunched over his knees. The boy was so absorbed in his work that he didn't notice our presence only a few feet away across the mud bed. There was no one else on the boat.

Suddenly, he turned his head in our direction and was stunned. I couldn't see his face, but it was clear that a pair of strangers watching him silently had terrified the boy. Acting on an impulse, he swept aside the net and crawled inside the boat's canopy. We continued to watch, stupefied, hesitating whether to call out and reassure him.

And then, through a gap in the canopy, I caught sight of an intense eye peering at us.

I recognized it instantly. I had seen this eye splashed across the silver screen countless times; I could never mistake it. In an unforgettable scene in *Pather Panchali*, Durga lets her exploring fingers into a hole in the quilt and uncovers an eye, closed and feigning sleep. And then, suddenly, as she is about to pull them open, the eyelids unfurl and there's this wide-awake, limpid eye filling the screen. It signals the first screen appearance of young Apu.

It is also his first day in school.

THE BEGINNING OF THE END

On 26 May 2009, three years after I visited Seshergram, Cyclone Aila devastated Dulal's world. It battered the mud cottages on the island, tore the bunds, and sent farm plots and homestead lands under salt water. There was no fatality in his family, but tidal waves swept away their cow. The villagers rushed to the high embankments to save themselves from the fury of the floods and camped there in unspeakable conditions. It took ten days for the rescue teams to reach out to this remote island. Before that, robbers came in the guise of relief workers. They took away whatever valuables the hapless people could salvage from the cyclone's fury. But they didn't kill or physically harm anyone. The most harrowing news, however, was that the entire Adivasipara, the portion of the island jutting south, had vanished under the raging waters. It had just dropped off the map. The two dozen families who had their homes there could never be traced. They included Dibash Kotal, his wife and their younger son. Seshergram pulled through, but it was not what it had been. It would never be.

As I scanned the horrific reports that trickled in weeks after the catastrophe, I remembered the afternoon we had spent at Dibash's place. His family had been among the longest continuous inhabitants in the Sundarbans, Dibash had claimed, and then had added, 'But for how long? That I don't know.' The grim tone that had weighed his words now haunted me.

Cyclone Aila brought back to focus the predictions of the experts. For many years, they have been warning that we'd lose the Sundarbans sometime soon, that it would be the end of one of the most fascinating places on earth. How soon will that 'soon' be? I have no idea. As I write these lines, another cyclone, Cyclone Amphan, has battered the Sundarbans again. But for me, the erasure of Adivasipara on 26 May 2009 marks the end of the Sundarbans. On that day, a cyclone wiped out the community of a mangrove tribe before anyone could strike off their names from a citizens' register.

Meanwhile, Dulal and I had fallen out of touch. The education department transferred him to an engineering college in north Bengal. But on a grey winter's afternoon, I ran into him in College Street.

We were meeting after a long time, and I noticed that the intervening years hadn't been kind to Dulal. His hair was now completely grey, and deep lines creased his brow. He had a knapsack on his shoulders.

'After such a long time!' I exclaimed, embracing him.

'Yes, two years and three months,' Dulal replied with a smile.

'Come, let's sit somewhere,' I said, catching his arm.

Dulal hesitated. He waved a piece of paper and said, 'Actually I have come here to buy a few books. I have an evening train to catch.'

'Are you going back to north Bengal this evening?'

'Yes, by Kanchan Kanya Express.'

'Then there's enough time for a cup of coffee,' I said. 'But first you must finish your shopping.'

In the fading light of December, amid the usual hum of voices echoing in the high-ceilinged hall of Coffee House, I learnt that Dulal's mother had died of typhoid a few months after Cyclone Aila; that Manik had shifted with his family to his in-laws' place in the uplands; that their father now stayed with them; and that their family had been splintered. This was the picture in most households on the islands. Aila had even changed the character of the soil on the island: almost nothing grew there now.

I couldn't find suitable words of sympathy. I could sense that for Dulal, it was not just the loss of a parent or a family, it was the loss of an address where he could return.

An odd object popped up in my memory.

'What happened to the window frames your mother had got from the refugees of 1971? Did you lose them in the flood?' I asked.

For the first time, Dulal's face beamed.

'No, we have made good use of them. We have built a pucca house, finally. Gour and his wife live there now with our grandmother.'

'Oh! How is she?' I asked. I had completely forgotten about the ancient woman.

'She's okay, carrying on. She has seen so many wars and riots. What can a cyclone do to her?' Dulal replied, and after a pause, said, 'But people are leaving the Sundarbans in search of a livelihood elsewhere, particularly the men. The villages are being emptied out. If it goes on like this, the forests will soon take over.'

With the menfolk staying away from the villages for long months, women traffickers were now stalking the islands, I learnt. An entire generation had dropped out of school.

'Do you remember Pocha, Gour's son?' Dulal asked.

'Of course I do.'

He was a lively boy with heat rashes on his skin, always smiling. His teeth were stained yellow with the iron in the water. I remembered him as a ball of coiled energy, always jumping off the porch, doing cartwheels in the courtyard and running with Bhulo over the edge of the bund. The words he uttered were like quick stabs in the air. But he talked very little, like his father, and watched the guest with unabashed eyes.

'Yes, that's him,' Dulal said.

'What about Pocha?' I was apprehensive.

'He is now staying with me, studying in the government school in Jalpaiguri. He'll appear in the higher secondary examination next year. These books are for him,' he said with a smile and pointed to the packet of books on the table.

I breathed a sigh of relief. I studied Dulal's face and tried to imagine how he had looked when he himself was Pocha's age. Had he, too, jumped around the village with the radiant energy of a coiled spring? But it was impossible to evoke a mental image beyond those premature wrinkles and sad, intelligent eyes. I remembered that afternoon in the green labyrinth of the forest. Had Dulal ever fallen madly in love, ever felt the reckless itch of youth? I didn't know how uprooting and migration stamped a community, how deep a mark they left on the mind of an individual. As one rebuilds a life brick by brick, perhaps the family grows inside – like a banyan growing out of a date-palm trunk. One can never view oneself as an individual. It carries no meaning really. The same pull, the bhitayer taan, that would bring Dulal every weekend to the Dharmatala bus terminus, that made him turn back from the road to the US, had now brought him here to College Street.

'And what about Suchismita?' I asked. 'Are you still in touch?'

Dulal nodded. 'She was in India last winter and came to north Bengal to visit the forests. She has left her job. Now she's a full-time homemaker and the mother of two growing kids.'

～

The urban bhadralok in Bengal have their origins in rural landed gentry. Their rural connections were still intact during the 1930s, when Bibhutibhushan wrote the novels. They still maintained their sprawling country houses, organized the Durga Puja, and patronized various social activities in the village. The less well heeled among the aspiring classes kept their families in their village homes and lived in the city, in workmen's hostels known as messbari. They usually returned home on weekends. One of the most enduring symbols of the bhadralok class's rural connection was the schools they set up.

By the time Ray was making the films, that connection had eroded because of two catastrophic events: the Bengal Famine of 1943, which took over thirty lakh lives and ravaged the old social systems in the countryside, followed by Partition. In two decades, the rupture of the bhadralok Bengali's bhitayer taan, and a concomitant identification with the city of Kolkata, was complete.

Apu is more of a bhadralok in the films than in the novels. But Dulal was not Apu.

VI

HOOGHLY

A MUSEUM OF MEMORIES

Bibhutibhushan movingly described Apu's yearning for his lost village home, for the long-past afternoons that lingered in the scent of tar and caulking glue on tugboats, for the slender bamboo shoots that fanned out against sunset skies like a lyrebird's tail, for wild creepers that exhaled a piquant scent into the choir of crickets, and for the moonlight upon coconut fronds on a breezy summer's night. I never had such a bucolic home where I, or my memories, could return.

Except, in a metaphorical sense, my old school in my hometown of Gouripur. It was a museum of my saddest and happiest memories. It housed, among a thousand other precious relics, the unforgettable taste of my own blood trickling down my broken nose, together with the sensation of the warm, penitent, loving arm of my attacker around my neck.

Words cannot fully describe the mixture of feelings that accompany a visit to the school where one has spent twelve of the most intense and delicate years of one's life. As he enters its portals after a gap of many years, after sufficient time has elapsed for the memories to turn into nostalgia, the school building insinuates into his consciousness like vintage wine, or an old, forgotten lover. Or both, together. The corridors greet him with their distinctive smell of ink, sweat and dust; and laced with them, during the tiffin hour, the mouth-watering whiff of alukabli (spiced potatoes), churmur (chickpea fritters), and a strange savoury known during our times as current noon (electric salt). This was probably table salt mixed with some black powdered acid that produced a tingling sensation on the tip of the tongue.

Next come the classrooms. Each room has its own variation of ambient light at different hours of the day, and their unique associations of terror and joy. The worn steps on the staircase, the odour of hydrochloric acid emanating from the chemistry lab, the familiar weeds growing in the cracks of paving blocks on the compound, the grim portraits of men on the walls of the teachers' room (who lose their lively essence when one learns who they were), the dark splotches left by generations of oil-slicked heads on the back walls of classrooms – these are like tiny electric sparks shooting into the folds of brain cells in a complex mnemonic therapy. One cannot have a more unnerving and a more delightful experience.

That was why, when my alma mater invited me to be a guest on an annual prize distribution programme, I grabbed it. But I also braced myself for disenchantment. I was going back there after a gap of thirty years.

The school was set up in 1875. Gouripur was then a mofussil town well known for its schools of Sanskrit learning. A string of jute mills had also come up here around this time. In fact, an odd coupling of classical scholarship and modern industry shaped my hometown. There were several tols and chatuspathis, traditional seminaries, where a new branch of Vedic philosophy known as Navya-Nyaya emerged through the scholarly works of its resident pundits. This was also the time when ripples of the Industrial Revolution were reaching these parts and, like a high lunar tide, were moving up north of Kolkata along the river Hooghly. Scottish entrepreneurs were setting up jute mills along its banks. They drove away the low-caste fishermen and farmers who had been living on these lands for centuries, but spared the powerful Brahmins and landowners. In this way, mills and other factories encircled Gouripur.

My family had lived here for nearly four centuries. My ancestors were Sanskrit pundits and priests until, two generations ago, they embraced English education. At the turn of the twentieth century, Gouripur's fame as a seat of Sanskrit learning waned. It coincided with the rise of the new manufacturing industries, particularly jute. The Sanskrit seminaries dwindled for lack of patronage and made way for formal schools under the colonial education system. The prudent sons of pundits and priests set up this school so that their own children could make the best of changing times. Their landed, middle-caste disciples donated the land. Here, too, as elsewhere, remnants of feudalism fed the engines of the so-called Bengal Renaissance.

Teaching in the seminaries and writing astrological tracts had been part of my family's calling. But that was a long time ago. The town in which I grew up didn't have any vestiges of that past. Gouripur was practically a shabby old suburb surrounded by factories and a railway marshalling yard. Three-fourths of the town's population lived in industrial slums. The centre of the town, where we had our home, was a warren of narrow lanes around tall, decrepit houses that resembled the old neighbourhoods of Benares. There were small private gardens hidden inside the alleyways, shaded with neem, mango and jackfruit trees, inner courtyards with terracotta temples and quiet, hyacinth-lined ponds. A superannuated community inhabited these spaces, holding on to memories of better times. Most of the younger generation were leaving Gouripur in search of better prospects and settling in the metropolises.

I, too, would eventually follow in their footsteps. And then, every time I returned, I'd see the mould of decay and loss seal my memories of my hometown.

When Ma was alive, my only other connection with Gouripur was Anil Kaka. But his health steadily deteriorated after he suffered the stroke. He was shifted to a hospital in Kolkata and put under the treatment of a team of specialist doctors. It was his ex-comrades from the Party he had left who made all the arrangements. After his death, following his wish, we donated his body for medical research. His final journey was brief, less than a hundred metres from the cabin where he had spent the last two months of his life, to the hospital's anatomy department. Before that, his comrades draped the red Party flag on his body and raised their fists in the air. They were all grey-haired men.

But my mother demanded a proper shraddha ritual, because although Anil Kaka was not a blood relation, he had become a part of our family. So we organized a shraddha ceremony in our home at 16 Vidyalankar Road. For this, the priest needed the names of seven generations of his ancestors. But Kaka had migrated from his home in East Bengal a year before Partition. It was now another country. All we knew was that a branch of his family still lived over there, in their ancestral village in Barishal district. Anil Kaka had no contact with them. When the CPI(M) came to power in 1977, the Bangladesh High Commission invited senior party members to visit the new country and their ancestral homes as state guests. Anil Kaka had turned down the offer.

'Dhush!' He had curled his lips with his customary insouciance. 'Let the bhadralok have their nostalgia. I am a communist.'

With the help of his old friends, we located his family in Bangladesh and contacted them. A day before the shraddha, an airmail containing Anil Kaka's family tree, harking back to seven generations, reached us. We performed all the rituals to Ma's satisfaction. We even cremated a straw effigy of him and offered a rice-ball pinda to his ancestral spirits on the riverbank at Gouripur. It was a scorching afternoon in July. That year, eastern India was reeling under an unusual dry spell, and the Hooghly, wasted and barred with grey sand, perfectly resembled Anil Kaka's nightmare.

All the old residents I had known in Gouripur were passing away. Those who replaced them had unfamiliar tastes and habits. They tore down the cool, sprawling houses with their thick walls and high, latticed ceilings, and erected garish concrete structures lined with ceramic and glass. My yearning to return to my hometown, that much-celebrated take-me-home feeling, was fading. That was why when I received the invitation from my old school, my first reaction was one of suspicion.

But on arriving there, when I pushed open the heavy iron gates of Gouripur Uchchomadhyamik Vidyalaya and stepped inside the walled compound, my first reaction was one of delighted shock. Not only had time stood still all these years but, in fact, it had also given the old L-shaped three-storeyed school building a weathering that was the most appropriate for nostalgia. A mysterious immutability was guarding my memories, I discovered, like our old durwan Ramsharan-ji.

Ramsharan-ji had died; his son guarded the school gates now. He was also a Ram, Ramsahay, and he sported the same thick, twirled moustache that his father had. But the uncanny thing was that the building was exactly as it had always been in my memory. No extension or modification and, perhaps, not even a coat of paint. The same clayish yellow colour common to most public buildings, which fades slowly and shades into the tint of underlying sand plaster to create the effect of wash painting. The row of tall deodars along the boundary wall had grown unchecked; their branches were now casting a shade over the cracked basketball court. Rusty basket posts, and an iron handpump in place of the quaint brass taps for drinking water. The old doddering ceiling fans in the teachers' room were still working. Everything was as it had always been, except that they appeared worn and mysteriously shrunken in size.

If I cast aside the blinkers of nostalgia, the truth would have appeared loud and clear: there was the stamp of neglect all over the building.

The underlying reason dawned on me when the names of the awardees were called out. The boys, dressed in blue-and-white uniforms, formed a beeline before the stage to receive their prizes. Bapan Duley, Sambit Gharami, Akhilesh Singh, Shankar Bagdi, Saifuddin Mondal – a Muslim, a Bihari, and the rest from the lowest rungs of Bengal's caste system.

I had a classmate named Sambit. But he was a Goswami, a Brahmin. During the twelve years of my school life, I never had a classmate with the title Gharami. Had there been a Duley or a Bagdi? I couldn't remember. But I was sure there had never been a single Muslim boy in the school. We had a Singh in our class, though – one Jitendra Singh. He used to come from the Mazdoor Lines on the periphery of town. Our teachers would tease him for the way he pronounced Bangla words. Jitendra had dropped out in Class 7. But we had Ghorai, Nath, Pramanik, Guchhait, and other boys from the Scheduled Castes. They never stood first or second in any examination. They were the so-called backbenchers, in fact literally so, because they always occupied the rear benches in the classroom. Most were from refugee colonies across the railway lines. During recess hour, they'd take out aluminium lunchboxes and eat rotis. Most of us – *boys like us* – would rush home during the break for a quick bite. Or else we would buy delicacies like yellow peas, fritters, spiced potatoes, candies and current noon outside the school gates. But sometimes, out of curiosity, we'd taste the contents of the lunchboxes of our backbencher mates. One of them lived in the railway quarters inside the marshalling yard; his father was a loco-engine fireman. His white cotton shirt would always be stained grey with soot, and the roti he brought every day had a smoky, salty flavour. In fact, many of them would bring rotis that had salt in them. When I told Ma this one day, she said, 'If a roti has salt in it, it needs no accompanying dish. Only a piece of onion or a green chilli can do. In some households they do it to save on food.' Much later would I learn that rotis first entered our household after the great Bengal Famine of 1943. But that is another story.

Memories of old schooldays were now forming a beeline in my mind, like those boys before the stage. Those days were over. The community that had patronized my school until about two decades ago had turned away. Now this institution served the children of the town's underclass: rickshaw-pullers, shopkeepers, housemaids and millworkers. I spotted a few of them sitting stiffly on red plastic chairs – gaunt figures dressed in their best clothes. Their weather-beaten faces glowed when their sons walked up to the dais to collect prizes.

The only thing that hadn't changed in all these years was the men on the dais. They wore black-rimmed glasses, spotless dhoti-panjabi and sombre expressions on their faces. They were the same Bhattacharyas and Chakrabortys, members of the school's managing committee and local dignitaries, remnants of the town's old elite who had converted their caste value into political currency. When the award-giving ended and the lectures began, they strode up to the lectern and addressed the distinguished guests in the front row in chaste Sanskritized Bangla, quoting liberally from Vidyasagar and Rabindranath, looking over the heads of the uniformed boys sitting cross-legged on the floor. Never once did they turn their eyes on the parents of the awardees, the men and women who pulled rickshaws and washed clothes for them.

But that didn't matter to these smiling men and women. It was their day. Their children had finally arrived. They had come from far away, from a town within the town, the obscure nooks and crevices of Gouripur. It had taken them quite a while to come this far. More than a century, in fact.

~

'Tell us, what do you do when you are caned?' he asked me.

I searched my memory.

'I catch my breath and stand still,' I said. 'That way I feel less pain.'

'You're right. *Good boy!*' he congratulated me.

'But when they pull you by the ear and cane blindly, you must raise your arms to save your face,' said the second boy.

'Now tell me, when they hit your elbow with a duster and there's this tingling pain, what do you do?'

I didn't have the answer for this one.

'That's easy,' the third boy said. 'You scratch the skin around it.'

Now it was my turn. 'Tell me, what do you do when you're ordered to kneel down on rough gravel?' I asked.

The three little boys looked at one another. They didn't know the answer. In fact, it wasn't possible for them to know. They wore shoes, and also white shirts and blue trousers. In our time, the school didn't have a dress code. We could come to school in any dress, and we usually wore rubber flip-flops. If the teacher ordered us to kneel on the gritty corridor floor, we'd discreetly slip the flip-flops under our knees.

But a few teachers never allowed us that luxury. They were not around any more, naturally. The ones who had replaced them, a few of whom I'd met in the pandal an hour back, were mostly young men. They were smart and well-dressed in shirts and trousers. Almost all the teachers in our time wore dhoti-panjabi. A few of them bore signs of penury on their clothes. They were not on a regular roll. Struggling to make ends meet with a meagre salary, sometimes they lost their temper for no obvious reason and beat us up indiscriminately. We could understand it even at that age. But sometimes, we also received unexpected gestures of affection. With all these contradictory traits, most of our teachers had been memorable archetypes. They occupied a prominent space in our young minds.

I was curious: were the teachers these days as colourful as their predecessors?

'Do all the teachers beat you?' I asked.

'Not all,' the tall one replied. 'Only Tuhin Sir and Ajay Sir beat us occasionally.'

'And Tathagata Sir makes us stand up on the bench if we talk in class,' another boy with a stammer added.

'What about Abhijit Sir?' I asked.

'Abhijit Sir never beats us, never even scolds us. Only when we don't remember a formula, he'll say – *Sillyfool*!'

'*Sillyfool! Sillyfool!*' the other two boys repeated, laughing.

I had met Abhijit Sir, their chemistry teacher, a short while ago. He was an astute young man pursuing a PhD at the Indian Association for the Cultivation of Science in Kolkata. Our chemistry teacher had been Satyen Sir – an eccentric bachelor who lived in a world of his own making. He was myopic and wore very thick glasses. Never afraid of him, we'd make the best use of his impairment by doing whatever we liked during his class. His back turned to a room full of cackling boys running around the benches and shooting paper missiles at one another, Satyen Sir would go on scrawling interminable formulas of chemical reactions on the blackboard. When the noise would grow too loud and spill out of the room, he'd turn around and face the class. His dim, unfocused eyes, curiously dilated by his thick glasses, had a strange chastising effect. We would fall silent, albeit temporarily.

Satyen Sir, I am sure, had never been as bright as Abhijit. Sometimes, as he solved the exercises in *Model Test Papers*, he'd be stumped by the tricky formula of an organic reaction. He would finish it the next day. Satyen Sir suffered from congenital myopia. And yet, by some miracle, he knew about the backbencher boy who couldn't buy the textbook because of a lockout in the jute mill where his father worked. He would call the boy discreetly after class and ask him to be present at a particular bookshop in the market on an appointed day and time. The following week, we'd find the boy with a crisp new copy of the book.

Did Abhijit Sir have such mysterious inner vision? I didn't try to find out. In fact, I didn't get the chance. The programme on stage went on until late in the afternoon.

A series of lectures on how important education is for building a strong backbone of society, imbibed for nearly two hours, is bound to give the listener a stiff back. I snuck out of the pandal to unstiffen it. Here, I met Abhijit. Spotting me loitering in the corridor, he came up promptly.

'Would you like to have something? Water, tea?' He beamed a smile. 'In case you need to go to the washroom, it's behind the teachers' room on the left.'

I thanked him. I had spent twelve years of my life in this building, I knew its layout like a nursery rhyme etched forever in memory.

I padded silently down the empty corridors with their honeycomb jaalis, stepping on remembered patterns of sunlight on the floor. It had all remained the same. The empty classrooms resonated like seashells with the microphonic bass of a speaker's voice in the pandal. I climbed the staircase to the second floor. At the far end of the balcony, I caught sight of the three little boys.

They had slipped out of the pandal unobserved and were now leaning over the railings to fly tiny paper planes. None of them had won a prize. But the programme had given them a delightful opportunity: to test their plane-flying skills from this height with unhurried freedom.

Seeing me appear at the head of the stairwell, they tried to run away. I had to show them how to fold an aeroplane with double sets of wings to coax them back to the balcony. And yet, they couldn't reconcile to the fact that the bald, hefty, middle-aged man standing before them had once been a student in this school, just like them, and loved to do the things they did.

They were from Class 6, section B. I led them to the corner room that had been Class 6, section B, during my time. I sat myself at my old place: third bench, corner left. The wooden benches were old, rickety, and covered with ink stains and etchings. I searched for a familiar scribble in the forest of graffiti. In vain. They showed me theirs: a Batman mask and the formula of $(a+b)^2$. In our time, we had pencils and fountain pens; ballpoint pens were making an entry. They used only ballpoint pens. The blackboard had turned grey with layers of chalk, with old, half-erased words of a Lucy poem by Wordsworth peeping through the circuit diagram of an electric calling bell.

One of them showed me how to fold a paper fan and mount it on the tip of a jotter. In our time, fountain pens had a tiny perforation in their caps. We'd place the pea-sized stone of a berry on them and blow into the cap. The stone danced on the needle of air for a few seconds before it dropped off. Those pickled berries were still sold outside the school gates, the classroom floor was littered with their stones. But ballpoint pens had no perforation in their caps. So I showed them how to draw the profile of Mahatma Gandhi with a single unbroken line of chalk. Then we exchanged titbits about the teachers, mine and theirs, and various methods of punishment and their antidotes.

Now we drifted to the far end of the balcony, where a brief flight of steps led to the building's roof. Broken furniture swaddled in cobwebs was stacked in a corner, like before. A rusty padlock hung on the door to the roof, like before. I told them the legend of the UFO that had landed on our school's roof once upon a time, and how the door had been kept padlocked ever since. The story was popular during our junior years. But none of the three boys had ever heard of it. Clearly, the legend had died. Otherwise, the spot was as it had been – the same darkness, the smell of sun-baked air, pigeon droppings on the landing, needles of sunlight streaming in through the rusted zinc roof. Only the needles had grown in number.

The boys played at catching the needles of the sun, exactly as we did in our time. We'd also stretch out our palms and let the spears of light impale them, showing through on the skin at the back of our hands in glowing spots of blood. I attempted to show them the trick, but age had thickened the skin on my hand. They tried to do it, but their skin was a shade too dark.

As I was about to return downstairs, they asked me to fold another plane with double sets of wings. I complied. By now the sun had dipped and a cool breeze was blowing from the direction of the river. As the paper plane glided cleanly over the topmost branches of the deodars, riding the breeze, I let out a squeal of joy that had been pent up within me for thirty years.

SEZ

Every night before the clock struck eleven, Sumita Pramanik would sit in the dark with her schoolbooks, waiting for electricity to return. As the tube light in the living room of their tiny two-room tenement flickered on, she'd race through her books before it went off again at 2 a.m. Sumita's Class 12 board examination was only six weeks away, and she was not dropping out.

Sumita's was one among the many stories of the other town tucked away in the crevices of Gouripur.

Welcome to the workers' quarters of a locked-out paint factory. Once a British-owned company, it made premium paints and urged the customers to remember them through a catchy slogan – 'If It's Colour, It's Us'. The only colour one could see here now was a rusted, moss-stained grey – the colour of decay and hopelessness.

'The management ordered suspension of work on a Friday in June, and in September, they cut off the power and water supply. That was four years ago. We ran from pillar to post, and now this is all we are getting – ten minutes of piped water twice a day and three hours of electricity during the middle of the night,' said Binoy Pramanik, Sumita's father.

These services, and a derelict two-room tenement were all that was being provided by the company where Binoy had worked as an electrician for twenty-two years. According to labour laws, when a factory declares closure or lay-offs, it must give the workers a monthly compensation until the Board for Industrial and Financial Reconstruction settles all dues. The workers are also entitled to receive their gratuity and provident fund. But since the company had declared a 'temporary suspension of work', it had no obligation to pay anything.

Four years on, most had vacated the staff quarters. Those who had nowhere to go, like the Pramaniks, were holding on. Weeds ran riot in the abandoned brick structures. Snakes proliferated.

Shobha, Sumita's mother, joined the conversation. 'I have been worrying myself to death. Sumita goes to a tuition class after school hours. But once darkness falls, this ghost town becomes a den of drug pushers. We're so scared, Dada.'

Fear stained young Sumita's face like a shadow. With rape, kidnapping and trafficking on the rise, this shadow was so familiar now.

At 3.30 a.m. every morning, when Sumita returned to bed, her parents would be up and about. Shobha would arrange the pots and pans before the water tap; Binoy would get ready for a five-kilometre trek to Jagaddal, a jute-mill cluster, in search of work. If he could reach there before the buses were on the road, he might find a place at the head of the queue before a mill gate. The morning sun would find the mother–daughter duo on the porch, plucking nylon threads from used car tyres. Two pairs of nimble hands could pluck twenty rupees worth of thread in two hours. By then, it would be time for Shobha to begin household chores and Sumita to leave for school.

For the twenty-odd families still living inside the staff colony of the paint factory, this was the daily routine. And yet, this was but a chapter from a larger story unfolding in this once-thriving industrial area, one of the oldest in the Indian subcontinent. A few hundred metres away from the premises of the paint factory was a big jute mill, one of the biggest in Asia, locked out for over a decade. Set up in 1885, the mill once had on its payroll twenty-two thousand workers. It even had its own thermal power generation unit. Tugboats laden with golden jute came from eastern Bengal via the Sundarbans. Next was a factory that manufactured shipping containers; this too was locked out. A paper mill, with about a thousand employees, stopped production more than a decade ago. Another jute mill that was famous for its production of gunny bags during the world wars lay abandoned, like many others in the area. A few thousand acres of land along the eastern bank of the Hooghly, forty kilometres north of Kolkata, told the story of a century-old saga of industry and commerce gone horribly wrong.

'Anyone will mistake this place for an ordinary slum cluster,' rued Subhasish, 'unless one knows the story.'

Subhasish was a member of the Association for Protection of Democratic Rights (APDR), a human rights organization that had come forward to assess the tragedy.

'This place was undivided India's first SEZ,' Subhasish muttered. 'Even now this is an SEZ. A Special Extinction Zone.'

The Hooghly was sick and scarred with sandbars. Water traffic had ceased, and the jetties with tall cranes on them were coming apart and dropping into the river. Row upon row of fine colonial-era buildings, decayed and overgrown with jungles, made it difficult to imagine that this had once been a bustling township, that life here cycled to the periodic bursts of the mills' sirens. The redbrick chimneys stood like ghosts from another era. There were minarets of mosques and temple spires, but it was these chimneys that dominated the skies. However, they didn't wear the banners of smoke any more. Tough trees, seeded by birds, were growing on their fluted tops. Nature was reclaiming this space, from above and from below.

'Most workers have returned to their villages in Bihar and UP. Those who are still around eke out a living by raising pigs or pulling rickshaws in town,' Subhasish informed me.

What we were witnessing had a fancy name: deindustrialization. The wheels of history were turning backwards, silently, unlike when it trundled forward with trumpets and drums.

We followed a disused railway track where once freight trains had rolled out of factories and gone to the dockyards. We walked past mounds of scrap iron and fly ash, past the padlocked rooms of the Mazdoor Lines, to a tea shop near the jute mill's locked gate. Brindavan Prasad was waiting for us here.

In his early sixties, Brindavan-ji had craggy features and grey, close-cropped hair. He was a senior shop-floor fitter and earned five thousand rupees a month before the lockout. He was entitled to receive compensatory allowances.

'But it took four years for my file to reach the babu in the labour department. By then, I was past fifty-eight. So they told me, "Now you're only entitled to retirement benefits." But how do you retire from work when there's no work?'

Brindavan-ji burst into laughter and slapped his knee theatrically. It was as if he had cracked a capital joke.

It *was* a joke. How do you retire from work that you don't do any more? How can you sit on a hunger strike when there's not a morsel of food? If one were able to detach oneself from one's circumstances, there couldn't be a more hilarious joke. It was a rare art and Brindavan-ji had mastered it, particularly after rheumatoid arthritis had twisted his bones. He walked with a stick.

But most of his compatriots hadn't mastered this art. Some had died of disease and starvation, and Subhasish's organization was compiling a list of them. There were others, still alive but too infirm to do any kind of work. They were starving, or barely surviving on the charity of their kin. Brindavan-ji had worked a few months at a security agency in Salt Lake's Sector 5, Kolkata's infotech hub, until arthritis forced him out of the job. His son had replaced him.

'He is a stout young man, and he's earning more than I did. Who needs the skill of an old fitter in a durwan's job?'

Again, he roared with laughter.

It had been ten years since the lockout. The employees had never received a single rupee from their own provident funds. A few crores were lying with the mill's trustee board. The owner had siphoned off much more than that amount, after lining the pockets of union leaders. Meanwhile, several factories had secretly changed hands and were waiting to morph into prime real estate. Laid-off workers now kept vigil from the tea shop all day. They joined in a bitter chorus to tell me how union leaders of all colours had led them into a labyrinth of false hopes. The faded graffiti on the mill wall provided an appropriate backdrop.

This particular spot had been the hub of these men's daily existence for more than half their lives. The hub had stopped wheeling. But they still gathered here out of old habit, and spent the morning hours on bamboo benches, sipping black liquor tea from tiny earthen cups. This was the only tea shop that was still open. Earlier, this place used to be a bustling bazaar lined with shops of all kinds.

'There's a perception popular among the middle classes that militant trade unionism has driven out the industries from West Bengal,' Subhasish said. 'But that is only a half-truth.'

'What is the other half-truth?' I was curious.

'Bengal has always been a haven for crony businessmen.'

I stared at him expectantly.

'Do some simple maths,' he continued. 'During the last twenty to twenty-five years, how many crores of workers' PF money was stolen? Have you heard of a fraud of this magnitude? And the interesting fact is, most of the crooks are still around. They've only changed their line of business, that's all. They have their men in media houses: they sponsor most cultural events in Bengal, from poetry recitals to art exhibitions. And I know of one jute-mill owner who has set up an art gallery in a posh south Kolkata neighbourhood. Whoever is in power, you'll always find these thugs by their side. From political leaders to intellectuals, painters to theatre personalities, everyone eats out of their hands.'

'What about the union leaders?' I prodded him.

'They, too, are doing fine,' said a thin, bearded man sitting across from us. 'The big leaders are beyond the reach of the masses, they live in the city. But the local ones are all here. Where will they go?'

'They have built palatial houses,' said another.

Subhasish continued, 'Some of these local leaders have been living in this mill area for two or three generations. Their grandfathers or even great-grandfathers were among the first who came from UP and Bihar. They worked as labour agents for Scottish mill owners and brought their kinsmen. They ruled the Mazdoor Lines like village chiefs. Most of these coolie sardars were upper-caste men, Thakurs or other Kshatriya castes. From left to right, all political parties banked on their descendants to organize labour unions. So a feudal caste system crept into the workers' movements here.'

Our adda was turning too theoretical, or perhaps too sensitive, to be discussed inside a tea shop. Brindavan-ji fidgeted with his walking stick and finally struggled to his feet.

'Please be kind and grace my humble dwelling with your presence for a minute,' he said in Bhojpuri, joining his hands in supplication. Rheumatoid arthritis had almost paralysed his left foot, I noticed.

Through a breach in the factory wall, we had a view of the officers' residences. Fine neo-Gothic buildings crumbling away and taken over by weeds. Rusted swings and see-saws peeped through thick brambles. We walked about two hundred metres and came to the workers' colony, rows of unplastered brick tenements. These had corbelled roofs fitted with curved terracotta air vents. Mounds of beaten automobile tyres were lying about. This was the workers' colony, or what remained of it.

'Two hundred families lived here thirty years ago,' Brindavan-ji said. 'Now only about a dozen do.'

His one-room tenement opened to a brick-paved community courtyard with a peepul tree at the centre. A tiny stone image of Hanuman, smeared with orange vermilion, sat in an alcove carved into the tree trunk. Flat boulders encircled the tree trunk.

'Phulmatia! Phulmatia re! See who I have with me,' Brindavan-ji called out in an affectionate voice into the open door of his quarters.

We helped him pull a charpoy under the tree.

'Please take a seat.' He gestured at us and lowered his bottom on a boulder.

A woman swaddled in a mustard yellow sari, her head veiled, appeared at the door. She had in her hand a brass plate with half a dozen thekua, fried wheat cakes, and water in a gleaming brass pot. She placed the brass plate on the charpoy and the water pot on the floor before us. Blue tattoos covered the crêpe-like skin on her arms.

'That's prasad from Chhat,' Brindavan-ji smiled. 'I know Subhasish-da loves thekua, so we saved these for him.'

Subhasish smiled back and picked up one. 'When was Chhat?' he asked.

'Last Friday, on the fourth of Agrahayana,' replied Phulmatia-ji. She had seated herself on her hams upon the ground, a few feet behind her husband.

Brindavan-ji spoke of the past, when people from all castes, faiths and languages lived here. It was a big workers' colony, one of the biggest in eastern India, and it comprised people from Bihar, Jharkhand, Odisha, Madhya Pradesh, Andhra Pradesh and even Tamil Nadu. They lived mostly in peace, and followed their own customs and rituals.

Brindavan-ji spoke a Bangla thick with Bhojpuri intonations. Phulmatia-ji couldn't speak a single word of Bangla.

'In the bygone days, I used to prepare ten to twenty kilos of thekua before the Chhat,' she reminisced, pushing back the sari over her forehead. 'A long jaloos of barefoot men and women would snake out of Mazdoor Lines in the early morning mist. Everyone carried offerings of sweets, fruits, incense and lamps on their heads. We sang holy songs and gathered at the ghats of Mother Ganga to worship the rising sun. Kahaan gaye woh din?'

Where have those days gone? She raised both her arms over her chest and delivered the last sentence with a sigh. I can never hope to put into words the despair it evoked.

'In the month of Fagun, we'd have Holi, in Magh, Pongal, and after that came Eid.' Phulmatia-ji counted the seasons on her fingers. 'We'd take part in each of them. On hafta days, the men would have heavy pockets and they'd turn the mill maidan into a big fairground. People even took the ferry from across the river to join in the fun. Kahaan gaye woh din?'

A soundscape was returning to me. The aerial distance between this place and my house at 16 Vidyalankar Road couldn't be more than two kilometres. I had never set foot here before, but every day at the silent hour of dawn, a muezzin's piping call and a recorded voice singing the Hanuman Chalisa would reach me through the folds of sleep. At other times of the day, these notes would be lost in the welter of noise, and the only sounds we heard were the mills' high-pitched sirens. These were like intimations of another world. But they were so much a part of everyday reality that I never paid any attention to them, except on winter afternoons, when the muezzin's distant calls were like a summons to rush back home after a neighbourhood game of cricket.

'This is a haunted place now,' Phulmatia-ji sighed. It seemed as if she was hearing her voice after a long time, and the words emanating from within were casting a spell on her. 'Nobody is around, not a soul with whom I can talk. Everything is so silent and still. No mill's siren, no workers filing past. Such a sannata. From dusk the jackals begin their call – hookka-hooa. It feels like a cremation ground. Life now has turned us into ghosts, living ghosts.'

Jinda bhoot. Living ghosts. She rolled the words on her tongue a couple of times and crashed into laughter. The sari slipped off her head, her silver nose-stud gleamed. Phulmatia-ji pressed the pallu on her lips to stop the laughter bubbling up from inside.

I didn't know where it came from, but I could see that this laughter held the old couple fast to each other and would continue to do so till death did them part.

~

Brindavan-ji led us down a rutted path along the factory wall, past two-storeyed community latrines, towards the river. The well-ventilated latrines, built at least a century ago, displayed a concept of workers' welfare that was out of place in the age of postcolonial labour unionism. The latrines stood amid inky pools teeming with pigs.

We came to the Hooghly riverfront. A mound of sand covered with vegetation offered the best view of the jute mill's abandoned power plant.

'This is the captive plant that once produced seven megawatts of electricity and fully served the needs of this industrial zone,' Subhasish said.

A forest of banyans, wild figs and thick lianas had taken over the ruins. We could still glimpse skeletal remains of giant machinery, massive pipes and girders. A trolley track went from the riverside jetty into the dark sheds smothered with roots, thick and mottled with moss, and resembling pythons. The surreal landscape reminded me of Andrei Tarkovsky's film *Stalker*. In that film, three characters travel on a trolley into a mysterious, cordoned-off place called the Zone. And here I was, standing before an unknown zone I had never known existed on the border of my hometown.

'Jackals live inside with their families,' Brindavan-ji said. 'They feed on animal carcasses that the tides deposit on the riverbank.'

Hillocks of garbage blocked the view of Hooghly town across the river. This town, a trading post that the Portuguese had built in the sixteenth century, had given its name to the river.

'There's a green bench ban on municipal waste dumping on riverbanks,' Subhasish said bitterly. 'But who cares?'

'Right. Who cares?' Brindavan-ji erupted into his trademark laughter. 'This river was once this region's nara, its umbilical cord. It was the lifeline of the industries here. The nara is now shrivelling up, but who cares?'

A dead industrial zone, a dying river – who cares? In a place where a few hundred families eked out a living by plucking synthetic threads from discarded automobile tyres, everything was up for sale. Even death. A scrap-recycling business was thriving. It employed children and workers of closed factories. Plastic lean-tos and giant weighing scales suspended on wooden posts shimmered on the heat-hazed bank.

'Wooden door frames, cast-iron railings, galvanized pipes, asbestos sheets ... you'll get everything here. Brass and copper machine parts from British times are being stripped out of factories in broad daylight,' Brindavan-ji said.

'Scrapping and recycling is the only viable industry now,' Subhasish added.

An industry would usually have its own downstream industry. Tramping about the riverfront, we wandered behind the bustle of the scrap market to a stretch of bare chocolate-coloured earth. Not a tree or a blade of grass was growing here; not a pig or a dog roamed about. A desolate silence prevailed. Under the strong late-afternoon sun, about twenty men and women sat hunched on the ground, busy doing something. From a distance, they appeared like a flock of vultures. Up close, they turned out to be wizened old people, all skin and bones. Each had a bamboo basket by his or her side.

'Here they sift the dirt dug out of factory shop floors and pick bits of iron,' Brindavan-ji explained in a hushed voice.

Ancient grease had turned the dirt a deep chocolate brown. These old people were running magnets attached to discarded microphone speakers through it and catching tiny nuts, twisted screws, washers and bolts. Each basket had a small pile of scavenged metal.

They were working ceaselessly, wordlessly. Their groping fingers, some bandaged with rags, seemed to belong to blind people.

Brindavan-ji knew most of the men. Once skilled workmen like him, they now worked here from eight in the morning to four in the afternoon, earning fifty rupees a day.

'Would you like to ask them anything?' he whispered in my ear.

The sun had dipped and our elongated shadows striped the turned-up dirt. But they never looked up at us or even stopped their hands once. I could detect a pulse of tension in their bony fingers.

What could I ask? Many years ago, someone had told us about a UFO landing on our school's roof. We were kids then, and I could remember the endless hours we had spent discussing the event. What excited us most was the possibility of an encounter with aliens and the questions we should ask them. That time, we had failed to come up with any that would have been appropriate.

This time, too, I failed.

VII

BAY OF BENGAL

HERMIT CRAB

At first, it seemed his shabby clothes and unkempt appearance had roused the beach dogs. But on closer inspection, the fact turned out to be different: he was stealing their food. Using a twig, he was digging into the sand, teasing the crabs out of their burrows, and in one swift motion of his fingers, breaking off their claws and stuffing the thrashing creatures, red as pomegranate flowers, into a polythene bag. We had seen the hunting ritual of the dogs. They did a lot of running and chasing about all over the beach, shoved their muzzles into crabholes, and dug heaps of sand with their forepaws. But after all the effort, their success rate was pitiful. In contrast, this man's technique was smart and graceful. In no time, the polybag was full of the crustacean harvest. And that was why all the beach dogs had formed a gang and were snarling at him.

But the man was unflappable. He walked to the water's edge on unhurried feet and stood gazing out at the horizon. The foamy sea swirled around his feet, the breeze scattered the clamour of dogs. After a long time, he bent over the rolling waves, scooped water into the polybag and carefully washed off the sand. He tossed the crushed claws to the crows. Then he shuffled across towards the casuarina grove. Large-scale erosion was taking place there, the breakers were nibbling away at a residential colony, vacated and surrendered to the whims of the sea. Salt water, sand, barnacles and marine creatures had laid siege to the empty concrete structures.

Erosion affected this side of the island too. The public works department was building embankments to protect Baroli, the newborn tourist resort on the seaboard of the Bay of Bengal.

We'd been camping here since last week. But we were not tourists. After the day-long fieldwork in the villages around the mangroves, we would return to the beach by a boat or a vano, a motorized rickshaw-van with a flat board to carry passengers and also goods. We would watch the sun dip dutifully into the sea. In the evening, the food stalls on Beach Road would open and transform the seafront into an open-air mall.

But that was during the weekends. The crowd would swell on a Friday evening, reach its peak on Sunday, and by Monday morning it would subside and return the beach to its solitude. The creeks and rivers here had high tide twice a day, Baroli had it once a week. From hotel owners to shopkeepers, vano drivers to coconut sellers on the beach, everyone hung on this weekend tide from Kolkata. Since we were neither tourists nor locals, these details engaged our attention.

And that was how we spotted the crab hunter on the beach.

Was the man a vagabond or simply out of his mind?

Every evening we dropped in at a seafront stall to imbibe tea and local gossip. Tapan, the owner, was a twenty-something man whose smart features and smooth manners complemented the trim look of his stall. It was built with coconut trunks and nipa-palm leaves, like the other beach stalls here.

I described the man and his activity on the beach, and enquired about his whereabouts.

'So many types of *public* come here, Kaku.' Tapan gave a shrug. 'It's impossible to keep track of each one of them. But he's a loony, I'm sure. Who else would catch red sea crabs?'

'Aren't they edible?' I asked.

'Ugh!' Tapan made a face. 'If you wish to taste sweet-water crabs, just ask me. I'll get them for you. They are *soooo tasty*, you'll never want to touch a lobster!'

'What else can you get for us?' Amitava teased, a mischievous smile fluttering on his lips.

'*Anything*, Kaku!' Tapan replied promptly, looking directly into Amitava's eyes.

'Tiger milk?'

Tapan chuckled. 'Yes, that too.'

'What other *anything* do your customers demand?' Amitava persisted.

'Oh, a lot! They come here to *relask* after a hectic week in the city.'

I made a mental note of the items laid out on bamboo racks inside the stall. Biscuits, chips, chocolates, candies, cheese cubes, condoms, soda-water bottles, instant noodles, shampoo sachets, gutkha, pencil batteries, film rolls, fruit-juice cans, Gelusil strips, tinned rasagolla, sanitary napkins, Hajmola tablets, torches…

These were on display. There were other items inside the red baby fridge nestled in an alcove cut into the mud wall. What other *anything* was there, behind the palm-leaf screen at the back of the stall, or beyond it, in the lantana bushes, around the garbage heaps, across a ditch clogged with crushed PET bottles and plastic wrappers, and even in the mud-and-thatch settlement beyond it, we had no idea. How far did Tapan's stall really extend?

That was a difficult question, no less difficult than the other big question: where did the Sundarbans begin? After Cyclone Aila, Tapan had migrated here from down south, like many other settlers in Baroli. Before that, he had worked on many islands, and even on the mainland, until he came to know about this new 'spot' being developed as a weekend tourist destination. Tapan was an early bird, and he had grabbed prime shop space on the seafront. The ditch behind the newly settled village was, in fact, the dead end of a creek clogged by sand, the same sand that had created the beach and had made the place viable for tourism. People drifted in here from nearby islands, battered by Aila or sinking under the rising sea levels. Tapan knew most of them personally. He addressed them as kaka, jyatha, boudi, pishi, bhaipo – all terms of familial relationships. He was calling us kaku – uncle.

In Bengal, one can address a stranger as kaku, depending on the number of grey hairs on the latter's head. But sometimes, this term is used to address a visibly younger person from a higher social rank – a bhadralok, that is. This phenomenon is not very old. During the colonial times and later, the usual form of address for a male stranger, irrespective of his age, was moshai, sir, for someone of equal social rank, and babu for one of a higher rank. In the Bangla films and novels of the 1950s and '60s, we find these to be the common forms of address. When and how did this change creep into the culture? Possibly during the 1970s. That was when large human groups migrated and settled in an already overpopulated land and sought networks of kinship for support. They even made it a habit of forging temporary kinship bonds where none existed, in a desperate bid for a share of the meagre resources of livelihood. New settlements and small business establishments flourished on clan networks; old caste relations were recast to deal with the pressing needs of the time. In the Sundarbans, with extensive areas sinking or becoming uninhabitable every day, this social phenomenon took on a new poignancy.

The island of Baroli had a mix of old and new population groups. There was the old fishermen's village, and a new settlement on newly reclaimed land, whose inhabitants were dependent on tourism. They drove vanos, ran beachfront stalls, and found seasonal employment in hotels and lodges.

As the evening ripened, under-the-counter sale of liquor picked up at Tapan's stall. The off-licence shop was three kilometres into the island. For city slickers, the time spent on getting the stuff from there was dearer than the few extra rupees Tapan charged. Cans of Kingfisher Lager slept inside the red baby fridge like a harem of seals.

The bird species printed on the beer cans were plentiful in Baroli. They perched all day on fishnet frames, and from time to time, flashed rainbow-hued lightning across the air and water. A second later, they'd be back on the perch, a silvery wriggle caught between their chopstick beaks. Did such a rainbow flash inside one's head when one slipped behind the steering wheel, the Kingfisher fizzing in the stomach, and raced the vehicle along the beach? The races would begin late in the evening, when the beach was deserted. The cars would swerve down to the wet sand slapped by the waves, to get better traction, and pick up maddening speed. They'd belt out ear-splitting beats and lacerate the raging, foamy-mouthed waves with their headlights. By then, all the trinket and fish-fry stalls would have closed and the green coconut sellers would have vanished. A damp sea wind would churn the distant mangroves. On the empty beach, bathed by orange sodium lamps, the day's accumulated litter – chips packets, PET bottles, aluminium cans, teacups, plastic wrappers and straw – would spin and drift across the sand. The beach dogs would chase them to the stands of casuarina trees, where the litter would accumulate through the night.

∼

On Sunday, Baroli received a decent-sized crowd. On Monday, late in the afternoon, I spotted him again inside the casuarina grove. He was busy rooting through the weekend's harvest of litter. Next day, at around the same time, I saw him again. This time, he was walking rather blithely, his feet barely touching the sand, into a brilliant sunset. The dogs were barking behind him and a lone crow was wheeling over his head. Two days later, at dawn, he was back hunting – a twig, a polybag, the same technique. Another afternoon, I caught sight of him at a handpump behind the beach stalls. Bare-chested, a pair of frayed trousers held up at the waist by a length of coir rope, he was pushing the handlebar and drinking water by putting his mouth directly to the faucet. I noticed deep scars on his shoulder blades.

~

The Sundarbans islands are arranged on the seaboard of the Bay of Bengal like loose pages from a manuscript. It is a fantastic novel, being written and erased and again being written. The island of Baroli sat on the sea mouth of the Hooghly. Ten years ago, its margins were covered with the mangrove plants and mud – soft curd-like silt studded with spores and exposed tree roots. Bathing, or even a walk along the beach, was out of the question. And then a mysterious geomorphological phenomenon occurred. Masses of sand drifted in with the tides and, in two years, created a fine beach. The public works department replaced the rickety wooden scaffold that connected the island with an all-weather concrete bridge, and another new tourist spot was born. A string of hotels and lodgings came up in no time, cocking a snook at the Coastal Regulation Zone guidelines. The tourism department laid concrete pathways and lit up the beachfront. A string of palm-leaf stalls, plastic chairs, beach umbrellas and pyramids of green coconuts completed the picture of a trim little beach resort – as trim as it could be on a strip of land between a mangrove forest and an old fishing village.

But in another part of Baroli, land was being eroded by contrary currents on the tidal mouth of the Hooghly. To protect the newborn resort, they were laying along the coast a guard wall of giant polymer tubes filled with sand. This was another costly technology imported from Japan. Behind Amitava's camp office – a plain two-storeyed building where I had put up – giant machines with lobster claws worked day and night. They churned up sand and water, and injected the mixture into the inflatable tubes.

The spectacle reminded me of the construction of the power plant on Ayodhya Hill. For Amitava, that was a distant memory now. These days, his mind seemed to be steeped in muddy waters and salty air. It could not survive the aseptic world of academia. After his stint at Visva-Bharati University was over, this camp office became his address. Here, Amitava was in charge of a livelihood project spread over seven islands. Twenty-two men worked under him.

Cyclone Aila had woken up the world to the dire situation in the Sundarbans. Aid was pouring in from all corners of the country and the world. 'This,' Amitava reminded me, 'is not a new phenomenon. If you factor in the number of NGOs working in the Sundarbans against its population, the ratio is unmatched anywhere in the country. But the plight of the people here has never entered our political discourse, although this place is so close to Kolkata. Everyone is convinced that the Sundarbans is a lost cause.'

～

From Tuesday to Thursday, I did not see him even once. The stall owners and vano drivers on the beach couldn't give me any information. It was the middle of the week, and the beachfront was deserted. One could easily spot a lone figure from a distance. Perhaps he had gone away elsewhere. There were so many islands here, many of them inhabited. He could have slipped away to any of them on a fishing boat. Or did he swim across the creeks, as tigers do? The BSF, the BGB or the Border Guard Bangladesh, the Indian Coast Guard, the maps, the borderlines, the barbed wire, the watchtowers – all the signs and insignia of nations got blurred in this tide country. Like the statutory national flag on a fishing boat – limp, faded and indistinguishable from the gamchha the boatmen would hang out on the rudder to dry.

From the moment I first laid my eyes on him, this man had taken a hold of me like an unrelenting tune buzzing inside one's head. How old would he be? Fifty? Forty? How did a life spent outdoors among the elements leave its marks on a person's physical appearance? Salt lined his flaking, sun-scorched skin, and the matted hair around his face and head was the colour of jute; it was impossible to tell whether they had greyed. The deep lines on his brow could have been caused by years of looking for food in the glinting sand.

If his age was anywhere between forty and fifty, then he had been a boy in 1979. It wasn't impossible for a young adult to move from island to island, sleeping out in the open or inside an abandoned boat, begging and foraging for food, alone or in the company of a group of vagabonds. Most of them must have died since, and perhaps he was one of the last wayward survivors. I wasn't sure.

∽

A swathe of mangroves, protected by barbed wire, from a time when these plants ruled this island. Now, only this much had remained – the last stunted survivors of the tide-country species. Inside the fencing was the forest department's beat office: log cabins on stilts, sweet-water ponds and a coconut plantation. A government tourist lodge was coming up in the vicinity. It was a big three-storeyed structure of glass, granite and stainless steel designed like a Gothic castle, complete with turreted roofs and fake buttresses. There was a paved driveway with smiling fibreglass tigers, standing like kangaroos on their hind legs to greet the visitor, their stomachs shaped into litter bins and a sign painted on their chests – USE ME.

A brick-paved pathway curved away from the enclosed area towards the old fishing village. It passed a large rural development project area set up with foreign funding. It was a ten-acre sunflower farm dotted with wind turbines. The plant was yet to produce electricity, but the donor agency was buying up all the seeds from the farmers, I learnt. A sea of bright yellow sunflowers rolled in the wind, the blades of the turbines wheeled slowly.

∽

The older inhabitants of the tide country would never be mistaken about them, Dulal's father had told me, they'd never turn them away. But Tapan belonged to the new generation.

I made a discovery: the man never accepted charity, at least not from a stranger. For two consecutive days, I saw him on the deserted beach at dawn, hunting crabs. On the second day, I advanced and tried to engage him in conversation. He didn't respond, but neither did he turn away his alert, animal eyes from my face. I was carrying a camera, and I intended to take his picture. I pulled out from my purse a ten-rupee note. But he didn't accept it. He looked at the banknote for a few seconds, without expression, and then spun around to face the sea. He peeled off the tattered cardigan, which clung to his torso like a second skin, and stepped into the rolling waters. I watched his bare back, the rope-like muscles strung along the knobby spinal column, the pair of old scars on the shoulder blades, taut and shining.

He had dropped the cardigan on the sand. I noticed assorted items stuffed inside its many pockets: a flattened matchbox wrapped in a polybag, a rusty pocketknife, a roll of nylon thread, metal washers, bits of aluminium foil, pebbles, a film-roll container, a plastic straw, and balls of crumpled paper.

He waded into the chest-deep water and stretched his arms sideways over the gentle waves, like outspread wings. The image was imprinted in my memory.

∼

From the beach resort, keeping the sea on the left, a broken asphalt road ran alongside a battered habitat. It was abandoned and partially reclaimed by the sea. A string of prawn farms lined the road. They had been shut down after the global economic meltdown in 2008; prawn production here had been wholly export-dependent.

Rattling along the brick-paved path in a vano, we had a view of the abandoned ponds. Tiny pools of water, silted up and drying, standing in the middle, still as mirrors and framed with the spidery roots of dead trees.

A forest had once thrived here. Men cut down trees, embanked the floodplains and staked out prawn farms. Rusty sluice gates, concrete-lined canals, bone-dry, broken electric poles, bougainvillaea and other urban garden plants running wild. Left to itself, a new ecosystem would form here. But the old mangroves would never return.

~

A carbuncle would leave a permanent scar on the skin. But he had them on both his shoulder blades, exactly at the same spots, about three inches from the arm joints. When I first noticed them, he was pushing the handlebar of a handpump. Each time he flexed his arm, the scars came alive like fluttering eyes. A thought formed in my mind: could these be wounds from a tiger attack? If the animal had attacked from the rear, as it habitually did, its front paws would probably land on these spots upon the shoulder. Or, they could have been from deep gashes left by an axe or any such heavy instrument. In that case, the attacker was positioned above him – on a tree or a horse. A boat? If one had swum to a boat and had clutched on to its side, and if the attacker had wanted to dislodge him, it was likely that the axe would have descended on the shoulder blade...

There was no way of knowing. Sometimes, the marks on a body are as inscrutable as an excavated seal, unless one can decipher the language. What was his mother tongue? Did he still remember it? Or had the life of a hunter-gatherer in remote mangrove islands taught him the language of crows and winds rustling in nipa palms?

THE BIRTH OF A NOVEL

We were preparing for a long trip, a visit to seven islands on the mouth of the Hooghly. It would take four days on a boat, a narrow vessel with a six-cylinder engine, a tiny cabin and a tarpaulin-shaded deck. It took us two days to stock it up with fuel, potable water and provisions, and to get the permits from the forest department and the Port Trust. Now we were waiting for a researcher who'd join us from the city. He was working on the impact of climate change on the Sundarbans islands.

Amitava's organization offered internships, but the young researcher had a university fellowship. Also, his area of study was different, although it encompassed the same field. A joint field trip was mutually beneficial: it saved time and money for the researcher, and for Amitava, whose organization would bear the expenses of the trip, it meant access to advanced data on the islands and the river system. My old friend's appetite for learning was as active in the tide country as it had been in the Purulia hills or the flat plains of Birbhum. I was happy to know this.

But I also seemed to know the six-foot-plus bearded researcher whom I was meeting for the first time. Something about his features told me I had seen him before, although I couldn't remember when or where. Amitava introduced him.

'Here's Wrik. He is a junior research fellow at the School of Oceanographic Studies in Jadavpur University. He's working on the sinking islands of the Sundarbans. Wrik has another identity…'

Amitava turned to me and squinted; the young man flashed a demure smile.

'Wrik is my son.'

Now I remembered. Wrik had his mother Nandita's face, but I had never seen him before. Among all our friends, Amitava had been the first to settle in a job and get married. He had joined the corporate world and had married a girl from a family that folded seamlessly into that world. Nandita's father was a rich businessman and a leading exporter of leather products.

We, his friends, were distressed at Amitava's corporate lifestyle and shared a complex feeling of betrayal. This would later strike me as odd, but in those days, we still considered ourselves to be the legatees of an earlier, ill-fated generation. Our minds were filled with the tendrils of smoke from the trail the young Calcutta Naxalites had blazed in the 1960s, the decade in which we were born. In a few years, Amitava would chuck his plush job and go to work in the Bastar region. The news was like a slap across our faces; we smarted but felt strangely happy. For me, there was also a twinge of self-pity: I had lost faith in man's capacity for renewal. By then, Wrik had been born, and Amitava's marriage had broken off.

~

'In the next twelve years, nine islands on the Hooghly estuary will sink,' Wrik declared matter-of-factly as he unrolled a sheaf of maps on a rough wooden bench. These were the latest satellite pictures accessed from NASA's website. He tapped his index finger on a mud-grey patch. 'Already two have vanished, Bedford and Lohachara.'

'Nine islands. That means sixty to seventy thousand people,' Amitava muttered. 'They'll lose land and livelihood.'

'What about Bedford and Lohachara?' I asked.

'Bedford didn't have a human settlement,' Wrik said. 'It had a thin scrub forest. But Lohachara had villages on it.'

I faintly remembered the news that appeared in the media. Lohachara had made international headlines as the first 'inhabited' island on earth to fall victim to global warming and the rise in sea levels.

'Nobody in Kolkata or even in the Sundarbans had ever heard the name of Lohachara until it disappeared,' Amitava said. 'By vanishing, the island suddenly became visible.'

Wrik pulled out a tab from his knapsack, flicked his finger on the screen a few times and turned it towards us.

'Look, this is a picture from the 2007 Academy Awards ceremony in Hollywood. The awardees received replicas of Lohachara Island as part of a global awareness campaign against climate change.'

I could recognize Leonardo DiCaprio and Jennifer Lopez on stage, alongside other glittering men and women.

'But what about the people on the island?' Amitava asked. 'It would have made more sense if they had flown a few victims and put them up on stage.'

Wrik laughed indulgently.

'The situation is bad,' he said. 'A few centimetres rise in sea levels will render vast areas uninhabitable. At present, the sea is rising globally at a rate of three millimetres every year. Add to this the silt that is being deposited on the riverbeds here, raising them five millimetres annually. Altogether it is eight millimetres, the highest in the world, and speeding up.'

'It sounds like a losing battle against nature's own scheme of things,' I said.

'True.' Wrik nodded. 'But human intervention isn't negligible either. For the last two hundred years, men built bunds around these Sundarbans islands to claim the land. But the paradox is that the silt-carrying rivers had created these islands. As the bunds stopped the dispersal of silt, and further formation of land, it is now being deposited directly on riverbeds.'

'So, what's your solution?' Amitava demanded. 'Bombard the bunds?'

Wrik laughed.

'A country like China could probably do such a thing,' Amitava continued. 'They'd deploy the army, evacuate all the people, plant dynamite into the embankments and blast them.'

'But we are a democracy, *brother*,' I said and put my arm around his shoulder.

'And then there's the question of resettlement,' Wrik said. 'Where will you put forty lakh people?'

'They never thought about it when they got together and cut up this subcontinent in 1947,' Amitava quipped.

The formation of deltas and other fluvial processes of the river systems consumed Wrik's thoughts. Amitava's concerns, on the other hand, were with the inhabitants and their struggle for survival. One of them dealt with deep time, the other with cyclical time. And yet, the movements of waterborne lands connected their concerns, just as a bloodline connects a father and son.

Amitava had told me that the uprooted people were moving to higher islands in the Sundarbans, upsetting the ecosystem of these islands. Many had migrated to Kolkata and even to other cities outside the state. It was a disaster unfolding in slow motion. But then, our democracy permitted, even sanctioned, such slow-motion disasters. Like malnutrition, for example.

Our boat's sareng, driver, was a cheerful young man named Tarak Bhuiyan. He had a deep tan, rugged features and a corrugated forehead that had given him a prematurely ancient look. Tarak's family had lived on Lohachara Island for three generations until it started to sink. Now he lived in a refugee colony on Sagar, a large sea-mouth island where the famous Gangasagar Mela took place every winter.

'Tarak's surname Bhuiyan has its root in "bhuin" – land,' Amitava had said, introducing him. 'But these days he spends eight to ten months a year on water. Isn't that so, Tarak?'

Tarak had smiled, drawing out the deep lines on his brow. The sunlight reflected off the rippling waters had etched them. Like tree rings, they displayed his experience as a sareng.

Or were these wrinkles the result of unceasing worries about waters eating away the land? The same water that gave Tarak employment had also driven him out of his island home. One half of him worked on the boat, the other half was with his family living in the resettled colony. Late in the evening, when our boat moored for the night close to a bank, Tarak would call up his family if the mobile signal was available. I overheard him talk at length in a gloomy, intimate voice, possibly with his wife and children, enquiring about mundane household affairs. The deep parallel lines on Tarak's brow constantly brought to my mind the imagery of a tree. Each man here was a tree. I could only see the top half, branching out under the open skies, while the roots reached out below, unseen, continually interacting with a network of other roots, other trees.

'Bhuiyan is a title,' Amitava informed me, 'not a caste surname. In the Sundarbans, you'll find many Muslims having this title after their usual surnames like Khan or Ali.'

'Actually, we are the descendants of Baro Bhuiyan, the twelve zamindars who had once ruled Bengal,' Tarak said with a hint of pride in his voice and added quickly, 'But I have heard all this from my grandfather who couldn't read and write.'

It was late winter, the estuary was calm. Under the morning's misty haze, the water had the colour of green grapes. But as the day advanced, it slowly turned to a muddy bronze. Our boat traced a route along the bank that funnelled out to a small fishing harbour. It was busy at this season of the year. There would be a big lunar tide in a day or two, Tarak told us, and the trawlers were getting ready to set sail. Men were moving about, storing ice, nets, and drums of fuel. The blowing of conch shells and the ululation of female voices reached us from the bank, above the din of a dozen revving engines.

As our boat came closer, I spotted a group of village women, their heads covered in saris, standing in the forest of boats, crates, and bales of rope. They were bending over the water to float lighted leaf lamps. A saffron-robed priest was chanting a mantra hurriedly, balancing himself in knee-deep mud.

'A puja for the safety of their men,' Tarak explained as he inspected the scene from the wheel bar. 'They will be away for up to two weeks, fishing in the coastal waters.'

He steered the vessel close to the harbour for us to get a better view. I saw faces glistening with anxiety and hope. The men were having a quick last-minute talk with their wives, a few of them cradling babies in their arms. Intimate indoor scenes, being enacted under the wide expanse of the sky. The sad, elongated eyes painted on the prows of the trawlers kept watch.

The harbour receded, and now the wind turbines came into view above the line of casuarina trees. The blades were wheeling in slow motion, the fields of blazing yellow sunflowers stretched into the distance. I had seen them from the land, but the perspective from the estuary gave the scenery a picture-postcard quality. It was like an exotic, high-class tourist destination, out of sync with muddy waters and fish-smelling air. The state tourism department had been using photographs taken from these angles to promote Baroli.

'Do you know who's funding this project?' Wrik asked Amitava, pointing to the fields of sunflowers.

'Astika Agro,' Amitava answered, without looking up.

'Yes, and they are funded by Maserio, a big Italian corporation. Maserio has investments in a variety of sectors: agro-industry is one of them. It is they who are buying up all the sunflower seeds the farmers are producing here.'

Wrik now turned to me. 'You know something? Maserio was an equity partner of the five-star luxury resort project right here in the Sundarbans.'

When Sahara India Parivar had proposed the few-hundred-crore tourism project in the Sundarbans, it had become big news. From a floating luxury hotel to golf courses on the island, from scuba diving to helipads, they had plans to plant a piece of Phuket or Pattaya right here in this tide country. The picture postcard of casuarina trees, windmills and sunflower fields would have been of a piece with that plan. Concerned citizens and environmentalists wrote protest letters to the chief minister, and author Amitav Ghosh wrote an article in *Outlook* magazine, titled 'A Crocodile in the Swamplands'. That was in 2004.

'But by that time the government had signed the MoU,' Amitava said.

'Thank god Sahara went under.' I exhaled a sigh of relief.

'But that's not why they abandoned the project,' Wrik said. 'Other big companies would have stepped in. It was Cyclone Aila that played spoilsport. For long, environmentalists had been crying hoarse about this crazy project in a cyclone-prone zone. And then Aila struck, and they were proved right.'

'The *so-called* environmentalists!' Amitava winked at me.

'What's that?' Wrik asked.

I snickered.

For many years, in Kolkata's leftist intellectual circles, it was common practice to dub all activists who spoke for the environment as '*so-called* environmentalists' and dismiss them. It created a political culture where something like a Purulia Pumped Storage Project could be built without a murmur of protest. It reached its high point when a Kolkata-based environmentalist named Subhas Dutta pleaded with the judiciary to issue an order for shifting the venue of the Kolkata Book Fair from the heart of the city, away from the Maidan grounds. The Left Front government had breathed fire, and a prominent minister had threatened to gherao Dutta in his house.

But it wasn't possible for Wrik to know all this; he was too young then.

'Days before the government signed the MoU,' Amitava said, 'the Supreme Court directed it to stop all fishing activities on Jambudwip. They put up police pickets and demolished the shacks the fishermen used to dry fish. I don't think this was just a coincidence.'

Jambudwip was a two-thousand-two-hundred-and-fifty-hectare uninhabited island on the sea mouth of the Bay of Bengal. Thick mangrove forests covered it and wide beaches of fine yellow sand ringed it. A deep inlet had split it open to create a natural harbour. For centuries, coastal fishermen of both the Bengals used its wide sunny beaches to dry their winter catch. The mangroves served as wind barriers and sheltered their boats. During the three months, ten thousand men lived and worked on the island. A Supreme Court order had put a ban on this activity. But the fishermen returned after they scrapped the project, and nobody was complaining.

Soon, the grey haze of Jambudwip drifted into view. Under a pale blue sky, the rolling deep shaded from grey-green to tan. Jambudwip appeared on the horizon, a mass of mangroves cleft by an inlet. As we neared it, the trees on the island untangled themselves from the dark, formless splotch, and a smell of drying fish smacked the nostrils. We discerned silvery streamers of Bombay duck flashing on lines strung along the beach. Pyramids of fish gleamed under the noonday sun. Workers shovelled them into wheelbarrows and carried them to nipa nipa-palm sheds. The men wore thongs, displaying gaunt, charcoaled limbs dusted with sand. It was a mirage colony that would vanish before the onset of summer. Only the nipa-palm sheds would remain standing.

Would the crab hunter move in then? Jambudwip was barely three kilometres from the coast. It wouldn't be too difficult for him to ride the pre-monsoon currents on a DIY raft of driftwood to get to the island. There were sweet-water ponds on the island, and small animals too. And with all the fish drying, surely birds would keep coming to scavenge the leftovers. Besides, of course, there was no dearth of red crabs.

Over the steady thrum of the boat's engine, Amitava's voice reached my ears from another time:

'For many years, Jambudwip was a prickly point between various government departments. It's a designated reserve forest area, but a few thousand men also depend on it for their livelihood. A Supreme Court order changed all that. They barricaded the harbour mouth with wooden poles. And then one day, a cyclone hit these parts. The fishermen out at sea rushed to take shelter in the inlet, as they had always done. But this time, armed forest guards repulsed them. Forty men perished, seven trawlers sank. Twelve days later, the police tore down the temporary sheds and destroyed a large stock of fish. I remember that day. I was in nearby Fraserganj, attending a conference of NGO workers. It was 16 October 2003, World Food Day.'

In silence, we watched the island blur in the distance as our boat now headed towards the Hooghly's tidal mouth. The water turned muddy again and the engine's hum dropped. I could hear the waves slapping the hull.

'I was in Class 6 that year,' Wrik said, looking into Amitava's eyes, a faint smile curling the corners of his lips.

Amitava turned his head away and gazed into the distance, where a flock of gulls was flying in wide spirals along the line of the horizon where the water met the sky, as if hemming in the two elements.

~

I saw him in a dream. His wings, severed from the shoulder blades, were buried somewhere, and he was searching for them all over the islands. A gentle rocking of the boat awakened me. The tide was turning. Amitava was sleeping by my side, stretched on his back, his left arm across his eyes. His right arm was resting on his son's shoulder. Wrik had curled himself up like a foetus to fit his tall frame on the cramped cabin floor. It was 3.20 a.m. on my watch. I raised my head and peered through the slats. The dim light from the stars drew outlines of trees and their exposed roots. Plastic litter tangled on low branches glimmered like surreal flowers. The river, warm and full, exhaled vapour, which instantly turned into wisps of mist and drifted over the dark polished surface. I watched the phenomenon for some time until I nodded off.

I woke up at dawn. Amitava was sleeping in the same posture, but Wrik wasn't there. Our boat glided like a sleepwalker, emitting a deep hum. I climbed on to the deck and found the universe covered in dense fog. A weak glow was oozing in the east, but I wasn't sure if it was the sun. The search lamps on the wheelhouse blinked intermittently. The shafts of light, yellow and mottled with tendrils of mist, melted a few feet away. It appeared as if there was not a soul on this grey planet besides the few humans on this boat. Except for its gentle rocking and the engine's muffled hum, it was impossible to tell if we were moving. A beedi glowed on Tarak's lips inside the dark cubbyhole.

Wrik sat on the foredeck in the lotus posture, hooding his head with a wrapper. I crept up to him. A GPS monitor glowed on his lap. On the blue screen, a red line was squirming like a horsehair worm in a forest of numbers and meshed lines. The boat's pointed prow churned up the fog as it glided forward. My head turned damp and groggy. I climbed down into the cabin and stretched myself on the cold polypropylene mat.

For the past four days this boat had been our home. We'd return here after a day of fieldwork on the islands. The long stay on the vessel seemed to have aligned our body's equilibrium with its movements. It was as if we ourselves had metamorphosed into limbs of the boat. The wisps of mist the river was exhaling before dawn were the words we had been listening to on the islands. Everything that the islanders narrated to us was weaving itself into an impenetrable haze. Uprooted people, drifting from island to island, or leaving the tide country forever. They were leaving the bhitay where they had been born and had lived for generations, where a lifetime's labour had gone into clearing the forests, embanking and taming the islands, and making them fit for humans. Lohachara had sunk with huge international fanfare. But there was Ghoramara, a larger island that thirty years ago had two dozen villages and eight thousand families living on it. The island was shrinking every year, every hour in fact, its fields, orchards and homestead lands dissolving into the swirling waters like lumps of jaggery.

Three years ago, when Amitava joined the project, seven villages stood on Ghoramara. Now, most of them were only names alive in the memory of the uprooted people – Mandirtala, Chunpuri, Bagpara, Khasimara … Only a chunk of Khasimara was still standing: a row of date palms, a clutch of cottages huddled on a rise, encircled by grey water. Freestanding mud walls, cracked and flaking, mimicked the maps of the Sundarbans. The notched date-palm trunks told a story of winter tapping, of chill mornings, weak straw fire and cold-benumbed hands reaching out from under cotton wrappers, of rooster calls and the scent of warm jaggery, of a settled way of life that was no more.

Islands vanishing, turning into memory ghosts.

~

I was wallowing in a light sleep when I heard excited voices on the deck. The boat was crawling and stopping, crawling and stopping, moving forward with great circumspection. I climbed again on to the deck to find the fog had thinned. The pale disk of the sun had turned a stretch of water into molten copper. The two enginemen, the cook and the guard deputed by the forest department, had all assembled on the front deck. They were peering at the blazing water about two hundred metres ahead. Wrik had taken position on the steering bridge, beside Tarak. The GPS tracker's bluish glow lit up his chin and a field glass that hung from his neck. Tarak sat clutching the wheel, his face tense with excitement. When we made eye contact, he waved his hand and directed me to look ahead.

At first, I couldn't see anything. The sheet of water glowed an opalescent pink. Then I spotted a flock of whiskered terns flying low over the surface of the water, so low that their wing tips almost brushed it. As the birds cut a diagonal path across the waterway, they ascended together at a particular spot, as if riding an invisible roller coaster, their white underbelly briefly aglow, and then they dipped again. Now I saw it: in the middle of the watery expanse, a sandbar had risen above the tides. It was shining like metal. Suddenly, the boat vroomed and wrenched to a halt.

The evening before we set off, Wrik was telling us about this. Lohachara Island continued to sink, and shrink, during the 1990s, until it vanished from satellite pictures in 2006. That was when it hit international news headlines as the first inhabited island to pay the price for global warming. But since last year, satellite cameras had been picking up images of a mysterious speck at exactly the same coordinates where Lohachara had sunk. Local fishermen, too, were regularly spotting a sandbar here, particularly during winter. Brimming with excitement, Wrik explained to us how, if this speck on the estuary turned out to be the rebirth of Lohachara Island, it would add a new spin on the effect of climate change on the Sundarbans' geomorphology. I didn't understand all the technical details of what he said, and their scientific implications, but I felt a strange stirring inside me when he showed us photographs of the new char accessed from NASA's global monitoring system. It resembled a stingray floating with its wings outspread over the blue water.

From the deck, however, its shape wasn't clear. By now, the men had lowered into the water a long, narrow gangplank with pieces of wood nailed to it. Tarak and Wrik were the first to descend. They climbed down and slipped into the water, until they found a foothold on the submerged land. The river reached up to Wrik's thighs. Then Kalu, the engineman, dropped a long bamboo pole which they held at both ends, on the deck and in the water, like a railing. I rolled up my pyjamas, gripped the pole and stepped gingerly down the gangplank. As I released myself into the river and sank until I found land under the soles of my feet, I was flooded with an indescribable feeling. It was like the current noon that, during our schooldays, we'd put on the tip of our tongue. A similar sensation now passed through the soles of my feet and shot up my spine. The water flowing between my thighs was warm and sentient. As my toes tried to dig in, the sand seemed to slither away at first, bashfully, and then it clasped me around the heels. Floating twigs brushed past my knees as I waded to the raised land.

The tide was turning, wavy folds of sand glistened liquid gold. They were nicked with birds' feet. There were tiny pools of water with green crabs on them. The crabs had paddle-like feet. At the sound of human footsteps, they scampered up in a flash, built igloos with fine pellets of earth and closed them over their heads.

Tarak walked up to almost the middle of the raised land. It was the size of half a football field. He walked on light and bouncy feet, like a moonwalker, like the first human being on a virgin planet.

Now he spun around and faced us. He raised both his arms over his head and, receiving the delicate sun on his upturned face, beamed a smile.

~

How do I describe the smile I saw on the face of this proud descendent of Baro Bhuiyan, the twelve chieftains who had ruled Bengal during the era of the Delhi Sultanate? So many types of smiles I have collected on these field trips: the smile on the face of young Amin Singh in Hudisahi when he told us how a labour contractor had cheated him; the smile pasted on Uchiar Ali's lips when we asked him whether his son would drop out of school like other neighbourhood boys; the smile that Savitri Munda bit back when I asked her why she never helped the pupils with their studies; the smile that lit up Dulal Mondal's face when he told me that Pocha, his nephew, was staying with him, studying in a government school; the smile that shimmered on the faces of old Nabadwip widows when we gave them a packet of biscuits; the smile that spread across Mampi Das's face like the wings of a monarch butterfly when I asked her what she wanted to be when she grew up; the smile on Bharati Das's lips when she confessed that the husband who had walked out on her would ask her for money now and then; the smile that crinkled Gouranga Bauri's lips when he described how the TV reporters had asked him to lie down on the floor before they switched on their cameras; the smile that Nakul Sardar flashed when he complained that he could never stay away from the bitch of a river; the smile that Utpal Basak shared with his roommates like a cigarette stub when he told me how many PhDs had applied for the post of an office peon; the smile glinting on the craggy faces of rickshaw-pullers and housemaids during the prize-giving ceremony in school; the smile playing on Brindavan Prasad's lips when he asked me how a person could retire from a job that was no more…

Such a harvest of smiles.

~

It was early winter, the river was lean, but the tide hadn't sufficiently ebbed yet. This char was here to stay. The corrugated sand resembled the lines on Tarak's brow. Soon, particles of silt would be deposited in their folds, dark green algae would line the ridges, beach grass would sprout, waterfowl would come and drop more seeds. Around the sandbar's edges, the ebbing waters would leave behind shelled mangrove seeds that travel upon the tides. In the span of the few hours it takes for the tides to turn, the magic seeds would sprout and hook into the silt. In two days, a little hard stem would peep out. In five days, there would be a pair of tiny leaves on it.

And thus would begin *a fantastic novel.*

Here in this tide country, it takes two decades for a newborn island to get a mangrove forest, half a century for a human settlement to come up on it.

How long does it take to raze that settlement to the ground? How many hours to eject the settlers?

A human figure on the deck broke my reverie. It was Amitava. With the dazed eyes of a sleepwalker, he peered at us standing below on the newborn char.

'Come down, Baba,' Wrik called out to him.

Again, they hoisted the bamboo pole. Amitava, holding it with both his hands, shambled down the gangplank to the notch above the water, until he grabbed Wrik's outstretched hand.

This was the first time I heard Wrik call him father.

～

When the boat returned us to land, the sun had set. Dusk stained the sky and the waters. It was a Saturday. A weekend crowd was milling on the beachfront. The boat dropped us at the jetty and puttered away towards the fishing harbour, waving a ribbon of black diesel smoke. Amitava and Wrik sauntered towards Tapan's stall for a cup of tea. I lingered on the shore to unstiffen my legs. After four days on the water, the sensation of stable ground under the feet, accompanied with a mild loss of bearings, was interesting. I wanted to savour it for as long as it lasted. So many millennia ago, the forebears of our species had left the waters and migrated to land. Weren't the traces left in our cellular memories?

The sea was a dull mercury, the breakers foamed silver, a breeze murmured in the dark casuarina grove. Below the jetty, on a desolate stretch of sand, three minor girls were picking meen. They had spread a blue plastic sheet over a depression to build a shallow pool. From it, they were scooping the tiny prawn larvae with seashells and storing them in a tin can. The light had dimmed, and I could hardly see the microscopic strands of their catch.

The girls appeared to be between ten and twelve. They wore identical smoke-blue frocks, frayed and faded, with false neckties sewn between the lapels. The buttons at the back were missing and, with not even a safety pin to hold them in place, the frocks were constantly slipping off their shoulders. One of them had a silver nose ring, another had raw, newly pierced ears. They huddled over the blue plastic and lightly skimmed the water, as if it were a game they were playing.

Seeing a stranger, the girls grew self-conscious but didn't stop or turn to look.

When I asked them where they lived, one of them pointed a finger vaguely over the casuarina trees.

'Do you go to school?'

One of the girls, the one with the silver nose ring, poked the one by her side. 'There, she goes.'

The girl in question acted as if she were offended. 'No, no,' she protested. 'Here, she goes.'

And she slapped the one with the newly pierced ears on her knee. Now the three girls stabbed their fingers into one another and began to giggle. They made a show of it, as if this too were part of a game.

I laughed with them for no reason and continued to watch their antics. Soon, they forgot my presence and turned to their work. It was as if I, too, were a part of the landscape – like the dogs, the crows, and the speck of light from a lone fishing trawler bobbing on the horizon.

The plastic sheet had trapped countless tiny organisms. The girls picked each one of them and tossed them around for the flapping crows that were now almost invisible in the darkness. I moved on.

Another two hundred metres down the dunes, the coastline curved inwards. The waves crashed on a desolate beach. Attempts had been made to check the erosion with a fencing of wooden poles. They hadn't worked. The broken poles stuck out on a bed of soupy silt, like the raised fingers of drowning men. Barnacles were growing on them. Behind them, a colony of low, identical buildings lay abandoned and half-buried in the sand. These had once been the staff quarters of the fisheries department. Under the astral light, it was now impossible to tell whether these were the ruins of a settlement surrendered to the sea or an archaeological site surfacing from the depths. The contractors had stripped away the wood and metals; only the bare concrete shells were standing. The sea wind howled around them.

Here, I found him. He was standing on raised ground, facing the wind, contemplating the ruins.

His back was turned to me, and yet I recognized him. Did he live in one of these concrete shells? Like a hermit crab?

His long hair was blown back, the cardigan flapped like wings, the beach litter was hurled before him. The sand was slipping from under his feet, the wind propelled him backwards.

ACKNOWLEDGEMENTS

I cannot hope to acknowledge here my debt to all the persons who have made this book possible. Some of them appear in it. I have changed their names to protect their identities.

Among the others, I am indebted to Jatindra Kumar Nayak, eminent educationist and translator, for his unwavering support and for connecting me with the people working in the field of tribal education in eastern Odisha. I am also grateful to Anil Pradhan, the secretary of Sikshasandhan, Bhubaneswar, and Yamuna Samad, Birsa Singh, Pitambar Sankhua, Bhrugu Rath and Amar Ranjan Bhoy from its Nuasahi camp office, as well as Pradeep Kumar Sar, for all their help.

I must record my gratitude to Surai Hembram, respected tribal leader from Mayurbhanj; Amita Murmu and members of Sathi Shikshashram, Purulia; Debasish Sarkar, former secretary, West Bengal Council of Higher Secondary Education; Utpal Biswas and his family from Samsher Nagar, North 24 Parganas; Debashish Pal from APDR; Arup Biswas and his cousins from Palashipara, Nadia; Nikhil Ranjan Pramanik and his sister from Madhabpur, Howrah; Purnabha Dasgupta and Atanu Deb, formerly with Literacy India; Kanai Mondal and his family from Birbhum; Mintu Islam, Dolon Roy, Saptarshi Goswami, Manjari Ghosh and Dipankar Sengupta. They have helped me in countless ways, sometimes going out of their way and not always in favourable situations, showered me with affection and insight, and led me, literally and figuratively.

Saurabh Bhattacharyya has accompanied me on some of the trips, sharing the thrill and the pain with his trademark dry humour.

Shoma Bhattacharjee, Anurag Basnet, Soma Ray, Sreejith K. and Partha Chakraborty, my Bengali publisher, have assisted me at various stages of the writing. They are the kind of readers who sustain a writer. Some of the faces and voices in this book first appeared in a column I used to write for *The Telegraph*. I am grateful to Bhaswati Chakraborty for giving me that space.

I am greatly beholden to Ramachandra Guha for his encouragement and promptness.

Kanishka Gupta, my agent, rescued the project from limbo and found it the best possible home. Rahul Soni, my editor, nurtured it with the kind of insight and care only he can bring. Rinita Banerjee edited the copy with deep empathy and intelligence. My gratitude to them is exceeded only by my admiration for their skill and dedication.

Indrani and Isti, my wife and daughter, have remained, as always, an unfailing source of support and forbearance.

Two persons who have had a profound influence on the shape of this book are no more. They are Dhiraj Ghosh, alias Master-da, who dedicated his life to a non-formal school he built in one of the most backward regions in Purulia, West Bengal; and Asok Sen, eminent intellectual and editor of Kolkata's most respected Bangla magazine, *Baromas*. I cannot convey my gratitude to them from this space, just as I cannot thank all the children, spread across many districts in two states, for giving me some of the best moments in my life.

ABOUT THE AUTHOR

Parimal Bhattacharya, a bilingual writer and translator, teaches in the department of English, Maulana Azad College, Kolkata. He is the author of *No Path in Darjeeling Is Straight* and *Bells of Shangri-La*. *Nahumer Gram O Onyanyo Museum*, published in 2021, is his most recent work in Bangla.